HEAVEN
The Heart's Deepest Longing

PETER KREEFT

HEAVEN

The Heart's Deepest Longing

IGNATIUS PRESS   SAN FRANCISCO

Previously published by
Harper & Row Publishers
San Francisco
© 1980 Peter J. Kreeft

Cover by Riz Boncan Marsella

© 1989 Ignatius Press
ISBN 0-89870-228-3
Library of Congress catalogue number 88-83747
Printed in the United States of America

For Maria, especially on Mondays

Contents

Introduction

Our Guide on the Quest for Heaven: Our Society or Our Heart?

Our Society's Silence

Of all the questions the human mind can ask, three are of ultimate importance:

1. What can I know?
2. What should I do?
3. What may I hope?

The three questions[1] correspond to the three "theological virtues" of faith, hope, and charity.[2] Faith in God's word is the Christian answer to "What can I know?" Love of God and neighbor is the Christian answer to "What should I do?" And hope for God's Kingdom, the Kingdom of heaven, is the Christian answer to "What may I hope?" Just as faith fulfills the mind's deepest quest for truth and as love fulfills the moral will's deepest quest for goodness, so the hope of heaven fulfills the heart's deepest quest for joy.

It is the quest that moves irrepressibly through the world's great myths and religions, the masterpieces of

---

[1] Immanuel Kant, *Critique of Pure Reason,* trans. Norman Kemp Smith (New York: Macmillan, 1958), p. 635: "All the interests of my reason, speculative as well as practical, combine in the three following questions: (1) What can I know? (2) What ought I to do? (3) What may I hope?"

[2] Aquinas, *Summa Theologiae* I–II, 62, 3.

its greatest artists and writers, and the dreams that rise from the primordial depths of our unconscious. However different the heavens hoped for, wherever there is humanity, there is hope.

The question of hope is at least as ultimate as the other two great questions. For it means "what is the point and purpose of life? Why was I born? Why am I living? What's it all about, Alfie?"

Most people in our modern Western society do not have any clear or solid answer to that question. Most of us live without knowing what we live for. Surely this is life's greatest tragedy, far worse than death. Living for no reason is not *living* but mere existing, mere surviving. As Viktor Frankl found in a Nazi concentration camp, our deepest, rock-bottom need is not pleasure, as Freud thought, or power, as Adler thought, but meaning and purpose, "a reason to live and a reason to die".[3] We need a meaning to life more than we need life itself.

Millions all around us are living the tragedy of meaningless life, the "life" of spiritual death. *That* is what makes our society most radically different from every society in history: not that it can fly to the moon, enfranchise more voters, have the grossest national product, conquer disease, or even blow up the entire planet, but that it does not know why it exists.

Every past society gave its members answers to all three great questions. It transmitted the teachings of its sages, saints, mystics, gurus, philosophers, or gods through tradition. For the first time in history, society

---

[3] Viktor E. Frankl, *Man's Search for Meaning* (New York; Washington Square Press, 1963). Cf. John Powell, *A Reason to Live, A Reason to Die* (Niles, Ill.: Argus Communications, 1972).

no longer regards tradition as sacred; in fact, it no longer regards it at all. We are the first tree that has uprooted itself from the universal soil. If we are to find an answer to the question "For what may I hope?" we must find the answer individually; our society simply does not know. The only sound we hear from our noisy society concerning the most important questions in the world is the sound of silence.

How has this silence come about? How is it that the society that "knows it all" about everything knows nothing about Everything? How has the knowledge explosion exploded away the supreme knowledge? Why have we thrown away the road map just as we've souped up the engine? We must retrace the steps by which we have come to this dead end; to recapture hope we must diagnose the causes of our hopelessness before we begin to prescribe a remedy. Before we undertake the main task of this book, the exploration of the deepest hope of the human heart, the hope for heaven, we must first answer two preliminary questions: first, why our society is silent, and second, how our hearts can substitute for our society in being our teachers and guides on our quest for hope, our quest for heaven.

The History of Hope

From earliest times humanity has hoped for heaven. The earliest artifacts are burial mounds. The dead were always prepared for the great journey. However various the forms, belief in an afterlife is coterminous with humanity.

Among ancient peoples two stand out in this respect, as in most others: the Jews and the Greeks. These peoples are the twin sources of Western civilization, the two main tributaries of the river whose waters, blending in the medieval synthesis and separated again in modernity, still trickle far downstream through the swampy delta of the present. If a visitor from another planet had observed the face of the earth some twenty-five centuries ago with an eye sensitive not merely to external but also to internal energies, he would have singled out not Persia or Egypt but Greece and Israel as the waves of the future and the roots of history's civilized tree. They were the only two peoples who found modes of thought other than myth for answering life's three great questions. For myth the Jews substituted faith in a historically active and word-revealing God, and the Greeks substituted critical, inquiring reason. For this reason they developed different hopes, different heavens, from those of the myths.

The Hebrew conception of heaven arises in exactly the opposite way from the pagan one; instead of rising out of humanity's heart, it descends from God's, as the New Jerusalem descends out of the heavens at the end of the story in Revelation. From the beginning of the story, God tells humanity what he wants instead of humanity telling God what it wants. Instead of humanity making the gods in its image, God makes humanity in his image; and instead of earth making heaven in its image, heaven makes earth in its image. Thus the greatest Jew teaches us to pray: "Thy Kingdom come . . . on earth as it is in heaven."[4]

The Jews are "the chosen people"—through no merit

<hr>

[4] Matt. 6:10. Scriptural quotations are from the Revised Standard Version unless otherwise noted.

of their own, God insists—chosen to be the messengers of hope for the world, the world's collective prophet, God's mouthpiece.5 God teaches them, and through them the world, three things: who he is, what they must do, and for what they may hope. For the third, he promises many things, some obscure, some incredible, as when he says he will raise the dead.6 God says he will show them something (whether on this earth or not is obscure) that "eye has not seen, ear has not heard, nor has it entered into the heart of man".7

The good Jew therefore does not speculate about heaven. If it has not entered into "the heart of man", well then, whatever *has* entered into "the heart of man" is not it. Let God define it and provide it, not humanity. Only when God speaks do we know with certainty, and when God speaks obscurely, we know only obscurely. Jews, unlike Christians, do not believe God has spoken clearly about the afterlife (at least not yet), and they will not run ahead of God—a proper and admirable restraint when contrasted with the extravagant myths of the rest of the world, who succumb to the irresistible temptation to fill in with human imagination the gaps left in God's revelation.

The Greeks are the other root of the tree of Western civilization. The Jews gave us conscience; the Greeks, reason. The Jews gave us the laws of morality, of what ought to be; the Greeks gave us the laws of thought and of being, of what is. And their philosophers discovered a new concept of God and a new concept of heaven.

5 Deut. 7:6–8.
6 Isa. 25:8; Ezek. 37:12–14; Job 19:25–27.
7 1 Cor. 2:9; cf. Isa. 64:4, 65:17.

While the priests were repeating their stories of fickle and fallible gods with their Olympian shenanigans and imaginative afterworlds, underworlds, or overworlds, the philosophers substituted impersonal but perfect essences for the personal but imperfect gods and a heaven of absolute Truth and Goodness for one of pleasures or pains. Not Zeus but Justice, not Aphrodite but Beauty, not Apollo but Truth were the true gods: perfect unpersons rather than imperfect persons. (The Jews, meanwhile, were worshipping a Perfect Person, transcending the Greek alternatives.) The heaven corresponding to the Greek philosophers' theology was a timeless, spaceless realm of pure spirit, pure mind, pure knowledge of eternal essences instead of the priests' gloomy underworlds of Tartarus and Hades, earthly otherworlds of Elysian Fields, or astronomical overworlds of heroes turned into constellations.

Two of these heavenly essences stand out as ultimate values: Truth and Goodness. Even the gods are judged by these values and found wanting; that is why Socrates was executed, for "not believing in the gods of the State".[8] Plato asks, "Is a holy thing holy because the gods approve it, or do the gods approve it because it is holy?"[9] The priests say the former; the philosophers, the latter. For them the two eternal essences, Goodness and Truth, stand above the Greek gods. But they do not stand above the Jewish God, the God who *is* Goodness and Truth, *emeth,* fidelity, trustworthiness. The Greeks discovered two divine attributes; the Jews were discovered by the God who has them.

[8] Plato, *Apology of Socrates* 24b.
[9] Plato, *Euthyphro* 10a.

Hebraism and Hellenism meet—Hebraism in its Christianized form, Hellenism in its Romanized form. But these forms remain Hebraic and Hellenic in substance. Christ was not an alien import; he did not ask Jews to convert to a new religion but claimed to be their prophets' Messiah. And Rome remained a Greek mind in a Roman body. The Empire added emperors aplenty, the material accoutrements of roads, armies, and political power, but not one important new philosophy.

The meeting and blending of these two great rivers, the biblical (Judaeo-Christian) and the classical (Greco-Roman) produced the Middle Ages. Medieval thinkers were intensely conscious of being inheritors and synthesizers, preservers and blenders of two ancient foods. As medieval theology synthesized the personality of YHWH (incarnated in Christ) with the timeless perfection of the philosophers' essences, the medieval picture of heaven synthesized the biblical imagery of love and joyful worship of God with the Greek philosophical heaven of the contemplation of eternal Truth. The medieval heaven is thus the Beatific Vision of God.

But the Middle Ages are no longer. The Renaissance and the Reformation disintegrated the medieval synthesis, divorced the couple that had been stormily but creatively married. These two sources of modernity both harked back to premedieval ideals: the Renaissance longed to return to Greco-Roman humanism and rationalism, and the Reformation longed to return to a simple biblical faith.

From the Reformation emerged a Protestantism whose essential vision of human destiny was in agreement with medieval Catholicism, since both were rooted in biblical revelation. But from the Renaissance

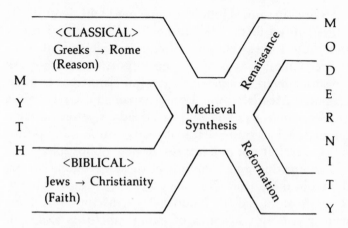

emerged something radically new in human history: a secular society with a secular *summum bonum.* Of the twenty-one civilizations Toynbee distinguishes in his monumental *Study of History,* the first twenty kept some sort of religious basis and purpose; ours is history's most unique experiment. It remains to be seen how long a civilization can survive without the use of spiritual energy, without a supernatural source of life.

What purpose is substituted for the service of God and the hope of heaven? The conquest of nature, first by the ineffective attempt of magic, then by the reliable way of technology. But the difference between these two means is minor compared to the difference between their common new end and the common old end: "There is something which unites magic and applied science while separating both from the 'wisdom' of earlier ages. For the wise men of old the cardinal problem had been how to conform the soul to reality, and the solution had been knowledge, self-discipline, and virtue. For magic and applied science alike, the problem is how to subdue reality to the wishes of men: the solution is a technique."[10]

This new purpose in life is logically connected with a new vision of the nature of reality, for one's life view and world view (*Lebenschauung* and *Weltanschauung*) hang together. As long as the nature of ultimate reality was thought to be trans-human—some sort of God or gods—our fundamental relation to reality was to conform, not to conquer. But once the gods drop out of view and "reality" comes to mean merely material nature—the subhuman, not the superhuman—our life's business is not to conform to it but to conquer it for our own purposes. Bacon trumpets the new age with slogans like "knowledge for power" and "Man's conquest of Nature".[11] These replace the "impractical" and "passive" traditional goals of knowledge for truth and of being conquered by God.

Think of humanity as a tube with two openings. The openings can be either open or closed, as we choose. Think of God, or superhuman reality, as above the tube, and nature, or subhuman reality, as below it. Traditional religious wisdom tells us to be open at both ends so God can flow in one end and out the other: in the receptive end first by faith and then out the active end by works. But if the top opening is closed, our business becomes exclusively human action in the world, without a plug-in to divine power. This is technologism, "Man's conquest of Nature".

---

[10] C. S. Lewis, *The Abolition of Man* (New York: Macmillan, 1965), pp. 87–88.

[11] Francis Bacon, *Magna Instauratio,* Preface; *Novum Organum* 2. 20.

Traditional Western Religion	Eastern Mysticism	Modern Western Secularism

There is a third possibility: the tube could be closed at the bottom and open at the top. This would characterize Hinduism and Buddhism, for which the world is illusion *(maya)* or temptation, and the sole end of life is the realization of oneness with trans-human ultimate reality. Oriental mysticism minimizes worldly action; modern Western secularism denies receptivity to God; and the classical Western tradition synthesizes the two, giving priority to the God-relationship, for we must first be directed by God before we can wisely direct our world.

Once modernity denies or ignores God, there are only two realities left: humanity and nature. If God is not our end and hope, we must find that hope in ourselves or in nature. Thus emerge modernity's two new kingdoms, the Kingdom of Self and the Kingdom of This World: the twin towers of Babel II. Judging by the outcome of Babel I, the prognosis does not look good.

The Two Modern Idol-Kingdoms

An idol is anything that is not God but is treated as God: any creature set up as our final end, hope, meaning, and joy. Anything—*anything*—can be an idol. Religion can be an idol. Religion is not God but the worship of God; idolizing religion means worshipping worship. That's like being in love with love rather than with a person. Love too can be an idol, for "God is love" but love is not God. Every divine attribute, separated from the divine person, becomes an idol. God is Truth, but Truth is not God. God is just, but Justice is not God. The first commandment is surely the one most frequently broken, and the apostle John does well to end his first letter with the warning, "Little children, keep yourselves from idols."[12]

Since an idol *is* not God, no matter how sincerely or passionately it is treated as God, it is bound to break the heart of its worshipper, sooner or later. Good motives for idolatry cannot remove the objective fact that the idol is an unreality. "Food in dreams is exactly like real food, yet what we eat in our dreams does not nourish: for we are dreaming."[13] You can't get blood from a stone or divine joy from nondivine things.

There are *two* idols, two false kingdoms, in the modern world rather than just one because the modern world is a split world, an alienated world, a world of dualism. Humanity and nature, siblings from a common Father, became alienated from each other when humanity, nature's priest and steward, became alienated from God. In the Genesis story thorns and thistles appear after Adam's Fall, and pain in childbirth for Eve.[14]

The alienation between humanity and nature begun at

[12] 1 John 5:21.
[13] Augustine, *Confessions* 3. 6.
[14] Gen. 3:16–19.

the Fall is exacerbated by Renaissance humanism, and its two forms herald the two modern idol-kingdoms. First, the southern European Renaissance places humanity in the foreground and God in the background; then the northern European Renaissance puts nature in the foreground and the road to utopia becomes the conquest of nature.

Descartes, the father of modern philosophy and child of both Renaissances, separates humanity and nature more sharply than ever before. Humanity's essence is merely mind and nature's is merely matter; and mind and matter are two clear and distinct ideas. For mind does not occupy space, but matter does; and matter does not have any consciousness, but mind does. The fact that we find the mind-matter distinction clear and self-evident is a measure of how influential Cartesian dualism is.

But the alienation is not merely between ourselves and nature but also within ourselves between mind and body. Descartes sees the human being as a "ghost in a machine", a pure spirit or mind in a purely material body, and we have no idea how a ghostly finger can push the buttons of a bodily machine.[15] We do not recognize ourselves in this picture of the ghost in the machine; yet it is the picture to which modern common sense naturally gravitates. We know we are not ghosts in machines, but we do not know what we are. We know reality cannot be two totally different and unconnected things, but we do not know what reality ultimately is— that is, if "we" are typically modern.

[15] The phrase is from Gilbert Ryle, *The Concept of Mind* (New York: Barnes & Noble, 1949).

The overcoming of dualism is monism—but a monism of what? Matter or spirit? Both solutions have emerged in modern philosophy. LaMettrie and Hobbes are early modern materialists; Spinoza and Leibnitz are early modern spiritualists. Materialism reduces spirit to matter; spiritualism reduces matter to spirit. Later, with Kant, spiritualism changes from an objective to a subjective spiritualism. Ever since Kant, the modern dualism has been not merely between matter and spirit but between objective matter and subjective spirit. The two idol-kingdoms are built in these two realms: the Kingdom of This World in the realm of objective matter at the expense of spirit and the Kingdom of the Self in the realm of subjective spirit at the expense of the objective. Subjective truth replaces objective truth; subjective values replace objective values. Both kingdoms are alternatives to the Kingdom of God, which is built in the realm of objective spirit. God is objective spirit, and when "God is dead", the objective world is reduced to matter and the spiritual world is reduced to subjectivity. That is our dualism.

To overcome this dualism and to relieve the anxiety its alienation causes, we take refuge in one or the other of the two monisms. We dare not see both halves of our split personality at once. Buber writes memorably about this in an image:

> At times the man, shuddering at the alienation between the *I* and the world, comes to reflect that something is to be done. . . . And thought, ready with its service and its art, paints with its well-known speed one—no, two rows of pictures, on the right wall and on the left. On the one there is . . . the universe. . . . On the other wall there takes place the soul. . . . Thenceforth, if ever the

man shudders at the alienation, and the world strikes terror in his heart, he looks up (to right or left, just as it may chance) and sees a picture. There he sees that the *I* is embedded in the world and there is really no *I* at all—so the world can do nothing to the *I*, and he is put at ease; or he sees that the world is embedded in the *I*, and that there is really no world at all—so the world can do nothing to the *I*, and he is put at ease. . . .

But a moment comes, and it is near, when the shuddering man looks up and sees both pictures in a flash together. And a deeper shudder seizes him.[16]

The only overcoming of that deeper shudder of alienation is in the common Father of *I* and world. Thus Buber's next line is, "the extended lines of relations meet in the eternal Thou".

The Deathly Consequences of the Death of God

When the eternal Thou dies, humanity and nature become alienated—worse, they die too. The death of God is the death of nature and of humanity.

First, of nature. Once heaven is no longer a Father, nature is no longer a Mother. "She" becomes "it", demythologized into dead atoms rather than living spirit. Her life forms are seen as merely external forms of merely physical life, evolving from the lifeless dust and returning to the dust again. The fundamental world-stuff is the dust of death.

Second, humanity in turn is reduced to a natural, not a supernatural being; highest among life forms, we too

[16] Martin Buber, *I And Thou*, trans. Ronald Gregor Smith (New York: Charles Scribner's Sons, 1958), pp. 70–72.

are made of the dust, and our destiny is simply to return to the dust. A new unity between humanity and nature arises to replace the old spiritual unity: the unity of dust, physical unity. Humanity and nature are one in death. First God dies; then humanity and nature are alienated; then humanity and nature die and find their oneness in death. When God is dead, death is God.

"God" here includes objective Truth and objective Goodness. The extent to which the consequences of the "death of God" have permeated Western civilization can be gauged by the extent to which people feel uncomfortable with such phrases as "objective Truth" and "objective Goodness", "eternal verities" and "absolute values". Even the linguistic shift from speaking of "goodness" to speaking of "values" reflects the death of God, for "goodness" is an objective concept, while "values" is a subjective concept, especially when used in the plural. "Good" means what is *really* good, but "values" mean whatever I (or we) value—our "sense of values". Similarly, the shift from the use of the words "truth" and "knowledge" to the use of the word "consciousness" reflects the death of God and of objective Truth. For "knowledge" connotes a real, objective Truth—"knowledge" is always "knowledge *of*"—but "consciousness" can be a world unto itself without any objective Truth outside it to refer to or above it to judge it. "Knowledge" can be wrong (judged by objective Truth); knowledge can fail to reach its object, since it has an object. "Consciousness" need not have any object, thus is not judged, thus is never wrong.

Dostoyevsky saw with prophetic clarity that the death of God entails the death of objective Truth and objective values when he wrote, "if God does not exist, all things are permissible."[17] Nietzsche and Sartre, from the opposite (atheistic) point of view, agree. Nietzsche's *Twilight of the Idols* makes terrifyingly clear that when God is dead, "Truth" is dead too; and Sartre argues that "there can no longer be an *a priori* Good because there is no infinite and perfect consciousness to think it."[18]

What then is left? God is dead; truth is dead; goodness is dead; humanity is dead; nature is dead. We can only blow up the bubble of death, empty within and empty without but expanding in size and power. As Nietzsche saw, the "will to power" replaces the "will to truth". If there is no God to fill us with his life, we can still fill nature with ours. If we cannot be spiritually impregnated by God, we can still physically rape Mother Nature. The "conquest of Nature" is the first idol that arises from the death of God.

"The conquest of Nature" means two things: power over nature and power over society, physical and social engineering, technology and totalitarianism. Both are extensively present in the modern West, the democratic West as well as the communist West. Democracy is no sure bulwark against totalitarianism, for democracy and totalitarianism are answers to different questions, not mutually exclusive answers to the same question. Democracy is an answer to the question: *In whom* shall the political power be located? The answer is: the people at large, or the majority of voters. Totalitarianism is an

[17] Fyodor Dostoyevsky, *The Brothers Karamazov,* trans. Constance Garnett (New York: Random House, 1950), I, 2, 5; II, 5, 5; IV, 11, 6–8 (pp. 79, 313, 760).

[18] Jean-Paul Sartre, *Existentialism and Human Emotions* (New York: Philosophical Library, 1957), p. 22.

answer to the question: How much of human life shall be politicized, publicized, communalized? The answer is: all of it. Totalitarianism, though not as advanced in the democracies as under communism, is making inroads here. As the communist bloc is catching up to us in technology, we are catching up to it in totalitarianism, though more slowly. The two forms of humanity's conquest of Nature are joining forces. Thinkers like Heidegger, Solzhenitsyn, and William Barrett insist Russia and America are spiritually indistinguishable insofar as they pursue the same end (the conquest of Nature) by different means.[19]

Despite the popularity of the Kingdom of This World on both sides of the iron curtain, the Kingdom has cracks in its foundation. Once this is seen, three reactions are possible: (1) a turning to the true kingdom, the Kingdom of God, (2) a turning to another idol-kingdom, the Kingdom of Self, or (3) a turning to nothing, to despair, loud or quiet.

The cracks in the foundation of the Kingdom of This World all amount to this: the idol simply doesn't work. It does not deliver what it promises: heaven on earth, or even happiness. Pascal puts it very simply: "All men seek happiness. There are no exceptions. . . . Yet all men complain. . . . A test which has gone on so long, without pause or change, really ought to convince us that we

---

[19] Martin Heidegger, *Introduction to Metaphysics,* trans. Ralph Manheim (New York: Doubleday Anchor, 1961), p. 31: "From a metaphysical point of view, Russia and America are the same: the same dreary technological frenzy, the same unrestricted organization of the average man." See Solzhenitsyn's 1978 Harvard commencement address. William Barrett, *The Illusion of Technique* (New York: Doubleday Anchor, 1979), pp. xi–xii, 325–360.

are incapable of attaining the good by our own efforts
. . . this infinite abyss can be filled only with an infinite
object."[20]

The history of revolutions is most instructive here,
and most depressing. Nowhere, perhaps, is the gap
between promises and deliveries, the ideal and the real,
more astonishing. The only thing more astonishing is
the fact that we are not astonished by it, that we blandly
accept it with the words "Oh well, that's human
nature." Consider the difference between "liberty,
equality, fraternity" and the Jacobins, Robespierre, the
guillotine, and the eventual dictatorship of Napoleon;
between the "new order" National Socialism promised
and the old barbarian disorder it delivered; between "the
dictatorship of the proletariat" and the dictatorship of
the Kremlin. Then consider the fact that this discrepancy is the rule, not the exception. Our history is largely
the history of hypocrisy. All sane men and women
prefer peace to war, justice to injustice, understanding
to misunderstanding, love to hate, freedom to enslave-
ment; yet their history—our history—is a desert of war
and injustice with rare oases of peace and justice. In
heaven's name, why?

To reply that it is because history is determined by the
few bad guys oppressing the many good guys is impos-
sibly naive. However different the political structures,
the few necessarily emerge from, represent, and are
followed by the many. They are humans, not martians
or demons; they are we. Furthermore, those nations that
have overthrown the few by revolution are precisely the

[20] Pascal, *Pensées,* 148, trans. A. J. Krailsheimer (New York:
Penguin Books, 1966), pp. 74–75.

ones that best illustrate the discrepancy between the ideal and the real in the history of those revolutions. Every revolution has betrayed its ideals. (America never had a real revolution, only a War of Independence. Yet America, too, is increasingly betraying its original ideals.) Why?

I once had a dream that answered this question for me. It went like this. I had always thought that if I could only have adequate answers to two great questions, I would be wise: What is and what ought to be? What is the nature of reality and what is the purpose of human life? In the dream I realize that I (and everyone else) have answers to these two questions but not to a third question, and that is why we are not wise.

I find myself in the dream naked in a desert. There is nothing around me but sand—no trees, no lakes, no buildings, no animals. Everything is reduced to its lowest common denominator: stuff. And thus I know the nature of reality. Every form of stuff is made of stuff, matter; and I know matter because I too am made of matter. I know matter more adequately than a brilliant physicist who is an angel could know it: I know it from within. I also *know;* therefore there is mind as well as matter. That, too, I know from within. Finally, I know there is a God, for there is a sun in the sky (the sky seems to symbolize spirit, as the sand symbolizes matter, and the sun seems to be a God-symbol). However, I cannot see the sun, for every time I turn to look at it, it moves so as to stay behind my head all the time. But it always casts a shadow, so I know it is there.

So I know the nature of reality: sky and sand, "the sky above, the mud below", spirit and matter; and I am both. Now for the next question: What should I do?

What is the good, the end, the goal of my existence? As
soon as I ask the question, I receive an answer I know is
true, even though it sounds crazy, because it comes out
of the sun and simultaneously out of a large yellow disc
in my chest. The answer is, "Build the Taj Mahal." (The
Taj Mahal has always been to me the most beautiful, the
most perfect building, and here it seems to symbolize
the ideal society, the society we all want.)

I start to argue with the voice: How about a sand
castle? I can't build the Taj Mahal; I don't even know the
principles of architecture, and I have nothing but sand to
build with. But the voice says to me: You can't argue
with me, you *are* me, or rather I am you. Where do you
think I'm coming from, anyway? I look, and the voice is
coming from the yellow disc in my chest. My own heart
demands the Taj Mahal; it is I, not another, who demand perfection.

Then I realize the point: Even though I have adequate
answers to the first two great questions (and so does
everyone else), I am not wise because I do not have an
answer to the third, far more difficult question: How?
How does the naked ape build the Taj Mahal from sand?
Though I know what I am and what I must do, I have
no hope of doing it. It is the third question, the question
of hope, that stumps me.

I think I will wake up now, having learned my lesson;
but I don't. And as I begin to get bored, I fool around
with the sand and begin to think: There's nothing else to
do but to start building. Suppose I make some bricks
out of this sand and build a brick wall and then a brick
factory; and then I'll build harder bricks in the brick
factory and make a brick shovel to dig until I find some
stone. Then I'll build a stone smelter and smelt some

iron ore out of the stone, and I'll redo the Stone Age and the Iron Age and the Bronze Age—eventually I'll redo all of human history, learn the principles of architecture, and build the Taj Mahal. I'm Adam, and I'll do it right this time.

So I start making bricks. But I have no water or straw to mix with the sand. So I spit on the sand, and pull some hair from my head to mix with it, and the bricks hold together. I start to have optimistic dreams about the Taj Mahal, but the dreams are suddenly dashed. For as soon as I build the first brick wall up to six feet high, it collapses. Even when I build it three or four bricks thick, even when I dig a deep foundation for it, it always collapses as soon as it reaches six feet.

And that's the end of the dream. No Taj Mahal. Not even a brick factory. Just failure.

The symbolism and the lesson seem obvious. What I'm teaching myself in the dream is that I can't make something bigger and better than myself. I can't pull myself up by my own bootstraps. Like water, I can't rise above my own source. The first wall of what was eventually to become the Taj Mahal was built not just *by* me but *of* me: my hair and my spit was mixed with the world-stuff, the sand. Our societies come tumbling down because they are built of us: inferior material. *We* are the problem of war, of slavery, of injustice. The external war is just the outworking of the internal war. In the words of America's greatest philosopher, Walt Kelly, author of the Pogo comic strip, "we have met the enemy and he is us."

That's why the Kingdom of This World is as full of sand as the Kingdom of the Self; it is built by and for and of the Self. Self can no more find heaven in its world than in itself. To quote Pascal once again, "The Stoics say: 'Withdraw into yourself, that is where you will find peace.' And that is not true. Others say: 'Go outside; look for happiness in some diversion.' And that is not true: we may fall sick. Happiness is neither outside nor inside us: it is in God, both outside and inside us."[21]

Not only *may* we fall sick, but we will certainly die. The fact of death, life's only certainty, is the unanswerable refutation of both kingdoms. It is instructive that the most prominent representatives of the Kingdom of This World, the Marxists, have absolutely nothing to say, amid the tons of ink they spill on every other conceivable topic, about death except to condemn concern with it as "morbid". And Marxism is not the only philosophy whose ship of hope founders upon the rocks of death:

> Almost all our modern philosophies have been devised to convince us that the good of man is to be found on this earth. And . . . lest your longing for the transtemporal should awake and spoil the whole affair, they use any rhetoric that comes to hand to keep out of your mind the recollection that even if all the happiness they promised could come to man on earth, yet still each generation would lose it by death, including the last generation of all, and the whole story would be nothing, not even a story, for ever and ever.[22]

The turn from the Kingdom of This World to the Kingdom of the Self does not solve the problem of death, but it is popular nevertheless, especially in Amer-

---

[21] Ibid., 407.

[22] C. S. Lewis, *The Weight of Glory* (New York: Macmillan, 1949), p. 5.

ica. Our Declaration of Independence includes one of its most famous slogans: "the pursuit of happiness". It seems providentially fitting that the last published writing of the most brilliant and influential Christian apologist of the century, C. S. Lewis, was entitled, "We Have No 'Right to Happiness'."[23]

But wait. Didn't the Greek and medieval philosophers say that all we do we do for the sake of happiness, that happiness was the end of human life? Yes, but they meant by "happiness" something quite different than what we moderns mean; for them "happiness" was an objective rather than a subjective term. It meant the state of spiritual health, *eudaimonia,* literally "good-spirit-ness". It was not primarily a matter of feelings. For us, if we feel happy, we are happy; if we don't, we're not. The ancients, on the other hand, could feel happy and really be unhappy (for example, a successful tyrant), just as you can feel healthy and really be unhealthy. Or vice versa, as in the case of Job. A test question to distinguish the objective and subjective meanings of "happiness" is whether suffering can be part of happiness. In the modern, subjective sense, it can't (unless you're a masochist); in the ancient, objective sense, it can. Suffering is an occasion for wisdom, and wisdom is an essential ingredient in happiness. If happiness is objective, if it is not in us but we are in it, then its objective laws and principles may require subjective suffering on our part. Most great men and women of the past have both experienced and taught the

[23] *Saturday Evening Post,* vol. 236 (Dec. 1963), pp. 10–12. Also in *God in the Dock* (Grand Rapids, Mich.: Eerdmans, 1970), pp. 317–322.

creative value of suffering, the objective happiness of subjective unhappiness. Modern subjectivists cannot make that distinction.

The Heart as Teacher

We have seen how our idolatrous society cannot give us an answer to the question of heaven, the question of hope, the question of happiness; that its two kingdoms are idols; and that it is silent, hypocritical, or a failure in answering this crucial question. What can substitute for our traditionless society in teaching us what we may hope for? To what, you ask, can I turn now? Where am I to search? Which guru or authority or spiritual salesman should I listen to?

To your own heart. It is a teacher you can trust, for it will not despise you (it *is* you), and it is wiser than your head, wiser than you think. Listen to your heart. It will tell you for what you may hope; it will tell you "the meaning of life" if only you listen deeply. It will tell you of heaven.

Is heaven, then, in the heart?

By heaven, no! We have just exposed that idol, the Kingdom of the Self. Even though the heart's "inner space" is infinitely greater than all "outer space", heaven is infinitely greater than anything that has ever entered into your heart. Remember, "eye has not seen, ear has not heard, nor has it entered into the heart of man".[24]

What you will find in your heart is not heaven but a picture of heaven, a silhouette of heaven, a heaven-shaped shadow, a longing unsatisfiable by anything on

[24] See note 7.

earth. This book tries to raise that picture to consciousness.

What you will find in your heart is not heaven but a heavenly hole, a womblike emptiness crying out to be filled, impregnated by your divine lover. Heaven is God's body; earth is ours.

What you will find in your heart is not heaven but "the highways to heaven".[25] The highway is internal, not external; you can't get to heaven by rocket ship. But what is internal, what is in the heart, is only the highway, not the goal. Heaven is infinitely greater than your heart.

What you will find in your heart is not heaven but a finger pointing to heaven. The Zen masters say: A finger is excellent for pointing at the moon, but woe to him who mistakes the finger for the moon!

But though you do not find heaven *in* the heart, you do find heaven *with* the heart. The heart is the gate of heaven and of hell:

> ZEN MASTER: I will show you the gates of heaven and hell.
> (He smacks the disciple from behind with his sword.)
> DISCIPLE *(unsheathing his sword):* You fake! I'll kill you!
> MASTER: Here open the gates of hell.
> DISCIPLE *(sheathing his sword):* I see.
> MASTER: Here open the gates of heaven.[26]

Do you see? The heart is a great teacher. Listen to your heart. This book aims to help you do just that. It is

[25] Ps. 84:5–6: "Blessed are the men whose strength is in thee,/ in whose heart are the highways to Zion./ As they go through the valley of Baca/ they make it a place of springs."

[26] Paul Reps, *Zen Flesh, Zen Bones* (Rutland, Vt.: Charles E. Tuttle Co., 1957), p. 71.

a tour guide for your spiritual spelunking, your exploration of the heaven-shaped cave in your heart.

Many books have explored the heaven-shaped hole in
the modern head, the meaninglessness of atheist and
secularist philosophies. But there is not a single book in
print whose main purpose is to explore the heart's longing for heaven. For the heart is harder to explore than
the head and has had fewer explorers. The field of the
heart has largely been left to the sentimentalists. But
sentiments are only the heart's borders, not its inner
country. We must discover this "undiscovered country".

It is an undiscovered country because of the mistaken
assumption that the heart's business is not to see but
only to feel. Pascal's famous dictum, "the heart has its
reasons, of which reason knows nothing", is usually
misunderstood—in fact, it is turned upside down—and
interpreted as irrationalism.[27] But it says exactly the
opposite: The heart has *reasons*. We must not patronize
them or explain them away. The heart sees, and we must
look with it, not only at it, if we are to see. When our
eyes are healthy, we look with them, not at them; when
they are diseased, we look at them or ask a doctor to
look at them. We should do the same with the heart, our
inner eye, our third eye. The psychiatrist looks at it
when it is malfunctioning, but when it is functioning
naturally, we look with it.

The activities of the heart are to believe, to hope, and
to love. Each of the three has eyes. Take love. Look at
the difference between looking at love and looking with
love. When you read the verse from the Song of Songs

[27] Pascal, *Pensées*, 423, trans. A. J. Krailsheimer (New York:
Penguin Books, 1966).

in which the bridegroom says to the bride, "Behold, you are all fair, my love; there is not a spot or wrinkle in you",[28] do you think this is delightful but foolish? That love is blind? Then you are looking at love, not with it, and looking at it as something pathological: a blindness. The lover insists on exactly the opposite: that he is *not* blind, that he sees something that is really there. Not the lover but the loveless one is blind; he sees only the caterpillar, while the lover sees the butterfly. Love has X-ray vision. In the Song of Songs, according to the wisest interpreters, the bridegroom symbolizes God and we are the bride. God believes in our butterfly, hopes for our butterfly, loves us as butterflies. We see the present sinner; God sees the destined saint. Dare we call God a fool? His judgments are not blind but clear-sighted, accurate, and exact. Love is the highest accuracy. How can love be blind? God is love. Is God blind?

So we had better believe him when he calls us "all fair". Human lovers share the divine secret; they also see with the heart. Only one who loves you really knows you, and the deeper the love, the deeper the knowledge. The nonlover may know everything *about* you, but only the lover knows you. Everyone agrees with this in practice, if not in theory. Whom do you trust to understand you best, a genius who hates you or is indifferent to you, or a simpleminded person who loves you?

Take Dante, poetry's greatest lover. No woman has ever been so extolled in verse as his Beatrice. Now suppose you told Dante, in your reasonable, "realistic" way, that his Beatrice was really only a very ordinary girl, the daughter of a Florentine merchant, and not the

---

[28] Song of Songs 4:7.

goddess his poetry makes her out to be; that he was only "projecting" his own poetic beauty onto Beatrice. I think he would challenge you to a duel to defend the honor of his beloved; and then, much more important, if you both survived the duel, he would challenge you to a debate. He would argue and insist that his seeing of Beatrice is objectively true and the whole world's seeing is false.[29] The lover's X-ray vision sees through the beloved's body, temperament, and behavior into the heart; heart sees heart; "deep calleth unto deep".

According to the Greek philosophers, reason is the highest thing in us. Reason should judge love; we are to love and live according to reason. But according to Christianity, we are to love beyond reason, as God does, with *agapē*, nonjudgmental love, love that does not follow worthiness but creates it. Reason follows love rather than love following reason; only if we love will we know. When asked how to understand his teachings, Jesus replied, "If your will were to do the will of my Father, you would understand my teachings."[30] On another occasion he said, "Blessed are the pure of heart, for they shall see God."[31] What we see, what we understand, of God and each other, depends on our heart, on our faith and hope and love.

This must be dismissed as nonsense in science, of course, for science operates on the principle not of trust but of mistrust, systematic doubt—like a prosecuting attorney. It cross-examines nature, "puts Nature on the

[29] Cf. Charles Williams, *The Figure of Beatrice: A Study in Dante* (New York, 1972: Farrar, Straus & Giroux), pp. 47–48.

[30] John 7:17, AV.

[31] Matt. 5:8.

rack and compels her to bear witness", as Bacon puts it.[32] But in personal relations the opposite holds; we know only when we trust and love and hope for the other. You can't understand a person as an object of inquiry, as you can understand nature, for the very good reason that a person is not an object, therefore not an object of inquiry. What makes a person is precisely being a subject, not an object. To know a person you must get within, you must "walk in his moccasins". This is the work of the heart.

The heart, then, has eyes. Its deepest love and longing, the longing that nothing earthly can satisfy, is an eye. It sees something; it tells us something. It is not merely a psychological fact, a piece of flotsam or jetsam on our inner psychic sea. Instead of looking at it and explaining it, or explaining it away, let us look with it. This book is the thought-experiment of looking with the eye of the heart and exploring what we see of the deep desire hidden there, the desire for heaven.

It is an obscure and dangerous journey. The deeper we go, the less clear we become to ourselves. Heidegger gives a devastatingly honest answer to the fear that if I take this journey, "I hardly know anymore who and where I am": "None of us knows that, as soon as we stop fooling ourselves."[33] What lamp lights up our interior well as we descend to where the surface daylight no longer shines? We find a glow emanating from the depths, an interior source of light: the eye of the heart. Where head-lights fail, the heart lights up itself.

[32] Francis Bacon, *Novum Organum* 2. 20.
[33] Martin Heidegger, *Discourse on Thinking,* trans. John M. Anderson and E. Hans Freund (New York: Harper & Row, 1966), p. 62.

Our strength to make this descent is our vulnerability. To ascend the sky of reason we must become hard: doubting, critical, endlessly testing and proving. We need hard heads but soft hearts. Here in the depths, our strength is our softness. We must become little children, for only a little child is strong enough to open the greatest gate, the gate of the Kingdom of heaven. That gate is the heart, and who can open your heart like a child? The child in us is called by three names: faith (trust, openness), hope (idealism, wonder), and love (adoration, yea-saying). These are all terribly vulnerable things, quickly laughed at by a cynical, sophisticated world.

> In speaking of this desire for our own far-off country, which we find in ourselves even now, I feel a certain shyness. I am almost committing an indecency. I am trying to rip open the inconsolable secret in each one of you—the secret which hurts so much that you take your revenge on it by calling it names like Nostalgia and Romanticism and Adolescence; the secret also which pierces with such sweetness that when, in very intimate conversation, the mention of it becomes imminent, we grow awkward and affect to laugh at ourselves; the secret we cannot hide and cannot tell, though we desire to do both. We cannot tell it because it is a desire for something that has never actually appeared in our experience. We cannot hide it because our experience is constantly suggesting it, and we betray ourselves like lovers at the mention of a name.[34]

[34] C. S. Lewis, *The Weight of Glory* (New York: Macmillan, 1949), p. 4.

Read that wonderful quotation a second time—slowly and thoughtfully and heartfully this time—and ask yourself honestly: Is this true? Is this the secret in me?

If it is, we'd better start exploring it.

Chapter 1

The Beginning of the Quest:
The Heart's Hunger for Heaven

The Question: What Do You Want?

"There have been times", says C. S. Lewis, "when I think we do not desire heaven but more often I find myself wondering whether, in our heart of hearts, we have ever desired anything else."[1] Is this true? Let's find out. Let's look into our "heart of hearts".

In the broad sense of the word this is a scientific thing to do, for science in the broad sense is nothing other than careful and methodical looking—looking in the right places and with the right instruments and experiments. In this case the right place is our own hearts; the right instrument is honest introspection; and the right experiment is asking your heart the question: What do you want?

Take an hour or so to do this experiment, not just read about it. (The simple act of taking an hour away from external diversions for inner confrontation with your heart, no matter what comes of it, may be the hardest part of the experiment—and also the most valuable and desperately needed in your hectic life.) Ask your heart what it wants. Make a list. The sky's the limit. Now

[1] C. S. Lewis, *The Problem of Pain* (New York: Macmillan, 1962), p. 145.

43

imagine you are God; there is no limit to your power.
Design your own heaven and then give it to yourself.

First imagine what you want. Then imagine getting it
all. Finally, imagine having it for eternity. How soon do
you think you would grow bored or restless?

Suppose your first list wasn't very profound. Try
again. Go deeper this time: not pleasure and power and
fame and money and leisure, say, but good friends and
good health and intelligence and a good conscience and
freedom and peace of mind. That might take a few more
millennia to bore you, perhaps. But aren't all imaginable
utopias ultimately boring? In fact, aren't the most
perfect ones the most boring of all? Doesn't every
fairy tale fail at the end to make "they all lived happily
ever after" sound half as interesting as the thrills of
getting there?

Can you imagine any heaven that would not eventually be a bore? If not, does that mean that every good
thing must come to an end, even heaven? After eighty or
ninety years most people are ready to die; will we feel
the same after eighty or ninety centuries of heaven?
Would you have to invent death in your ideal, invented
heaven? What a heaven—so wonderful you commit suicide to escape it!

But if we don't want death and we don't want boredom in heaven, what do we want? If heaven is real, what
real desire does it satisfy? And even if it is unreal, only
wishful thinking, what is the wish? What do we want?

We want a heaven without death and without boredom. But we cannot imagine such a heaven. How can
we desire something we cannot imagine?

Our desires go far deeper than our imagination or our
thought; the heart is deeper than the mind. "Out of the

heart are the issues of life", says Solomon.[2] It is our center, our prefunctional root.[3] At this center we decide the meaning of our lives, for our deepest desires constitute ourselves, decide our identity. We are not only what we are but also what we want.

This is not true of our surface desires. Wanting an ice cream cone does not make us an ice cream cone. But at our center the want decides the wanter rather than the wanter deciding the want.

Another way of seeing this strange truth about ourselves is to notice that we are double selves. We identify with, or find our identity in, not only what we are but also what we want to be, not only our present, actual selves but also our hoped for, future, potential selves. Our hearts are always a beat ahead of our bodies. We have one foot where we are and the other where we are not yet. Yet both feet are ours. We are stretched between heaven and earth, and it is our hearts that stretch us into heaven even while our bodies are on earth.

But we don't know what heaven is. We can't imagine it: "Eye has not seen, ear has not heard, neither has it entered into the heart of man." We don't know what our hearts want. Therefore we don't know who we are (once we stop fooling ourselves).

This is awful as well as awesome. Because it is awesome, we wonder; but because it is awful, we rationalize. We quiet our hearts by pretending we know who we are. We mouth ridiculous bromides like "Accept

[2] Prov. 4:23 (AV).

[3] This is the central concept of the anthropological philosophy of Herman Dooyeweerd, *A New Critique of Theoretical Thought*, trans. David Freeman et al. (Presbyterian and Reformed Publishing Co., 1953).

yourself as you are"—a piece of advice that no one on earth can possibly follow without ceasing to be human because our very essence as human runs ahead of itself, falls over its own feet, and asks, "Is that all there is?" Our divine discontent is our humanity.

Even the atheist Sartre saw this and rose to the dignity of despair. Pop psychology, infinitely inferior to honest existential anxiety, offers a prescription fit for cabbages and pigs, not men and women. "It is better to be a human being dissatisfied than a pig satisfied, better to be Socrates dissatisfied than a fool satisfied."[4] Unless we are so fatuously arrogant as to believe we are already perfect, so there is nothing left to desire, we are dissatisfied until we are full-grown in spirit as well as body, until we are perfect. "Be ye perfect even as your Father in heaven is perfect."[5] Jesus speaks these words to us not only from without, from Palestine or from the Bible, but also from within, from our own hearts. Deep down, we are all perfectionists. If we weren't, we would simply stop doing anything: "The more I examine myself, the more I discover this psychological truth: that no one lifts his little finger to do the smallest task unless moved, however obscurely, by the conviction that he is contributing infinitesimally (at least indirectly) to the building of something definitive—that is to say, to your work, my God."[6]

If there were no ultimate end, no *summum bonum* to

[4] John Stuart Mill, "Utilitarianism", in *Essays on Ethics, Religion and Society by John Stuart Mill,* ed. J. M. Robson (Toronto: University of Toronto Press, 1969), p. 212.

[5] Matt. 5:48 (AV).

[6] Pierre Teilhard de Chardin, *The Divine Milieu* (New York: Harper & Row, 1960), pp. 55–56.

hope for, at least unconsciously, we would have no motivation to desire any means, for means are only means to the end. Of course "the end justifies the means"—what else ever could? Not every end justifies every means, and a morally good end does not justify morally bad means; but nothing but the end justifies the means to it. "Means" *means* means to the end.

What then is the end? What do we want? This is the very first thing Jesus asks in John's gospel.[7] First things first. It is the Socratic demand to "know thyself", for our heart's desires constitute our self, our identity. Jesus comes to us with an answer, but he must first test us with this question: What do you want? It means "Are your questions the questions to my answers?"

What do we want? A political savior? A superstar? A Superman? If so, Jesus is not our answer. He does not fit our expectations. "He is the great iconoclast. . . . The Incarnation is the supreme example; it leaves all previous ideas of the Messiah in ruins."[8] Our hearts are too small for him. He gives us more than we want, and he wants us to want more than we want so we can want what he gives us. Is it perhaps a new birth, a new being that we want? Divine life? The seed that will grow into being "perfect as my Father in heaven is perfect"? If that is what we want, Jesus is our answer. It is to this desire that he says, "Seek and you shall find . . . all who seek, find."[9] All other things can be sought and not found: money, pleasure, power, fame, health, peace, security, or worldly success. Only God is guaranteed. *All* who

7 John 1:38.
8 C. S. Lewis, *A Grief Observed* (New York: Seabury, 1976), p. 76.
9 Matt. 7:7–8; Luke 11:9–10.

seek him find him. But *only* those who seek him find him: "You will seek me and find me; when you seek me with all your heart, I will be found by you, says the Lord."[10]

Finding him is heaven. Seeking him is heaven's door. Not finding him is hell, and not seeking is the door to hell. The road to hell is *not* paved with good intentions but with no intentions, with "I don't give a damn" or "the hell with it".

The question "What do you want?" is also the starting point of the Hindu way. It is the first thing a guru might say to a prospective disciple. Like Socrates' and Jesus' disciples, the guru's disciples come looking for answers and instead get a question. To answer it they must go deeper into their hearts, for the heart is bigger on the inside than on the outside. They discover there four levels—"the four wants of Man": Pleasure, Power, Duty, and Enlightenment. If they persevere with honesty and courage, they eventually find that all other desires except the deepest one disappoint them when satisfied. Through experiencing success and disillusionment with success, they discover that what they really want is enlightenment, *mukti* (liberation from finitude), *sat-chit-ananda* (infinite reality, infinite understanding, and infinite joy).[11]

Of course this is God. Hinduism's name for God is "Brahma". Like a rose, a God by any other name will smell as sweet, though not, perhaps, sound as clear. In other words, although the Christian has important

[10] Jer. 29:13–14.

[11] Cf. Heinrich Zimmer, *Philosophies of India* (New York: Pantheon Books, 1951); Huston Smith, *The Religions of Man* (New York: Harper & Row, 1965).

theological disagreements with Hinduism, the Hindu experience of Brahma is apparently a real experience of God.

Great Western thinkers like Solomon (or whoever wrote Ecclesiastes), Plato, Aristotle, Saint Augustine, Saint Thomas Aquinas, Pascal and Kierkegaard see the same thing and structure their philosophy around the search for our ultimate end, the satisfaction of our deepest desire. They pass in review essentially the same three lesser answers as Hinduism does and conclude, "Thou hast made us for thyself, and [therefore] our hearts are restless until they rest in thee."[12]

The great Augustine, who penned that sentence, one of the most profound in all human writing, also proposed the following little thought experiment to show you, his reader, that your deepest desire is indeed the desire for God.[13] Imagine God appeared to you and said, "I'll make a deal with you if you wish. I'll give you anything and everything you ask: pleasure, power, honor, wealth, freedom, even peace of mind and a good conscience. Nothing will be a sin; nothing will be forbidden; and nothing will be impossible for you. You will never be bored and you will never die. Only . . . you shall never see my face."

Did you notice that unspeakable chill in your deepest heart at those last words? Did your surface desires leap after the first part of God's deal and your deepest desire freeze in standstill shock at "you shall never see my face"? Your surface mind, which is in touch with your surface desires, may not admit it, but your deepest

[12] Augustine, *Confessions* I. 1.
[13] Augustine, *Ennarationes in Psalmos* 127.9.

mind, which knows your deepest desires, knows it: you want God more than everything else in the world. Your heart too is restless until it rests in him.

You may not consciously realize it because this is the truth the human race keeps very, very busy hiding twenty-four hours a day by a million diversions. It is the terrible truth of Ecclesiastes, the truth that apart from the experience of union with God, apart from the satisfaction of the deepest and craziest of all desires, everything "under the sun" is "vanity", the shadow of a shadow, the chasing of the wind. It is the truth that making life "meaningful" in the short run by human artifice does not make it meaningful in the long run, that even though we fill our cities, minds, bellies, wallets, and wombs, if we remain unfulfilled in our hearts, our lives are "full of sound and fury, signifying nothing".[14]

If life on earth is not a road to heaven, then it is a treadmill, a merry-go-round minus the merry. It is like an old Mutt and Jeff cartoon that shows little Jeff standing next to a pile of stones in the center of a busy highway at night. There's a lantern atop the stones. Mutt comes along and asks, "Hey Jeff, did you put that lantern there?" "Yes, Mutt." "Why?" "To warn the cars away so they don't crack up on this pile of stones." "Good thinking, Jeff. But did you put the stones there too?" "Yes, Mutt." "What for?" "Why, to hold the lantern up, of course."

We laugh, but we laugh at ourselves. Every ingredient in our lives has a purpose: the stones are there for the lantern and the lantern is there because of the stones. But why is the whole thing there? All the cogs in the

---

[14] Shakespeare, *Macbeth,* act 5, scene 5.

civilizational machine are there for the sake of the machine, but why is the machine there? Is it like one of those little black boxes sold in joke shops? They make assorted noises, and lights blink on and off when you turn them on, and they wiggle back and forth . . . until the battery goes dead. "Full of sound and fury, signifying nothing." Is that what we are?

Take an hour sometime and sit under a bridge or major traffic artery until the traffic noise seems to be in your soul, not just in the road. Then, when it all seems necessary and reasonable, suddenly wake yourself up and ask WHY? Why is that bridge there? Well, it brings commuters from the suburbs to the city in the morning and back home in the afternoon. Why? Why do they go to the city? To work. To work at what? At all sorts of meaningful and necessary jobs. Like what? Like financiers, architects, policemen, construction workers. . . . And what do they do? Well, financiers finance bridges, architects design bridges, policemen police bridges, construction workers construct bridges. . . . You see? The lantern is there because of the stones and the stones are there because of the lantern.

Is that all there is? What is it all there for? We desire things like bridges as means—means to what end? Merely to more means? What is it *all* for? What is the end of life? What do we want?

The Nightingale in the Heart

Of course it is God we want. But not everyone knows that. How does one come to know it? Not merely by being preached at, nor by rational argument, but by experience—the Augustinian experience of the restless heart and the Ecclesiastes experience of the vanity of everything else. We find the presence of God by first finding the presence of the absence of God, the God-shaped hole that nothing else can fill. Everyone, not just "religious people" (whoever *they* are), is born, built, and designed to feed on God-food; and when we try to feed on other food, we starve.

There lives in us, deep down in the heart, a little nightingale that keeps calling for its birdseed. It is a bothersome but infinitely precious little bird. The nightingale lives way down under a host of larger, louder animals, each demanding its food; so it is easy to ignore. It has a "still, small voice".[15] But when we ignore it, even if we feed all the other animals (which is impossible), we are not satisfied, because we *are* that nightingale and we are starving.

We cannot vomit the nightingale up, as the questing knight in Ingmar Bergman's cinematic classic *The Seventh Seal* tries to do:

KNIGHT: Why can't I kill God within me? Why does he live on in this painful and humiliating way even though I curse him and want to tear him out of my heart? Why, in spite of everything, is he a baffling reality that I can't shake off? Do you hear me?

DEATH: Yes, I hear you.

KNIGHT: I want knowledge, not faith . . . I want God to stretch out his hand toward me, reveal himself and speak to me.

DEATH: But he remains silent.

KNIGHT: I call out to him in the dark but no one seems to be there.

DEATH: Perhaps no one is there.

[15] I Kings 19:12.

KNIGHT: Then life is an outrageous horror. No one can live in the face of death, knowing that all is nothingness.[16]

So we try to quiet this terrible, tiny voice. We feed the nightingale dog food and cat food and monkey food (especially monkey food). But it keeps crying for nightingale food, and we cannot find nightingale food. Yet, though we do not feed it, it does not die. We can muffle it, but, like Bergman's knight, we cannot kill it.

This is our deepest failure, the failure to satisfy our deepest desire. To cover up our failure, we compensate with other successes: we feed the other animals. We have a wonderfully efficient animal-feeding machine: that prolific diversion factory, that endlessly self-perpetuating game we call our modern technological society. It keeps us too busy ever to hear our nightingale, for we hear that voice only in silence.

> Faces along the bar
> Cling to their average day;
> The lights must never go out,
> The music must always play
> Lest we know where we are,
> Lost in a haunted wood,
> Children afraid of the dark
> Who have never been happy or good.[17]

If we are clever enough, we can muffle the nightingale's voice for a whole lifetime with surface noises (it

---

[16] Ingmar Bergman, "The Seventh Seal", in *Four Screenplays of Ingmar Bergman,* trans. L. Malmstrom and D. Kushner (New York: Simon & Schuster, 1960), p. 150.

[17] W. H. Auden, "September, 1939", in *The English Auden: Poems, Essays & Dramatic Writings,* ed. Edward Mendelson (New York: Random House, 1977).

is, remember, a "still, small voice")—if we are unfortunate enough to be clever enough. Clever indeed are the mechanisms of self-deception, and no one is more deceived than the one who feels free from self-deception.

In us is not only self-deception but also inner truth, and truth is stronger. That's why we are ultimately dissatisfied with all the monkey food, all the successes and diversions of the world. The issue is not whether worldly success will make us lastingly happy—it won't—but whether we are honest enough to question this unhappiness, to utter the word of power, the word "why", the word that moves mountains. If we are unfortunate enough to conquer the world, like Alexander the Great, we weep like him because we have no more worlds to conquer. Why? If we are as pitiable as Ecclesiastes, who says "I have seen everything under the sun", we despair, like him, at life under the sun as "vanity of vanities".[18] Why? What more do we want? There is great beauty and value and goodness and meaning in life under the sun—why do we want more? Why do we keep asking: Is that all there is? We are like children opening a thousand beautiful Christmas presents and asking after each one: Is that all there is? It sounds so greedy and ungrateful, and so we pretend to be satisfied. But the pretense can't last. Eventually we must face our inner truth, our nightingale, and ask, What do you want? There is no escape in the long run from truth, only in the short run. Even hell is truth, known too late. "Even if I make my bed in hell, Thou art there."[19]

[18] Eccles. 1:9.
[19] Ps. 139:8 (AV).

So let's look while the daylight lasts. What do we want? What do children still search for even after opening their thousand Christmas presents? For more of the same? Does the nightingale want more monkey food? Do we merely want to live a little longer or a lot longer? No, we want a different kind of life. The child in us is not greedy; we have been promised something we have not yet received—something alive, like a pet. But so far we have unwrapped only a thousand dead things, a thousand mechanical toys. Monkey food.

Who ever put such a thought into our heads? Who promised us the pet? Who whispered in our ear the desire for heaven? And when? And even more mysterious, why do we understand it? We recognize it, that is, we re-cognize it; we cognize it again; we remember it. When did we first learn it? And when and how did we forget it? We have never experienced the object of this desire, only its absence in our heart, its silhouette, for the totality of objects we do experience does not satisfy this desire. Yet we recognize it in the faintest hints, in a thousand things that teasingly suggest it. We know the unknown as a long-lost friend. It is in our ken because it is our kin.

We know it as a race as well as individually. The nightingale is social, too, because society is built not only by people and for people but *of* people. We are society, therefore it bears our image. Its history is the nightingale's hunger writ large: "Why does man alone of all animals have a history? . . . the historical process is sustained by man's desire to become other than he is. . . . Mankind today is still making history without having any conscious idea of what it really wants, or under what conditions it would stop being unhappy; in fact what it is doing seems to be making itself more unhappy and calling that unhappiness progress."[20]

Freud asks a similar question in *Civilization and Its Discontents*.[21] He says that through the technological control of nature, we have fulfilled most of the desires past societies projected into imagined gods; we have become like gods. He then asks the wonderfully simple question: Why aren't we happy? And he gives the wonderfully simple answer: I don't know. (Thank God for honest atheists!)

Our Universal Unhappiness

There is a very old wisdom, quite out of fashion today, that says we are not *supposed* to be happy here. In fact no one is really happy here, and the "pursuit of happiness", which the American Declaration of Independence declares one of our "inalienable rights", is in fact the silliest and surest way to unhappiness.[22] This is not a wisdom

[20] Norman O. Brown, *Life against Death. The Psychoanalytical Meaning of History* (Middletown, Conn.: Wesleyan University Press, 1959).

[21] Sigmund Freud, *Civilization and Its Discontents,* trans. James Strachey (New York: Norton, 1961), pp. 38–39: "Science and technology . . . are in actual fulfillment of every—or of almost every—fairy tale wish . . . long ago he formed an ideal conception of omnipotence and omniscience which he embodied in his gods. To these gods he attributed every thing that seemed unattainable to his wishes, or that was forbidden to him. One may say, therefore, that these gods were cultural ideals. Today he has come very close to the attainment of his ideal, he has almost become a god himself. . . . But . . . present-day man does not feel happy in his Godlike character."

[22] Cf. Malcolm Muggeridge, "Happiness", in *Jesus Rediscovered* (New York: Doubleday, 1979), p. 179: "The sister-in-law of a friend

we like to hear, and for that reason we had better give it extra hearing. It is a wisdom not just from the past but also from within, from the soft spot in us that we cover up with our hard surface, from the vulnerable little child in us that we mask with our invulnerable adult. Our adult pretends to want pleasure, power, wealth, health, or success, then gets it, then pretends to be happy. But our child knows what we want—nothing less than infinite joy—and, as children, we know we don't have it. Romanticists are wrong: children are not happy. They're too honest with themselves for that illusion.

No one is really happy. The phenomenon is universal, not peculiar to some temperaments, for it is not a matter of temperament or feelings, which always undulate like waves. (We are all somewhat manic-depressive.) Beneath this surface, beneath the waves of satisfaction alternating with dissatisfaction of surface desires, the deep hunger of the heart remains unsatisfied.

Because it is not a matter of temperament, this deep unhappiness appears most clearly not when one would expect, when life is full of fears or sufferings. If it appeared mainly at such times, we might dismiss it as escapism. But it is precisely when life treats us best that

---

of Samuel Johnson was imprudent enough once to claim in his presence that she was happy. He pounced on her hard, remarking in a loud, emphatic voice that if she was indeed the contented being she professed herself to be then her life gave the lie to every research of humanity. . . . The pursuit of happiness, included along with life and liberty in the American Declaration of Independence as an inalienable right, is without any question the most fatuous that could possibly be undertaken. This lamentable phrase—the pursuit of happiness—is responsible for a good part of the ills and miseries of the modern world."

the deepest dissatisfaction arises. As long as we lack worldly happiness, we can deceive ourselves with the "if only" syndrome: If only I had this or that, I would be happy. But once we have all our thises and thats and are still unhappy, the deception is exposed. That's why rich and powerful modernity is not happier than previous cultures. That's the answer to Freud's question: "Why aren't we happy?"

Our greatest bitterness comes not only in the sham sweetness of riches and power but also in the middle of our truest earthly sweetness: hearing a symphony, seeing a sunset, complete sexual love. It is highest life that sets us longing for something more than this life:

"I have always . . . had a kind of longing for death."

"Ah, Psyche," I said, "have I made you so little happy as that?"

"No, no, no." she said. "You don't understand. Not that kind of longing. It was when I was happiest that I longed most. It was on happy days when we were up there on the hills, the three of us, with the wind and the sunshine. . . . And because it was so beautiful, it set me longing, always longing. . . . Everything seemed to be saying, Psyche come! But I couldn't (not yet) come and I didn't know where I was to come to. It almost hurt me. I felt like a bird in a cage when the other birds of its kind are flying home."[23]

At the heart of our greatest pleasures lies a still greater sadness, a sadness larger than the world, crouched there like a crocodile ready to devour the world like an apple. It's no wonder we "put on a happy face" and keep very

[23] C. S. Lewis, *Till We Have Faces* (New York: Harcourt, Brace, 1956), p. 74.

busy at the ridiculous task of trying to turn earth into paradise. It's no wonder, but it's no wisdom either.

Questioning

What would be wisdom? Questioning would be wisdom—questioning our universal unhappiness. *Why* are we unhappy? Socrates was declared the wisest man in the world by the god of the Delphic oracle because he alone knew he was not wise and therefore questioned.[24] The subsequent history of philosophy (and the sciences, its children) stems from this discovery of the power of questioning. Questioning distinguishes us most clearly from animals, from computers, and from gods. Animals do not question because they know too little; gods, because they know too much; and computers, because they know nothing at all. They merely store information, like books. Computers do only what they are programmed to do; that's why no computer ever thinks, because thinking means asking questions.

Hundreds of professors with Ph.D.s do not know this; they seriously believe computers think, though the evidence that they do not is as patent as a smile: Computers never ask questions. Even if a computer is programmed to ask a question, it does not question *that* programming. It obeys programmed commands to question but never disobeys commands not to question. We do. Our social programming tells us: X is true; do not question X. And our response is gloriously human disobedience: We question X.

[24] Plato, *Apology* 20c–23b.

We question because we are creators, as computers are not. Really to ask a question is to create it, to raise it from nonbeing to being. It is a dangerous business, this business of creating, especially when it is a case of creating a question, for what is created gets a life of its own and goes on living in unpredictable and uncontrollable ways, like Frankenstein's monster, or a newborn baby, or language. Questions cannot be killed, only muffled. They are spiritual, not physical: They have immortal souls.

The question of happiness is doubly dangerous because it is not only a question but a fundamental question. When we ask a fundamental question, we question our very fundament, our foundation. When we ask nonfundamental questions, we stand on our secure, unquestioned foundation as we dismantle and test our questioned superstructures. But when we ask a fundamental question, there is no place to stand. All that was once taken for "granite" turns to sand. The granite cliffs of certainty topple into the shifting sands of uncertainty. Asking a fundamental question is holding what is questioned out over an abyss: perhaps what seemed to *be* really is *not* after all.[25] What metaphysical terror lies in this nothingness! How positive and real is this nonbeing—like blindness, or death.

[25] Heidegger says, "the fundamental question, Why is there anything at all rather than nothing?, prevents us in our questioning from beginning directly with an unquestionably given essent (thing) and, having scarcely begun, from continuing on to another expected essent as a ground. Instead, this essent, through questioning, is held out into the possibility of nonbeing." ("The Fundamental Question", ch. 1 of *An Introduction to Metaphysics*, trans. Ralph Manheim [New York: Doubleday, 1961], p. 23.)

A fundamental question is a quest as well as a question; it involves the questioner. The question recoils on the questioner, and he, the asker, is asked.[26] Subject and object exchange places; the questioner becomes the one questioned, the one questionable. The abyss is within, not without: an abyss we not only see but are. No wonder we return to the surface quickly and keep very busy. Perhaps we will forget that awful sight. The first American Indian to see the Grand Canyon, according to legend, tied himself to a tree in terror. We tie ourselves to our little external worlds because we are terrified of our inner Grand Canyon, our abyss.

Those who will not abandon the quest to "know thyself" no matter what Oedipus-like terrors lie hidden in this abyss will explore further. Spelunkers of the heart, let us descend. Rabbits may scuttle home to bed.

[26] Cf. Gabriel Marcel's distinction between "problem" and "mystery": "Is there such a thing as being? What is it? etc. Yet immediately an abyss opens under my feet: I who ask these questions about being, how can I be sure that I exist? Yet surely I, who formulate this problem, should be able to remain outside it—before or beyond it? Clearly this is not so . . . a subject . . . cannot be, by definition, an object of thought . . . there exists well and truly a mystery of cognition: knowledge is contingent on a participation in being for which no epistemology can account because it continually presupposes it. At this point we can begin to define the distinction between mystery and problem. A mystery is a problem which encroaches upon its own data." "On the Ontological Mystery", in *The Philosophy of Existentialism,* trans. Manya Harari (Secaucus, N.J.: Citadel Press, 1956), pp. 15–19).

Chapter 2

The Time of the Quest:
Time of Exile

Evasion is always temporary, a matter of time. Truth is a matter of eternity, whether it is truth evaded or truth faced. In time there are three possible answers to every question: yes, no, and evasion. Death, the touching of time to eternity, removes the possibility of the third answer.

Let's practice eternity in time. Let's evade evasion. Let's look into, not away from, our deepest unhappiness. We may be surprised—even "surprised by joy".[1] We may find our greatest hope precisely in the middle of our deepest despair, our way home in the center of our exile, like the subterranean explorers in Jules Verne's *Journey to the Center of the Earth*, who find their way back to the surface only by pushing on toward the center. It is a perfect symbol.

Alienation: Our Greatest Blessing

Malcolm Muggeridge found his chief blessing in his deepest sorrow, what the existentialists call "alienation":

> For me there has always been—and I count it the greatest of all blessings—a window never finally blacked out, a

[1] Cf. C. S. Lewis, *Surprised by Joy* (New York: Harcourt, Brace & World, 1955).

light never finally extinguished. . . . I had a sense, sometimes enormously vivid, that I was a stranger in a
strange land; a visitor, not a native . . . a displaced
person. . . . The feeling, I was surprised to find, gave
me a great sense of satisfaction, almost of ecstasy. . . .
Days or weeks or months might pass. Would it ever
return—the lostness? I strain my ears to hear it, like
distant music; my eyes to see it, a very bright light very
far away. Has it gone forever? And then—ah! the relief.
Like slipping away from a sleeping embrace, silently
shutting a door behind one, tiptoeing off in the grey
light of dawn—a stranger again. The only ultimate disaster that can befall us, I have come to realize, is to feel
ourselves to be at home here on earth. As long as we are
aliens, we cannot forget our true homeland.[2]

Why does Muggeridge call this feeling of alienation
"the greatest of all blessings"? Because it is. It is the
greatest thing on earth because it leads us to heaven,
which is the greatest thing of all. Earthly dissatisfaction
is the road to heavenly satisfaction. It is not sufficient—
not all those who are dissatisfied with earth are guaranteed passage into heaven—but it is necessary. God is a
gentleman and will not force heaven on anyone who
says "No thank you". Implied in the encouraging words
"seek and you shall find" is a dire warning: If you do not
seek, you will not find. Earth is automatic, but heaven is
freely chosen and therefore can be freely refused. Physical birth is unfree, up to our parents; but spiritual birth
is free, up to us. Even God cannot force our free choice

[2] Malcolm Muggeridge, *Jesus Rediscovered* (New York: Doubleday, 1979), pp. 47–48.

(forced freedom is simply nonsense).[3] But he can and will do anything to "tempt" us to accept his invitation, especially by making us feel deep dissatisfaction with everything else, by the great gift of unhappiness.

That is the answer to "the problem of pain", the most powerful objection to belief in a loving God. Saint Augustine sees his pains as God being "mercifully hard upon me and besprinkling all my illicit pleasures with certain elements of bitterness, to draw me on to seek for pleasures in which no bitterness should be".[4] The prophet Hosea calls suffering a hedge that blocks our path to idols and makes us turn back to our first love and our true joy, God.[5] C. S. Lewis learns that "the hardness of God is kinder than the softness of men, and his compulsion is our liberation."[6] He calls even death "a severe mercy".[7] God fills our lives with many joys but no guarantees, many pleasures but no security, because "Thou hast made us for thyself" and therefore so arranged earth that "our hearts are restless until they rest

[3] Cf. the argument in C. S. Lewis, *The Problem of Pain* (New York: Macmillan, 1962), pp. 26–29: "You may attribute miracles to him, but not nonsense. There is no limit to his power. If you choose to say 'God can give a creature free will and at the same time withhold free will from it', you have not succeeded in saying *anything* about God; meaningless combinations of words do not suddenly acquire meaning simply because we prefix to them the two other words 'God can'. It remains true that all *things* are possible with God; the intrinsic impossibilities are not things but nonsense."

[4] Augustine, *Confessions,* II. 2.

[5] Hos. 2:6–7.

[6] C. S. Lewis, *Surprised by Joy,* p. 229.

[7] Cf. Sheldon Vanauken, *A Severe Mercy* (San Francisco: Harper & Row, 1977).

in thee."[8] Rest along the way, premature rest, is danger; the way to true rest is restlessness. The prophet denounces those who "have healed the wound of my people lightly, saying, 'Peace, peace', when there is no peace".[9]

There is a profound truth hidden in the fatuous song line "People who need people are the luckiest people in the world", but it is concealed beneath three mistakes.[10] First, it is not just people who need people but people who first of all need God; second, it is people who not only need God (that's everybody) but who know their need for God; and third, they are only the second luckiest people in the world. The luckiest are those who have found God. But the second luckiest are those who need and seek him, for all who seek, find. The profound point in the silly song is that our need is our hope. Pascal says, "There are only three sorts of people: those who have found God and serve him; those who are busy seeking him and have not found him; those who live without either seeking or finding him. The first are reasonable and happy, the last are foolish and unhappy, those in the middle are unhappy and reasonable."[11] It is obvious where the great divide is, even the divide between heaven and hell: not between finders and nonfinders but between seekers and nonseekers. Since our alienation spurs us to seek, it is our greatest blessing.

[8] Augustine, *Confessions*, I. I.

[9] Jer. 6:14.

[10] "People", words by Bob Merrill, music by Jule Styne, Chappell & Co., Inc.

[11] Pascal, *Pensées*, 160, trans. A. J. Krailsheimer (New York: Penguin Books, 1966), p. 82.

Let's explore our blessing. Let's open our strange present and play with it a bit. What does it mean?

Alienation is the opposite of being at home. If the Bible is not wrong when it calls us "strangers and pilgrims",[12] then that's why we feel alienation: We feel what *is*. When any organism is at home, there is an ecological fit with its environment, a harmony, a rightness. If the environment does not supply this, that environment is not its home.

A fish has no quarrel with the sea. Yet we have a lover's quarrel with the world. "If you are really a product of a materialistic universe, how is it you don't feel at home there? Do fish complain of the sea for being wet? Or if they did, would that fact itself not strongly suggest that they had not always been, or would not always be, purely aquatic creatures? Notice how we are perpetually *surprised* at Time. ('How time flies! Fancy John being grown-up and married! I can hardly believe it!') In heaven's name, why? Unless indeed, there is something in us which is *not* temporal."[13]

We have a homing instinct, a "home detector", and it doesn't ring for earth. That's why nearly every society in history except our own instinctively believes in life after death. Like the great mythic wanderers, like Ulysses and Aeneas, we have been trying to get home. Earth just doesn't smell like home. However good a road it is, however good a motel it is, however good a training camp it is, it is not home. Heaven is.

Play with that thought for a minute: Heaven is *home*. Experiment with the thought; feel the gem; look at the picture; explore the house before deciding whether to

[12] I Pet. 2:11.
[13] C. S. Lewis in Vanauken, *A Severe Mercy,* p. 93.

buy. Heaven means not just a pleasant place but *our* place, not just a good but a good place for us. We fit there; we are fully human there. We don't turn into angels (that's why there has to be the resurrection of the body; we don't change species).[14] "Your soul has a curious shape because it is . . . a key to unlock one of the doors in the house with many mansions. . . . Your place in heaven will seem to be made for you and you alone, because you were made for it—made for it stitch by stitch as a glove is made for a hand."[15]

It is our home because we receive there our true identity. We don't know who we are, remember; we are alienated not only from our home but from our selves. This is beautifully symbolized in Revelation 2:17: "He who has an ear, let him hear what the Spirit says to the churches. To him who conquers I will give some of the hidden manna, and I will give him a white stone, with a new name written on the stone which no one knows except him who receives it." George MacDonald explains this symbol as follows: "God's name for a man must be the expression of his own idea of the man, that being whom he had in his thought when he began to make the child, and whom he kept in his thought through the long process of creation which went to realize the idea. To tell the name is to seal the success."[16]

---

[14] This is suggested in 2 Cor. 5:2–4: "Here indeed we groan, and long to put on our heavenly dwelling, so that by putting it on we may not be found naked. For while we are still in this tent, we sigh with anxiety; not that we would be unclothed, but that we would be further clothed, so that what is mortal may be swallowed up by life."

[15] C. S. Lewis, *The Problem of Pain*, pp. 147–148.

[16] C. S. Lewis, *George MacDonald: An Anthology* (New York: Macmillan, 1978), no. 15, p. 8.

What does it mean that the name is a secret "which no one knows except him who receives it"? That "with every man he has a secret—the secret of a new name. In every man there is a loneliness, an inner chamber of peculiar life into which God only can enter. There is a chamber also (O God, humble and accept my speech)— a chamber in God himself, into which none can enter but the one, the individual, the peculiar man—out of which chamber that man has to bring revelation and strength for his brethren. This is that for which he was made—to reveal the secret things of the Father."[17] C. S. Lewis explains "that for which he was made" as follows: "For doubtless the continually successful, yet never complete, attempt by each Soul to communicate its unique vision to all others (and that by means whereof earthly art and philosophy are but clumsy imitations) is also among the ends for which the individual was created."[18]

That is what we were designed to do and that is where we belong. Until we are there and until we are doing it, we are, in fact, "strangers in a strange land".[19] Feeling like exiles is only feeling a fact.

Longing for Eden

Our feeling of exile is an inconsolable longing for an indefineable Something incalculably precious and irretrievably lost. "Nobody ever gets through the tiny gate into the secret garden. Nobody ever hears the horns of

[17] Ibid., nos. 17, 18, p. 9.
[18] C. S. Lewis, *The Problem of Pain*, p. 150.
[19] Exod. 2:22. (AV).

elfland, or finds the faerie sea. The closest we ever get to it all is some hint or echo in a face or a painting or a concerto or a woodland glade, and then it fills us with an infinite sadness, because we know that it is lost, and that we must turn back to our traffic jams and enemas and red tape."[20] The exiles remember home.

> By the waters of Babylon
> There we sat down and wept
> When we remembered Zion . . .
>
> Let my right hand wither! If I forget you, O
>   Jerusalem,
> Let my tongue cleave to the roof of my mouth
> If I do not remember you,
> If I do not set Jerusalem above my highest joy![21]

To some (especially Romantic poets like Wordsworth and introspective autobiographers like Proust), this longing seems to be a nostalgia for their lost youth, or lost youth of soul. But this won't do, for the events in our past that now fill us with such bittersweet longing as we remember them (feel it?) felt quite ordinary at the time. Why is their memory now touched with such potent magic? How can the mere passage of time confer value or significance?

It can't; but it confers distance, and distance is needed to appreciate value. A mountain seems ordinary to someone who was born on it and has always lived on it but extraordinarily wonderful to the tourist from afar. Before space travel, we took the earth pretty much for

---

[20] Thomas Howard, *Christ the Tiger* (Philadelphia: J. B. Lippincott Co., 1967), p. 128.
[21] Ps. 137:1, 5, 6.

granted, as children take their mothers for granted—until the astronauts' unforgettable photos of "spaceship earth" spinning like a precious little blue gem in black space. When we first leave home, we first appreciate home. In fact, only when we "can't go home again" do we long to.

What is home? What are we longing for? Not just our lost youth, but humanity's. Our individual past is a symbol of our racial past, not vice versa. We long not for 1955 or 1255 but for Eden, where we lost not just our youth but our identity. Who are we now? We're not sure; we all have amnesia. We feel like dethroned princes turned into frogs by a magic spell and awaiting another magic spell, the transforming kiss, to restore our true identity.

The frog kisser, of course, is God. Going around kissing frogs hardly fits the conventional picture of divine dignity; but that picture is human, not divine. God evidently has some very strange tastes. Anyone who doubts this has never looked an ostrich full in the face.

Not only the Frog Prince but many other fairy tales as well seem suspiciously amenable to crypto-theological interpretation. This should not be surprising, for if Jung is as right about them as he seems to be, their images come from the collective unconscious, that enormous inner sea that contains treasures of wisdom our conscious surface islands of ego have forgotten. And one of these is the memory of Eden.

Our nostalgia for Eden is not just for another time but for another *kind* of time. Time in Eden was the pool in which we swam. Time now is the river that sweeps us away. We do not feel at home in this river, even though "Time is our natural environment. We live in time as we live in the air we breathe. And we love the air. . . . How strange that we cannot love time. It spoils our loveliest moments . . . we had always been harried by time . . . we wished to know, to savour, to sink in—into the heart of the experience—to possess it wholly. But there was never enough time."[22]

Time feels like our enemy because it is our slippery slope toward death. We want to stop the slide, the river rushing over the falls, the whirlpool sucking a whole world down to the abyss, drowning the living present in the dead past. C. S. Lewis wrote after his wife's death: "I look up at the night sky. Is anything more certain than that in all those vast times and spaces, if I were allowed to search them, I should nowhere find her face, her voice, her touch?"[23] Time is this "nowhere", this nevermore. Even if there is life after death, "on any view whatever, to say, 'H. is dead', is to say 'All that is gone'. It is a part of the past. And the past is the past and that is what time means, and time itself is one more name for death."[24]

Memory is our only dike against the waves of time in this world. Like Crusoe's salvage from his sinking ship, our memories are precious because they are our living "dry salvages" from the dead, drowned past. But it is not enough; all dams and dikes fall in the end. Nothing "will delay the senility of the sun or reverse the second law of thermodynamics",[25] and "the whole temple of

[22] Vanauken, *A Severe Mercy,* pp. 202, 200.

[23] C. S. Lewis, *A Grief Observed* (New York: Bantam Books, 1976), p. 16.

[24] Ibid., p. 28.

[25] C. S. Lewis, *The Weight of Glory* (New York: Macmillan, 1949), p. 6.

Man's achievement is destined to extinction in the debris of a universe in ruins."[26]

The "night sky" that terrified Lewis, like the "eternal silence of these infinite spaces" that terrified Pascal, is not just space but time.[27] The spatial emptiness is a symbol of temporal emptiness, of the past as empty of life, of presence, of presentness.

Yet time and death are our friends as well as our enemies; they frame our lives and make them precious, as outer space frames spaceship earth and makes it precious. How heightened is the sense of life's preciousness when we think we are soon to die! At the moment of death, according to widespread testimony, we review our whole lives with new appreciation. But we need not wait for death; we can make an experiment of the imagination right now. First, remember some ordinary past event in your life. Then imagine—really enter into it— that you have only a few minutes to live. Now remember that same event again. How different, how incalculably precious it seems!

Now do this with your entire life: remember your life as a whole as if it were past, as if you are at the point of death. See how death gives life to pastness as well as giving pastness to life, gives preciousness to the dead past as well as giving death and pastness to everything precious. The experience of longing for the past that is unattainably gone is our deep nostalgia brought about by the knowledge of death. It is seeing our past with the eyes of death before we die.

[26] Bertrand Russell, "A Free Man's Worship", in *Mysticism and Logic and Other Essays* (London: Allen & Unwin, 1917), p. 47.
[27] Pascal, *Pensées,* 201, p. 95.

But this is not enough. Time and death make life precious, but they do not make it eternal. But that is what we long for ("thou hast put eternity into Man's heart"[28]), even if we do not know what it is. We are not satisfied with this reasonable world of cycles, this cosmic tool bench with a place for everything and everything in its place ("thou hast made everything fitting for its time . . . a time to be born and a time to die, a time to break down and a time to build up"[29]). We rejoice at "a time to be born" but not at "a time to die"; we do not weep at births or laugh at funerals. We love creation but not destruction. We care. We discriminate. We judge.

The universe does not. Utterly indifferent to our passions, it simply does not give a damn:

> A man said to the universe:
> Sir, I exist.
> Nevertheless, replied the universe,
> That fact has not created in me
> The slightest feeling of obligation.[30]

Take a poll of the universe. Universe, how many living things have you brought to birth, from atoms to apes to agnostics, from guppies to girls to galaxies? Let the total be X. Now universe, how many living things have you brought to death or are you now in the process of bringing to death? The number is X. Precisely the same. Not $X + 1$ or $X - 1$, but X. The universe does not prefer life to death by one iota. Even the stars are not, as

[28] Eccles. 3:11.

[29] Eccles. 3:11, 2, 3.

[30] Stephen Crane, "A Man Said to the Universe", in *The Poems of Stephen Crane, A Critical Edition,* ed. Joseph Katz (New Jersey: Cooper Square Publishers, 1966), p. 102.

the ancients fondly supposed, immortal. The law of the whole universe is the law of *samsara,* as Buddha called it, the cycle of birth-and-death, the river of time. "Whatever is an arising thing, that also is a ceasing thing." This is "the pure and spotless eye of the doctrine".[31]

No, Buddha, you are wrong. With the awe and respect due to a spiritual giant, I must insist that you forgot something. *We* are arising things but not ceasing things. We transcend *samsara.* Not "we" the invisible, impersonal cosmic mind known only in mystical experience, but we human beings, we I's, you and I. Our heads stick out of time's river (or rather, our hearts do); we demand something more than time. We the desirers whom you, Buddha, declared to be illusions, we human beings who are arising things, are not ceasing things. We are born, and we die. But we desire, we demand with infinite passion, to live after death. What we long for lies on the other side of the river of time and death. If we cannot cross that river and live, if we cannot see God's face and live, our deepest desire is thwarted; our lives are failures at their depth and height.

The universe satisfies all our other desires but this one, our deepest desire and highest aspiration. The universe is a giant wishing tree, an Aladdin's lamp, a gourmet smorgasbord—until it comes to the main course. After whetting our appetite with dozens of delicacies, it trots out its main course—eternal nothingness. If that is all there is, then the universe is no more run by chance than by a good God; it is run by a bad God, a

[31] From "the Sermon at Benares"; cf. E. A. Burtt, *The Teachings of the Compassionate Buddha* (New York: Mentor Books, 1955), p. 31.

cosmic sadist who carefully arranges all the come-ons to let us down in the end.[32] The ultimate truth beyond the walls of the world is either the good God or the bad God; there is too much of a plot in the world for no God. There is design; the only question is whether the designer is good or bad.

The surest way to find out is through experience, through meeting the designer. But how do we get there? Time is our country of exile; how do we get home to eternity?

Four Roads from Time to Eternity

Four roads have appeared in human history, four answers to the question how to get from here to eternity. The first leads backwards through time, through the past, to Paradise, or the Golden Age when the gods were on earth. It is the path of myth. The myths enable us to time-travel from secular time to sacred time, to live in the eternal past from which we primordially fell into the ever-shifting present.[33] The second leads out of time altogether, not through it. It is the path of Eastern religions, which declare time to be *maya,* illusion, and with it the ego and its thoughts and desires. The third path leads through the future, through hope and promise, to eternity. It is the biblical path, the path of messianism and the Kingdom of God, of eschatology and

---

[32] Cf. C. S. Lewis, *A Grief Observed,* pp. 31–35.

[33] Cf. Mircea Eliade, *The Sacred and the Profane: The Nature of Religion,* trans. Willard Trask (New York: Harcourt, Brace, 1959), p. 68: "by its very nature sacred time is reversible . . . it is a primordial mythical time made present."

expectation. Finally, modern secularization of the biblical path also leads through the future, but only to more future, to some sort of "heaven on earth", whether via the dictatorship of the proletariat, human engineering by behavior modification, the control of nature by technology, or just a little bit of love.

In comparing the four paths, note that we really have only two that lead through time to eternity; for the Oriental path does not lead through time and the secular path does not lead to eternity. But all four paths can be included in a comparison between the two basic directions, past and future. The biblical and secular paths are both futurist; while the Oriental path, like the mythic, can be classified as nostalgic because of its frequent use of the imagery of return (to the innocence of pre-birth, pre-ego-consciousness, the oneness with the world of the unborn child, the uncarved virgin block).[34] Both myth and Oriental mysticism are past-oriented; both Judeo-Christian theism and modern secularism are future-oriented.

It is often difficult for a modern Westerner, whether religious or secular, to understand the appeal of myth and mysticism. Hope for the future is our soul food, our requirement for meaning. Though the Christian hopes for heaven and the secularist for earth, both hope. Both the Bible and Madison Avenue know the appeal of the word "new". In the modern world we boast that "progress is our most important product", and there must always be something new under the sun. In the Bible, even if there is "nothing new under the sun",[35] there is

---

[34] Cf. Lao Tzu, *Tao Te Ching* 32.
[35] Eccles. 1:9.

something new beyond the sun, and that (or rather, he) makes everything under the sun new.

But the Bible also includes the nostalgic note of a Fall from Eden, an exile from the bliss of the intimate presence of God "walking in the garden in the cool of the evening".[36] And this doubleness fits us. Whatever the objective truth of the matter, both roads are subjectively true; they fit our hearts. We long in both directions; we feel both nostalgia and hope, fallen from the heights and on the upward road, exiles from Eden and apprentices to heaven. Even those who do not believe still feel; even those who do not hope for heaven still hope.

In reading this riddle of double direction, remember that the image of the road is just that: an image. An image extended in time is a myth, a larger-than-life story that structures or explains life, uses an ingredient *in* our lives to overarch and explain the whole of our lives (for example, "the whole universe is a gigantic egg" or "life is a battle"). Images, unlike concepts, are not mutually exclusive. One cannot argue via the law of noncontradiction that life is a love affair and a battle is not a love affair, therefore life is not a battle, or that the universe is a bubble and a bubble is not an egg, therefore the universe is not an egg. Opposite and even contradictory myths (such as love and battle) can both be true.

In pre-Christian times the myth of Paradise Lost, the Golden Age, and universal devolutionism gave ancient cultures a meaningful vision of history. In modern culture the opposite myth, the myth of progress and universal evolutionism, has taken its place, buttressed by Renaissance humanism, the Enlightenment's faith in

---

[36] Gen. 3:8.

science, and popularized Darwinian evolution. Christians are often torn between the two, the conservative temperament leaning toward the ancients and devolutionism, the progressive temperament leaning toward the moderns and evolutionism.

But both visions of history are myths. They spring not from empirical data, which can be verified or falsified simply by historical research, but from the heart; not from external evidence but from internal desires. As C. S. Lewis pointed out, universal evolutionism was popular among Western intellectuals *before* Darwin looked for and found empirical data to support biological evolution of species. The hearts of Goethe, Keats, Shelley, and Wagner demanded it before the head of Darwin supplied it.[37] And the same is true of the opposite myth. When ancient sages bewailed the degradation that had polluted the purity of earlier times, they selected appropriate evidence from their complex history to prove their simple thesis. (Many of them are still at it.) It is as profound a half truth as universal evolutionism. The point is that *after* you see history as rise or fall, you find examples to prove it. History and statistics are like a nose of wax, twistable into almost any shape. "Figures don't lie, but liars figure." A myth is like a map: a simplification. A myth about history is a *guided* tour of history.

The more detail you know about history, the more it looks *neither* like a falling stone nor like a rising balloon but like a yo-yo. We move both up and down, in different ways, often at the same time. Thus it is just as

[37] C. S. Lewis, "The Funeral of a Great Myth", in *Christian Reflections* (Grand Rapids, Mich.: Eerdmans, 1967).

fallacious to think the evolution of biological species disproves the biblical story of the Fall as to believe contemporary American decadence disproves utopian hopes.

The lesson of our little excursion into comparative mythology seems to be that it is the heart that uses the head. Modern culture created the myth of evolution because the myth of devolution had died; and once the old myths die, the culture must find new ones or die itself, for a culture needs meaning to go on living, and myths give a culture meaning. We are not demythologized; we are remythologized. To be demythologized is to be spiritually dead.

Another consideration to help in reading the riddle of a double direction through time to eternity is that the two halves of a seeming paradox can be reconciled only from a higher, more inclusive point of view. For instance: A lives on the north side of a mountain and (truly) calls the mountain cold; B lives on the south side and (truly) calls it warm. Only from the top, or from a distance, can you see how both are right. Another example: no three-dimensional object can be in two different places at once, but it can be in two places at different times. Move it through the fourth dimension, and you escape the laws of the third.

Similarly, what is new and what is old are logical contradictories. Time flows one way; the older anything is, the *less* new it is. But suppose there is something that transcends but includes time, as time transcends but includes space—the fifth dimension, eternity. It is not merely very old or even everlasting; it is not *in* time, as time is not in space; time is in it, as space is in time. If such an eternal thing were to show itself somehow in time, it might appear both new and old, both beyond the beginning of time and beyond the end of time, infinitely old and infinitely new. And its lover would cry out, "Late have I loved thee, O Beauty so ancient and so new!"[38]

We long for the infinitely old and the infinitely new because we long for eternity. Even if we reached the mythical Golden Age of the past, even if we reached the moment of the creation of the world, we would long to take one more step, off the edge of time itself into the eternal mind of God, through the whole creation to the Creator. And if we ever reached the mythical future utopia on earth, we would still long for the ultimate end of the whole story, the end of the world, the death of time, swallowed up in eternity. We long to ride the river of time right into the ocean of timelessness, to reach the God toward whom all history moves.

What about the Oriental orientation to time, or rather away from time? Like the Vermont farmer pondering directions to the city slicker and concluding, "You just can't get there from here", the Oriental mystic says you can't get to eternity from time. For time is seen as a circle, not a line. In the West, both biblical and secular, time is seen as a line, with a beginning and an ending. Thus the two Western roads to eternity through time, the alpha and omega roads. The reason for the difference is that as Westerners, we read time from our lifetime, which has a real beginning (birth) and ending (death). We are humanists; we read time as human time. Orientals read time as natural time, and nature moves in cycles. Instead of moving from birth to death, it recycles

---

[38] Augustine, *Confessions* 10. 27.

the dead to fertilize the living. Eternity for the Orient is not at the end or the beginning, for a circle has no end or beginning; it is *off* the circle, off the "wheel of rebirth".

What reading can we give this myth? What desire of the heart does it reveal? (For remember, what we learn from myths is not the nature of the empirical world but the nature of the heart.) Don't we want more time, not less? What does this myth of time as a meaningless and even illusionary cycle teach us about what we want?

If we listen carefully to ancient sages like Buddha or modern teachers like Krishnamurti, we can see the point of this myth.[39] Time is the condition for all fear; that's why time is the enemy. For fear is always of the future, fear of what might happen next, not of what is actually happening now. Some psychologists think as much as nine-tenths of pain is mental, not physical, induced by fear and removable by fearlessness. Timelessness means fearlessness and painlessness.

The Buddhist word for timelessness is *nirvana*. It means, literally, "extinction". Yet Buddha said of it not that "it is not" but that "it *is* . . . there *is*. O monks, an unborn. . . . If there were not, then no escape could be shown for what is here born."[40] What is extinguished in *nirvana* is *samsara,* which means birth and death, coming into being and passing away—in other words, time. *Nirvana* is bliss because by extinguishing time it extinguishes desire *(tanha)* and by extinguishing desire it extinguishes fear.

[39] Cf. Jacob Needleman, *The New Religions* (New York: Pocket Books, 1972), pp. 143–163.

[40] E. A. Burtt, *The Teachings of the Compassionate Buddha,* p. 113.

To Westerners, whether secular or religious, this seems more negative than positive. The price of *nirvana* is the extinction of the individual self, its desires and its hopes. It sounds like spiritual euthanasia, curing the disease of egotism by surgically removing the patient's ego.

Whether or not it is what it seems, it is not the Western road. Whether the Western road is better or just different, it is different. Whether the Eastern road is true or not, that is, whether it leads to the true God or not, I cannot know, for I do not walk that road. Those who have walked both roads come back with widely different reports: Some say they lead to the same place; some say they do not.[41] I think we are not told about others' roads for the same reason Jesus did not satisfy the disciples' curiosity about the comparative population statistics of heaven and hell when they asked, "Are few saved?" He replied simply, "Strive to enter in."[42] Bud-

[41] There seem to be three positions on this issue (as on most issues):

1. essential oneness, represented by such writers as Aldous Huxley *(The Perennial Philosophy)*, Huston Smith *(Forgotten Truth)*, Frithjof Schuon, and the middle period of Alan Watts *(The Supreme Identity)*;

2. essential otherness, represented by such writers as the later Alan Watts *(Beyond Theology)*, R. C. Zaehner *(The Comparison of Religions)*, D. T. Suzuki *(Mysticism East and West)*, G. K. Chesterton *(Orthodoxy)*, and Teilhard de Chardin, all coming to this conclusion from different and even mutually opposed starting points;

3. a middle position, represented by such writers as the early Alan Watts *(Behold the Spirit)*, Raymond Panikkar *(The Unknown Christ of Hinduism)*, Dom Bede Griffeths *(Christ in India)*, Dom Aelred Graham *(Zen Catholicism)*, and Thomas Merton.

[42] Luke 13:24.

dha, too, refused to answer merely speculative questions, "questions not tending to edification".[43]

Our road is forward, not backward; that much is certain. In Genesis God sent the seraphim with the flaming sword to bar Adam and Eve from returning to Eden once they had fallen. Their road to God is now ahead, "east of Eden",[44] through the world of time and history and struggle and suffering and death. Our "home is behind the world ahead".[45] You can go home, but "you can't go home again". No return to the womb. Ejected from Eden's eastern gate, we travel through and around the world, from west to east, forever seeking the rising sun (the Rising Son!) and find him standing at the western gate of Eden, saying, "I am the door."[46] The man who claimed to be God stood there neck-deep in the river of history and called out from the moving molecules of a human mouth, "Before Abraham was, I AM . . . I am the way, the truth, and the life; no man comes to the Father but by me."[47]

Through the Incarnation the eternal God has added time to his nature by adding humanity to divinity; and we are invited to enter divinity not stripped of our humanity and temporality but clothed with it. Our

[43] E. A. Burtt, *The Teachings of the Compassionate Buddha,* pp. 32–36.

[44] Gen 3:24, 4:16.

[45] This is a providentially apt misreading of the hobbits' walking song at the beginning of Tolkien's *Lord of the Rings,* resulting from only a comma being overlooked. The original reads, "Home is behind, the world ahead." J. R. R. Tolkien, *The Fellowship of the Ring* (New York: Ballantine Books, 1965), p. 115.

[46] John 10:7.

[47] John 14:6.

whole world "groans and travails" with us and is redeemed with us.[48] God does not fish us out of the sea of
time; his hook is wide enough to catch the whole sea.
Our destiny is to be in Christ, with two natures, not
Brahma, with one only. Eastern mysticism sees our
identity as merely divine and eternal; Western secularism
sees it as merely human and temporal; and Christianity
insists on the paradox of the two natures in one person.
The christological creeds are formulas for *our* nature and
destiny. God fell in love with us creatures of time, us
passing gusts of wind, us passing guests, and invited us
into the inner sanctum of the Master of the House
forever—all of us, lock, stock, and barrel full of time.
How dare we deny him his heart's desire? It is our heart's
desire too.

Why Heaven Is Not Boring

When we read our hearts, we find a picture of heaven
that has two natures, like Christ: temporal and eternal.
This is the clue to solve an absolutely crucial problem
that has vitiated the hope for heaven in the modern
world. The problem is not doubt so much as dullness,
not disbelief but disinterest. Most of us are not unbelievers; we are ready to believe almost anything that
turns us on; in fact, we are far *too* credulous. But heaven
will not turn us on if our head's picture of heaven does
not meet our heart's needs.

The popular head picture of heaven is one of
changeless perfection, sometimes in imagery of harps,
halos, and clouds, sometimes in imageless concepts of

[48] Rom. 8:22.

abstract spirituality. That may be heaven for angels, but it's more like hell for humans.

In reaction to this boring picture, modern thinkers often substitute a picture of endless progress. Lessing, for example, sounds the typically modern note (quoted approvingly by Kierkegaard) when he says, "If God held all Truth concealed in his right hand and in his left hand the persistent striving for the Truth, and while warning me against eternal error should say: "Choose!" I should humbly bow before his left hand and say, "Father, give thy gift: the pure Truth is for thee alone."[49] In other words, it is better to travel hopefully than to arrive.

No, it is not. C. S. Lewis demolishes this popular fallacy at one short stroke: "If that were true, and known to be true, how could we ever travel hopefully? There would be nothing to hope for."[50] Everyone now reading this book, sitting, standing, or lying down, is living testimony to the fact that we do *not* believe it is better to travel hopefully than to arrive, for we are not traveling now; we are staying put because we think it is better to have arrived.

But this arrival is only temporary; we get up again and move on. The dilemma stands: Is heaven mountain climbing or the view from the top? Frustrating or boring? Climbing is fun, but endless climbing is frustrating; we would be sometimes arriving home. But "home"

---

[49] Sören Kierkegaard, "Theses Attributable to Lessing", *Concluding Unscientific Postscript,* in *A Kierkegaard Anthology,* ed. Robert Bretall (New York: Modern Library, 1936), from Lessing, *Werke,* vol. 10, p. 53.

[50] C. S. Lewis, *The Great Divorce* (New York: Macmillan, 1946), p. 42.

soon becomes "domestication", and we seek new adventures. The most boring part of the fairy tale is the last, spectacularly unsuccessful line: "They all lived happily ever after." No one has ever described that happiness so as to satisfy the heart.

Perhaps we can find an answer in that most philosophical ditty, "The Bear Went over the Mountain": climb another mountain instead of sitting endlessly on the top. But this won't do either, for then each additional mountain becomes just one more foothill or bend in the road up the one overall mountain. We want to *arrive*. Yet we want to arrive at heaven, not Philadelphia. The question remains: How can heaven not be boring?

There are six things to be said in answer. The first is the longest, though its point can be put in one sentence: The point (eternity) is off the line (time), not one of the many moving points on it. It is transcendent. But it is also immanent in the whole line; in fact, it *is* the whole line looked at end-on. This is why God's eternal eye looking at our lives end-on from the point of their consummated perfection can say to us radically imperfect creatures in time: "Behold, you are all fair, my love; there is no spot or wrinkle in you." He is not speaking of what we are now, but neither is he speaking merely of what we will be, but about the whole of us, our lives as a whole. Only eternity sees time as a whole. Time is life spilled out, like a bucket of water spilled on the ground. Eternity is the togetherness of all the water in the bucket. It is time come home. Boethius gave the classic definition of eternity as "the whole, perfect and simultaneous possession of endless life".[51]

From this God's-eye point of view, "all things work

[51] Boethius, *The Consolation of Philosophy,* trans. Richard Green (Indianapolis: The Library of Liberal Arts, 1962), p. 115: "only that

together for good for those who love God, those who are called according to his purpose."[52] Nothing is missing; nothing is lost; nothing goes down the drain:

> I announce to you redemption. Behold I make all things new. Behold I do what cannot be done. I restore the years that the locusts and worms have eaten. I restore the years which you have drooped away upon your crutches and in your wheel-chair. I restore the symphonies and operas which your deaf ears have never heard, and the snowy massif your blind eyes have never seen, and the freedom lost to you through plunder, and the identity lost to you because of calumny and the failure of justice; and I restore the good which your own foolish mistakes have cheated you of. And I bring you to the Love of which all other loves speak, the Love which is joy and beauty, and which you have sought in a thousand streets and for which you have wept and clawed your pillow.[53]

We can't see that yet; our lives are not yet one, whole, finished. But we can believe it even though we do not see it because God tells us so. From eternity we appear "all fair", and though we do not see from eternity, God does and tells us, and we can at least *believe* from eternity. And as eternity itself includes all time, our vision of eternity includes a new vision of time, works backwards: "both good and evil, when they are full grown, become retrospective . . . all their earthly past will have been heaven to those who are saved . . . all their life on earth too will then be seen by the damned to have been hell."[54]

---

which comprehends and possesses the whole plentitude of endless life together, from which no future thing nor any past thing is absent, can justly be called eternal."

[52] Rom. 8:28.

[53] Thomas Howard, *Christ the Tiger,* p. 159.

[54] C. S. Lewis, *The Great Divorce,* p. 67.

Eternity includes time because it is the fifth dimension. A line includes points; a surface includes lines; a solid body includes surfaces; and motion through time includes solid bodies moving. As the fourth dimension includes the third, the fifth includes the fourth.

This is not merely a philosophical curiosity but has practical, personal application. It makes eternity interesting, not boring. The square walls of a house are rather boring when flat and detached from the house. But when the two-dimensional walls are part of the three-dimensional house, they come alive. And the three-dimensional house itself comes alive as part of someone's four-dimensional lifetime. Our four-dimensional lifetimes are the walls of our five-dimensional heavenly house.

Another application is this: Since eternity includes all time, it includes both the future with its newness and fascination and the past with its unchangeable security. That's why two opposite roads lead to it and why we experience it as "beauty so ancient and so new".

It also explains why it fulfills both the opposite desires of the heart. On the one hand, it is not boring because it is a drama to be lived, not a static, dead, or abstract thing like the past: "You cannot know eternal reality by a definition. Time, and all the events in time, are the definition and it must be lived."[55] On the other hand, it is not insecure or frustrating; it is not a future to be grasped at and missed, for it is an inviolable fact, already there in God's unchangeable plan. It is like the present experience of the Christian, both already redeemed and in the process of being redeemed, both eternally secure

[55] Ibid., p. 125.

and battling in "fear and trembling", both "working out your own salvation" and knowing that "it is God that is at work in you, both to will and to work".[56] It is like that because it is that.

Eternity including all time, both past and future, also explains the paradoxical experience of joy as both a standstill shock, as if time were frozen, and a rush forward with unimaginable energy, as if we were speeding to the very edge or end of time. At its height, this speedy time becomes one with frozen time; super-speeded time becomes superseded time; and the two temporal images of eternity meet: "if movement is faster, then that which moves is more nearly in two places at once . . . but if the movement were faster still . . . you see that if you made it faster and faster, in the end the moving thing would be in all places at once. . . . Well, then, that is the thing at the top of all bodies—so fast that it is at rest, so truly body that it has ceased being body at all."[57]

This casts new light on God's omnipresence: It is not static but dynamic, more like energy than like space. Nothing physical can move faster than light. But God moves faster than light and thus is in all places simultaneously, for God is spirit. Spirit moves with infinite speed.

Our spirit too moves with infinite speed. Thought takes no time to travel from mind to mind. The more spiritual any act is, therefore, the faster it is. The adoration of God is faster, and therefore more omnipresent,

[56] Phil. 2:12.
[57] C. S. Lewis, *Out of the Silent Planet* (New York: Macmillan, 1965), p. 94.

than thoughts derived from sense perception. When the psalmist calls on all creation to praise the Lord, it is not just pious sentiment but accurate metaphysics. Praise is omnipresent.

An act of spirit is so fast that time stops. But the *act* does not stop; it is not static or frozen. It is *time* that stops. For it was time that made the act less than infinitely active; it was time that made it somewhat static, somewhat past. To be infinitely dynamic, an act must transcend time.

Perhaps the Western vision of time as a line and the Eastern vision of time as a circle are not contradictory after all if the two ends of the line touch at eternity. Time *is* a line, as the West knows, progressing in a single direction from past to future, from birth to death, from creation to the end of the world, from a real and absolute beginning to a real and absolute ending. But that beginning and ending are one: the God who calls himself both alpha and omega.[58] From his point of view all the line is simultaneously present, and it is a circle because he touches its two ends together; he is the oneness of the beginning and the end.

We see time as a bloodstream of life and history pumped from the eternal heart of God. It flows from that heart through the arteries of the past and it returns through the veins of the future. All of history is a metaphysical circulatory system, with God at its heart. But our hearts, made in his image, also transcend time. The rest of us lies somewhere along the system, but our hearts are "at home with the Lord".[59] That is why they pull us home.

[58] Rev. 22:13.
[59] 2 Cor. 5:8.

Or, to change the metaphor, we are like trees rooted in the rock of eternity even as all our visible parts, trunk (ego, identity), branches (faculties), and leaves (actions) wave in the winds of time. We already have eternity in our hearts but find none in our world. We seek a mate fit for us, a corresponding eternity to love, as Adam sought an equal, not an animal, to marry.[60] We are not satisfied by the animal in us or in each other. We seek a not-spilled-out eternity in the other to be a fit mate for the not-spilled-out eternity in our own hearts. "Deep calleth unto deep."[61]

We find this in other people, but we find its source in God. The images lead us back to their model. *That* is why "our hearts are restless until they rest in thee". *That* is why "there comes a time when one asks even of Shakespeare, even of Beethoven, is this all?"[62]

Another reason we need the original eternity in God, not just the derived eternity in each other, is that we are not just individuals but a race, with a real unity, like a tree, a body, or a family. And the human race as a whole is lonely and unfulfilled unless it has a divine lover. If there is no God, we transcend individual egotism only to find racial egotism. The whole tree of human time longs for the eternal sun.

That was all part of the first answer to why heaven's eternity is not boring. There are five parts to come, but they are all shorter and simpler. (Nothing is more riddled with riddles than time and eternity.)

A second answer is that eternity is not changelessness

[60] Gen. 2:18–25.

[61] Ps. 42:7.

[62] Aldous Huxley, quoted in Huston Smith, *The Religions of Man* (New York: Harper & Row, 1958), p. 25.

(which *is* boring) because changelessness means time passes while nothing changes. Heaven is like Rivendell, "the Last Homely House" in *The Lord of the Rings:* "Time doesn't seem to pass here; it just *is.* A remarkable place altogether!"[63] Eternity is not a million years or a trillion millennia; it is not an unending line but a point.

The third answer explains the mistake of "better to travel hopefully than to arrive". This can be said only if we conceive of the end—truth, goodness, beauty, eternity, or heaven—as static and abstract rather than dynamic and concrete. It is not eternity but time that is abstract, as a surface is an abstract aspect of a concrete three-dimensional solid, and the solid itself is an abstract aspect of a historical event in which it is involved. There is a dialog between a confused ghost from hell and a heavenly spirit who is trying to teach him about the concreteness of eternity in C. S. Lewis' *The Great Divorce.*

> "Will you come with me to the mountains?"
>
> "I should require some assurances . . . an atmosphere of free inquiry . . ."
>
> "No . . . no atmosphere of inquiry, for I will bring you to the land not of questions but of answers, and you shall see the face of God."
>
> "Ah, but . . . for me there is no such thing as a final answer . . . you must feel yourself that there is something stifling about the idea of finality . . . what is more soul-destroying than stagnation?"
>
> "You think that, because hitherto you have experienced truth only with the abstract intellect. I will bring

[63] J. R. R. Tolkien, *The Fellowship of the Ring,* p. 305.

you where you can taste it like honey and be embraced by it as by a bridegroom. Your thirst will be quenched."[64]

A fourth, related answer uses the distinction between two activities of the will: desiring an absent good and rejoicing in a present good.[65] The latter is just as active as the former. Thus once heaven is attained, the will does not rest, in boredom. Nor does it work, in frustration. It rejoices, in play. Contemplation has traditionally been symbolized by play; divine Wisdom is pictured in Scripture as playing before God's face.[66] Work is like a river running to the sea; rest is like a calm sea; play is like a river running *from* the sea, or a great storm on the sea. Work is like filling an empty pail; rest is like a full, quiet pool; play is like an overflowing fountain.

Play images heaven by transcending time; it doesn't matter how long it takes because it has no goal beyond its own activity. It is not like climbing a mountain; it is like just walking or exploring or breathing or singing; better yet, it is *living*—you are quite happy never to come to the end.

But all play on earth eventually does get boring and we are happy to come to the end—if the play object is something finite and physical. But of an infinite object we neither can nor wish to come to the end:

> God, how hard it is to grasp your thoughts!
> How impossible to count them!

[64] C. S. Lewis, *The Great Divorce*, pp. 42–44.
[65] Aquinas, *Summa Theologiae*, Ia–IIae, 3, 4.
[66] Wisdom of Sirach 24:15. Cf. Josef Pieper, *Leisure the Basis of Culture* (New York: New American Library, 1964).

I could no more count them than I could the sand,
and suppose I could, you would still be with me.[67]

A fifth answer is that heaven is not static or boring because it is not the end but the beginning, not the evening but the morning, not a warm, womblike bath but a cold, birthlike shower. C. S. Lewis notes that every great tale is fascinating in its beginning, for the beginning touches something timeless that no events in time can grasp: "The grand idea of finding Atlantis which stirs us in the first chapter of the adventure story is apt to be frittered away in mere excitement when the journey has once been begun. . . . In real life, as in a story . . . we grasp at a state and find only a succession of events in which the state is never quite embodied. The titles of some stories illustrate the point very well. *The Well at the World's End*—can a man write a story to that title?"[68] Lewis's improvement on "they all lived happily ever after" is his heavenly conclusion to *The Last Battle* in the *Chronicles of Narnia:*

"You do not yet look so happy as I mean you to be."

Lucy said, "We're so afraid of being sent away, Aslan. And you have sent us back into our own world so often."

"No fear of that", said Aslan. "Have you not guessed?"

Their hearts leaped and a wild hope rose within them.

"There *was* a real railway accident," said Aslan softly.

"Your father and mother and all of you are—as you used to call it in the Shadow-Lands—dead. The term is over;

[67] Ps. 139:18 (JB).
[68] C. S. Lewis, "On Stories", in *Of Other Worlds* (New York: Harcourt, Brace & World, 1966), p. 20.

the holidays have begun. The dream is ended; this is the morning."

And as He spoke He no longer looked to them like a lion; but the things that began to happen after that were so great and beautiful that I cannot write them. And for us this is the end of all the stories, and we can most truly say that they all lived happily ever after. But for them it was only the beginning of the real story. All their life in this world and all their adventures in Narnia had only been the cover and the title page; now at last they were beginning Chapter One of the Great Story, which no one on earth has read, which goes on for ever, in which every chapter is better than the one before.[69]

Finally, a sixth answer is that even in our present experience we find two heavenly things that are not boring, two prophets or messengers ("angels") from heaven that have infinite depth so we can always experience something new in exploring them. They are wisdom and love. By wisdom I mean not just knowledge but understanding, and by love I mean not just liking but self-giving, "charity", *agapē*. These are the two things in our lives that are of heavenly substance, that are eternal, that are never boring, and that are stronger than death.

They are also the two values taught by all great sages, saints, philosophers, mystics, and resuscitated patients who catch a glimpse of heaven.[70] They say they will devote the rest of their lives to these two things, the only things that stand as absolutes in a world of petty though

[69] C. S. Lewis, *The Last Battle* (New York: Macmillan, 1956), pp. 173–174.

[70] Raymond A. Moody, Jr., *Life after Life* (New York: Bantam Books, 1976), pp. 88–93.

pretty relativities. The heavenly vision has clarified their perspective in this world, taught a heavenly model for earthly life. They know what it means to pray, "Thy Kingdom (= wisdom and love) come, Thy will be done on earth *as it is in heaven.*"

The life of heaven is the inexhaustible fountain of God's thought and God's love; how could it be boring? Time spilled out is the condition for boredom, and there time is swallowed up in eternity. Here eternity is usually swallowed up in time. But when we touch eternity in time, we smell the salt air of the sea even here, far upstream in time's river. Whenever we touch wisdom or love, we swim in salt water. Earth is God's beach, and when we are wise and loving, we are infants splashing happily in the wavelets of "that immortal sea".[71] But when we are spiritually full grown, gods and goddesses, we will buoyantly plow its breakers of wisdom and be borne up by its bottomless depths of love. Boredom, like pain, will be remembered only as a joke when we are "drenched in joy".[72]

---

[71] Wordsworth, "Intimations of Immortality from Recollections of Early Childhood".

[72] C. S. Lewis, "Man or Rabbit?" in *God in the Dock* (Grand Rapids, Mich.: Eerdmans, 1970), p. 112.

Chapter 3

The Place of the Quest:
Earth Haunted by Heaven

Have you ever felt it—the haunting of the world? You feel it with your "haunt detector". It is part of your heart. We have many different built-in detectors; we are instinctive detectives. Our five outer senses detect colors, shapes, sizes, sounds, smells, tastes, textures, heat, and many other things. But we have inner senses too. For instance, we have truth detectors and lie detectors, love detectors and hate detectors, beauty detectors and ugliness detectors, and right and wrong detectors (usually called "consciences"). These inner senses vary more from individual to individual than the outer senses do; for instance, a naive person's lie detector is insensitive and easily fooled, and a saint's conscience is more sensitive than a sadist's. So too with our haunt detector; everyone has one, but some are more sensitive than others.

The haunting has been called the sense of the "numinous".[1] It is the sense that the world we see is haunted by something we do not see, an unseen presence. It often inspires awe and fear because it is not humanly predictable and controllable, not definable and tameable. It seems to come from another dimension, another *kind* of reality, than the world it haunts. It is the

[1] Cf. Rudolf Otto, *The Idea of the Holy,* trans. John W. Harvey (New York: Oxford University Press, 1958).

primitive wonder that is the source of fairy tales and myths and also of the instinct to worship.[2] We invent preternatural or supernatural objects to incarnate it— elves and wizards and fairies, gods and goddesses—but none of them is *it*. We cannot objectify it. It seems to be behind us all the time; and when we turn to try to catch it, it disappears from view because it remains behind us even as we turn, like the back of our own head. Perhaps one day we will meet it (or its source) face to face; if we do, we will recognize it as an old friend/enemy/play-fellow/tease/lover: "So it was you all the time!" Above all, we long for it. Though we fear it, we love it. We are possessed by its magic, but we do not possess it. "You have never *had* it. All the things that have ever deeply possessed your soul have been but hints of it—tantalising glimpses, promises never quite fulfilled, echoes that died away just as they caught your ear. But if it should really become manifest—if there ever came an echo that did not die away but swelled into the sound itself—you would know it. Beyond all possibility of doubt you would say "Here at last is the thing I was made for."[3]

[2] Cf. G. K. Chesterton, *Orthodoxy* (New York: Dodd, Mead & Co., 1957), pp. 95–96: "This elementary wonder, however, is not a mere fancy derived from the fairy tales; on the contrary, all the fire of the fairy tales is derived from this. Just as we all like love tales because there is an instinct of sex, we all like astonishing tales because they touch the nerve of the ancient instinct of astonishment. This is proved by the fact that when we are very young children we do not need fairy tales: we only need tales. Mere life is interesting enough. A child of seven is excited by being told that Tommy opened a door and saw a dragon. But a child of three is excited by being told that Tommy opened a door."

[3] C. S. Lewis, *The Problem of Pain* (New York: Macmillan, 1946), p. 146.

The Haunting in the Human Face

One of the places we see it most strikingly is in the human face. The face is the most numinous, most magical matter in the world. For the surface of the face, like the appearance of the world, points beyond itself, beyond the surface to the depths—depths not of matter but of meaning. It cries out, "What you see is only a facade, the face of the deep, worlds within worlds." It points to "the beyond within".

The face is like a poem: it *means*. Archibald MacLeish wrote, "A poem must not mean but be."[4] Whatever he may have meant, the statement as it stands is absurd. A poem cannot merely *be,* as an object in the world, "palpable and mute as a globed fruit",[5] and still be a poem. It must mean as well as be; and if it is to be a good poem, its being must be part of its meaning, that is, it must exemplify what it means. For instance, the *Tao Te Ching,* that great Chinese classic *(ching)* about the power *(te)* of the Way *(Tao),* itself has great power. A poem about beauty must itself be beautiful. And a face, like a poem, must both be and mean, and must incarnate in its being what it means. A smile both is and means happiness; the word "happiness" only means it. There is no happiness *in* the word, as there is in the smile.

The magic of the face is that mind rules matter here. A human face is more than a part of the body, an object; it is a part of the soul, a subject, an *I*. It is the place where soul still transfigures body as its Creator designed it to. It is the part of the body most unaffected by the

4 "Ars Poetica", in *The Collected Poems of Archibald MacLeish* (Boston: Houghton Mifflin, 1917).
5 Ibid.

Fall—Eden's souvenir, the reminder that matter was once perfectly transparent to mind, obedient to the soul as the soul was obedient to God. When the soul rebelled against God, the body rebelled against the soul, for the soul's power over the body was a delegated power. The face is also our foretaste of the undoing of the Fall, when this power hierarchy will be restored: our resurrection bodies, our heavenly bodies will be all face.

Even infants detect the haunting in the face. Without language, without teaching, without acculturation, they instinctively know the meaning of a smile, a frown, an angry shout. They detect spirit, not just matter. Physiology no more explains it than you can explain the Mona Lisa by counting the dots of color.[6]

Adults, as well as infants, have face haunt detectors. Unless we are professionally committed to objectifying the face—unless we are beauty contest judges or plastic surgeons—we do not look merely at a face but along it. We follow the haunting.

But the whole world sometimes seems to be a face! And our "haunt detector" looks along the world-face at . . . what? What does everything point to? Whose face is it? Who haunts there?

To unsheet the ghost, to identify the culprit, let's gather more clues. There are other hauntings—one in particular that is even more fascinating than the human face. It is romantic love.

The Haunting in Romantic Love

Like the human face, romantic love is only a small part of the world but at the same time a symbol of some-

[6] The illustration is Bergson's, quoted by C. S. Lewis in *Miracles* (New York: Macmillan, 1955), p. 117.

thing true of the whole world. This particular fact has a cosmic meaning. It is like a sacrament in that way: a special sign of a general truth, a local reminder of a universal reality. The face is a very small part of the world. Less than a millionth, less than a billionth, of all the matter in the world is spiritualized in all the human faces in the world. Yet this small reminder symbolizes the whole world; the whole world is a face. Romantic love is almost as small, almost as rare a part of life as the face is a rare part of the world, as rare in time as the face is rare in space. For only a minority of cultures and a minority of individuals experience it, and even then it is usually fleeting, rarely lasting a lifetime.[7] Yet it is a cosmic epiphany, a powerful signal of "what it's all about", a lighthouse beacon from far across the waves of the world, a clue to the world's haunting.

Romantic love is not just a private experience between two lovers or *in* two lovers. For the beloved is seen not as one object among many in the universe but as the center of the universe, not as a point within the whole but as the point from which the whole flowers out. Alan Watts says, "The universe *humans* as a rosebush flowers."[8] The beloved appears as the universal rose.

Just as the face is the place where the person comes to revelation, comes to a point, so the beloved is the place where the universe comes to a point, the tip of the cosmic pen, the point of it all. As the face is the epiph-

[7] Cf. Denis de Rougemont, *Love in the Western World,* trans. M. Belgion (New York: Pantheon, 1956). But for a counterexample, cf. Sheldon Vanauken, *A Severe Mercy* (San Francisco: Harper & Row, 1977).

[8] Alan Watts, *The Joyous Cosmology* (New York: Vintage Books, 1965).

any of the person, the person is the epiphany of the universe, the universe's face as seen by the "haunt detector" called romantic love.

Even more than a revelation, it is an invitation, an RSVP, a call to "come further up and further in", to enter this "beyond within" that is "larger on the inside than on the outside".[9] The beloved appears as a passageway, a birth canal, a magic doorway, a hole through the world into other worlds, like birth and death;[10] and we are invited to pass through.

Let us look again at history's great paradigm of romantic love, Dante's love for Beatrice, to see this invitation. Beatrice appeared to Dante as an image of God, a mirror of Godlight. Beatrice became the outline, the shape of that Godlight. God appeared to Dante as a Beatrice-shaped glory. Yet Beatrice was not obliterated by the divine light. Dante did not merely pass *through* Beatrice to God; he found God *in* Beatrice. He did not love Beatrice less because he loved God more, just as another poet could say, "I could not love thee, dear, so much/ Loved I not honour more."[11]

In fact, the divine glory is so much *in* the beloved as well as shining *through* her that it is quite easy to idolize her. Dante was clear that God, not Beatrice, was his

[9] C. S. Lewis, *The Last Battle* (New York: Macmillan, 1956), ch. 25 and p. 133: "In our world too, a Stable once had something inside it that was bigger than our whole world. . . . Its inside is bigger than its outside."

[10] Cf. Peter Kreeft, *Love Is Stronger than Death* (San Francisco: Harper & Row, 1979), ch. 4, "Death as a Mother".

[11] Richard Lovelace, "To Lucasta, Going to the Wars", in *The Poems of Richard Lovelace,* ed. C. H. Wilkinson (Oxford: Clarendon Press, 1953).

ultimate beloved and his ultimate lover; but other romantic lovers often lack his clearsightedness and idolize their earthly beloved, not realizing that what attracts in her comes from beyond her, like light reflected in a mirror. The primal light, the attracting magnet, the haunter, is God seen "through a glass, darkly" in the finite form of the earthly beloved.

The ordinary romantic lover even more frequently misses a second, equally crucial point: Not only the beloved but everyone, even "ordinary" people, are such mirrors reflecting God. C. S. Lewis did not miss that point:

> It is a serious thing to live in a society of possible gods and goddesses, to remember that the dullest and most uninteresting person you can talk to may one day be a creature which, if you saw it now, you would be strongly tempted to worship, or else a horror and a corruption such as you now meet, if at all, only in a nightmare. All day long we are, in some degree, helping each other to one or other of these destinations. . . . There are no *ordinary* people. You have never talked to a mere mortal. Nations, cultures, arts, civilisations—these are mortal, and their life is to ours as the life of a gnat. But it is immortals whom we joke with, work with, marry, snub, and exploit—immortal horrors or everlasting splendours.[12]

Because romantic lovers usually miss these two points—that romantic love points beyond itself to God and beyond the beloved to all people—because romantic lovers seek joy *in* rather than through their loves, and

[12] C. S. Lewis, *The Weight of Glory* (New York: Macmillan, 1949), pp. 14–15.

only in their loves, they are always disappointed. Because romantic love is only a prophet, it breaks when turned into a god. Once idolized, the idol shatters. The worst disaster that can happen to romantic love is success. Once the beauty of the beloved is grasped, it disappears, like the rainbow or like light. The divine light cannot be trapped in the human mirror, only reflected. It lives only *en passant,* in passing. Try to bottle the light and you get only darkness.

The transcendent longing that inspired the romantic lover to jettison all prudence and calculation for the ecstasy of union with the beloved is always in the long run disappointed by that union. When the love is romantic and not merely physical, when it moves the lover from out of the heavenly beauty of the beloved and not merely from the earthly appetites of the lover, it always promises more than it can possibly deliver. It promises ecstasy; it delivers only intense pleasure. It promises a standing outside the self (this is what "ecstasy" literally means), a self-transcendence, a death and resurrection of the ego, a mystical transformation. But it delivers only a tiny intimation of this at best, which only whets the appetite for the real thing. C. S. Lewis "came to know by experience that it [our 'it', this desire we are exploring, which Lewis calls 'Joy'] is not a disguise of sexual desire. Those who think that if adolescents were all provided with suitable mistresses we should soon hear no more of 'immortal longings' are certainly wrong. I learned this mistake to be a mistake by the simple, if discreditable, process of repeatedly making it."[13]

[13] C. S. Lewis, *Surprised by Joy* (New York: Harcourt, Brace & World, 1955), p. 169.

Why do we keep repeating the mistake? Why do many people go through an endless succession of earthly loves (of persons or even of things) even after repeated experience tells them they are always disappointed? Pascal says, "A test which has gone on so long, without pause or change, really ought to convince us that . . . the infinite abyss can be filled only with an infinite and immutable object, in other words with God himself."[14] We keep trying despite repeated failures because we're looking for God. We can't help it; we have to have him. But we look in the wrong places. "Seek what you seek but not where you seek it", advises Saint Augustine.[15]

What we seek is joy, even when we don't know where it is. Aquinas says, "No one can live without delight and that is why a man deprived of spiritual joy goes over to carnal pleasures."[16] As C. S. Lewis puts it, "Joy is not a substitute for sex; sex is very often a substitute for joy. I sometimes wonder whether all pleasures are not substitutes for Joy."[17] Sheldon Vanauken says,

> Secretly we are all perhaps the Questing Knight. And yet, whatever the object of our quest, we learn when we find it that it does not ever contain *the* joy that broke our heart with longing. Thus, says Lewis, "if a man diligently followed this desire, pursuing the false objects until their falsity appeared and then resolutely abandon-

[14] Pascal, *Pensées,* 148, trans. A. J. Krailsheimer (New York: Penguin Books, 1966), pp. 74–75.

[15] Augustine, *Confessions,* IV. 12.

[16] Aquinas, *Summa Theologiae,* IIa–IIae, 35. 4, ad 2. *St. Thomas Aquinas: Philosophical Texts,* trans. Thomas Gilby (New York: Oxford University Press, 1960), p. 275.

[17] C. S. Lewis, *Surprised by Joy,* p. 170.

ing them, he must come out at last into the clear knowledge that the human soul was made to enjoy some object
that is never fully given—nay, cannot even be imagined
as given—in our present mode of subjective and spatio-
temporal experience. This, I think, is what C. S. Lewis'
life and writings are about; and mine, too.

Make it three.

I came to wonder whether *all* the objects that men and
women set their hearts upon, even the darkest and most
obsessive desires, do not begin as intimations of joy
from the sole spring of joy, God. One man's intimation
of joy through beauty may lead him to painting and
thence, the beauty half-forgotten, to advocacy of
nothing more than an artistic fashion; or that same desire
to be one with beauty may lead another man to cut-
throat art collecting or to flamboyant, Wildean excesses
in his personal life. Someone else may link the joy with a
glimpse of heavenly justice and then be led into law or
perhaps communism, justice in the end forgotten. . . .
The priest's vocation may spring from his glimpse of
God as joy, but that vocation may become episcopal
politics, God mouthed and forgotten. Even a Hitler may
begin with a longing for joy through peace and order.[18]

An image can easily become an idol, and romantic
love is an unusually powerful idol because it is such a
powerful image. We expect divine joy from this human
experience; that's why it ends in such bitter disappointment. We have heaped on the shoulders of the human
beloved a burden of joy-making that only God can
carry, and we are scandalized when those shoulders
break.

[18] Vanauken, *A Severe Mercy*, pp. 207–208.

Romantic love is a powerful image of the love of God because, unlike lust, it does not desire a possessable and consumable thing (like a body). It wants not to possess but to be possessed, not by the beloved but by love itself, the reality *in* which both lovers stand. Why do we say we are "in love" rather than saying love is in us? Why did the ancients spontaneously see love as a god or goddess entering into us from without rather than as a human emotion arising from within? Why does the silly old Hollywood cliche, "It's bigger than both of us", seem not silly but profound to lovers? Because it (love) *is* "bigger than both of us", and our desire is to be possessed by the god of love by enacting the divine mystery of two becoming one. We want to be one with the human beloved *in* divine love. Romantic love is an infinite passion because it is an unconscious longing for the infinite God who *is* love.

It is also an unconscious love of heaven. This answers one of the greatest mysteries of love: Why does *this* person fall in love with *that* person and not another? Why does just *this* face, *those* eyes, move us as lovers, work wonders in our heart, seem to be one we were born desiring? Why do we recognize (*re*-cognize, re-member) the beloved's beauty as what we were looking for all our lives? Why does Romeo fall for Juliet, of all people? Antony for Cleopatra? What in the world does Joe see in Mary?

Nothing in the world. But what in heaven does Joe see in Mary? That's it: what in heaven?

To him that overcometh I will give a white stone, and in the stone a new name written, which no man knoweth saving he that receiveth it. What can be more a man's own than this new name which even in eternity remains a secret between God and him? And what shall we take this secrecy to mean? Surely, that each of the redeemed shall know and praise some one aspect of the divine beauty better than any other creature can. Why else were individuals created but that God, loving all infinitely, should love each differently?[19]

Because our heavenly destinies (the "many mansions" Jesus spoke of) and identities (the "white stone") are unique, we are each unique lovers of unique facets of the infinite divine diamond. The earthly beloved is the mirror of that facet, the image of that unique aspect of God that we were created to love and appreciate as no other creature can.

So when, as lovers, we are haunted by a face that is just ordinary to everyone else, we are being addressed by a prophet, a messenger from heaven. We should not mistake the prophet for the god, the mouthpiece for the mouth. If romantic love is a true prophet, it must point beyond itself. It must point, like John the Baptist, to the Messiah: "He must increase, I must decrease."[20]

The Haunting in Pictures, Stories, and Music

A much more widespread example of the haunting than romantic love or the human face is simply pictures. Everyone has looked at pictures, but not everyone has looked into pictures, just as everyone has looked at people but not everyone has looked into people, as a

---

[19] C. S. Lewis, *The Problem of Pain*, pp. 149–150.
[20] John 3:30.

spiritual master does.[21] Look into a picture some time—not at it as a framed object in the world, but through the frame into its world. See it not as an opaque thing, like a stained glass window, but as transparent, like a clear window—a magic window, like Alice's looking glass, that takes us into another world.

Most pictures take us out of our part of the world into other parts of the world, other places or times. Some pictures take us out of this world entirely into other worlds, worlds of the imagination. But "the imagination" is usually misunderstood. A great work of imaginative art is more than an external expression of an inner, subjective state of consciousness; it is *real*. Our subjective consciousness enters into it, lives in it, conforms to its truth. We are in it; it is not in us.

The little artist merely makes; the great artist discovers. Small art is conventional; it could have been different. But there is a necessity to a great work of art. It seems as if it was always there and the artist has only pulled back the curtain a bit to reveal it to the rest of us—like the Eskimo ivory carver who carved better bears than any white man because they all tried to make the ivory into a bear while the Eskimo saw the bear already in the ivory and merely chipped away all the ivory that wasn't a bear.

What is true of pictures is also true of stories, for stories are verbal pictures. They have the same power as pictures, sometimes more: a word can be worth a thousand pictures if it is the creative word of the poet. Stories take us into other worlds, other times and places, just as

---

[21] Cf. John 1:42; Mark 10:21; Luke 22:61.

pictures do. They point beyond themselves and invite us to follow.

There is a real magic to great pictures and stories. They not only present you with other worlds; they take you there. They not only bring their worlds to you; they bring you to them. They do something to you. "What can you do with art?" asks the practical parent of the college art major. "Maybe nothing", is the reply, "but art can do something with you". The same is true of literature. Stories practice what they preach (in that sense, they are eminently "practical"!); they do to you what they say to you. When you read the *Iliad,* where are you? If the story's magic works, you are not in twentieth-century America in a chair; you are with Achilles before the walls of ancient Troy. If the story succeeds, you look out of it; if it fails, you look into it. [22] The same is true of art. When you stand before Van Gogh's "Peasant Shoes", you do not stand before it but in it—in fact, in *them,* in those shoes. You feel the earth, your tired bones, and the dying of the light.

Pictures and stories in our world move us to other parts of our world or to other worlds. But the world as a whole seems to be a picture of something: what? Is matter a picture of spirit? All its life and all its history seem to be a story about something: what? Is time a story about eternity? (Plato called time the moving image of eternity.) [23]

Perhaps the most mysteriously moving of all earthly hauntings is music—so powerful, the ancients spon-

[22] Cf. J. R. R. Tolkien, "On Fairy Stories", in *A Tolkien Reader* (New York: Ballantine Books, 1966), p. 37.

[23] Plato, *Timaeus* 37d.

taneously ascribed it to gods (the Muses), not to human beings. I know three intelligent, sensitive souls who were saved from atheism and despair only by the music of Bach. No one can tell me music is mere aesthetic pleasure, bloom or ornament. It is a lifeline, a prophet, a divine haunting. If there is a Bach, there is a God.

All the hauntings seem to come from the same source and point back to it, however diverse the media through which they come. Not only faces, romantic love, pictures, stories, and music, but also the sense of unimaginably remote lands hinted at in the smell of certain breezes, the fascination children have with colors (remember?), the unforgettable power of certain lines of poetry—all these and thousands more are hauntings that seem to say the same thing: There is something bigger than the world out there hiding behind everything in the world, and our chief joy is with it. The world is its mask; we must unmask it. We are outsiders, aliens, exiles; if only we could get *in!*

What more, you may ask, do we want? Ah, but we want so much more—something the books on aesthetics take little notice of. But the poets and the mythologies know all about it. We do not want merely to *see* beauty, though, God knows, even that is bounty enough. We want something else which can hardly be put into words—to be united with the beauty we see, to pass into it, to receive it into ourselves, to bathe in it, to become part of it. . . . At present we are on the outside of the world, the wrong side of the door. We discern the freshness and purity of morning, but they do not make us fresh and pure. We cannot mingle with the splendours we see. But all the leaves of the New Testament are rustling with the rumour that it will not always be so.

Some day, God willing, we shall get *in* . . . in through Nature, beyond her, into that splendour which she fitfully reflects.[24]

The Meaning of the Haunting: Reading the Signs

If the whole world is a sign, let's read it. What does it signify? We don't have to read it. We can look *at* a sign instead of looking along it.[25] We can see signs merely as things. Medieval Western society habitually looked at the world as a sign, one of God's two books ("nature and Scripture"). But the modern world has conditioned us to what C. S. Lewis calls a doglike state of mind.[26] When you point to your dog's food, he sniffs your finger because he does not understand the significance of the sign. We can do the same with the world's fingers. In fact, finger sniffing is the fashionable mode of thought for "realistic", worldly modernity.

But there is a culturally independent child in us as well as a culturally conditioned adult. Children want to know "What's that?" and do not put limits on the kinds of answers they will accept, as modern adults do. Modernity *trusts* scientific explanations (you have to have faith in *something*); it feels they are the real, objective explanations and spiritual ones are subjective, private matters of opinion or products of the imagination.

This is a most unscientific superstition. To take the scientific method as the paradigm for all objectively true

[24] C. S. Lewis, *The Weight of Glory*, pp. 12–13.
[25] For this very useful distinction, cf. C. S. Lewis, "Meditation in a Toolshed", in *God in the Dock* (Grand Rapids, Mich.: Eerdmans, 1970).
[26] C. S. Lewis, "Transposition", in *The Weight of Glory*, p. 28.

knowledge is unscientific, for it cannot be proved by the scientific method! It is a dogma of faith, not a discovery of science, that only the discoveries of science are objectively true and not the dogmas of faith.

The scientific method confines itself, quite properly, to looking *at* the world-sign, not along it. Thus it finds a certain kind of truth, indeed; it is true that the sign on the street corner, for instance, is a rectangular piece of metal, twenty-four by three inches, with an arrow at one end and with eight letters and two numbers two inches high. But it is also more than that. (In fact, everything is "more than that", more than all the things we can say about it; "there are more things in heaven and earth than are dreamed of in your philosophies".[27]) It is a sign, and it means Boston is twenty miles in that direction.

As scientists we want to know what things are made of and how they work, but as human beings we want to know what things *are*—their meaning. If we are neurophysiologists, we must discover the laws of brain chemistry; but as human beings we must also wonder at the brain as evidencing astonishing intelligence in its design, far more complex and efficient than any computer. Does not the human brain shout the praise of a divine design? As scientists we ask only what the signs are made of and how they work; as human beings we read the signs. The scientist tells how the clock ticks; the human being tells the time.

Not everyone is a scientist, but everyone is a human being. Everyone therefore should read the signs, should ask what the world-sign signifies; and some people—the

[27] Shakespeare, *Hamlet,* act 3, scene 1.

scientists—should also look at it and say how the world-clock ticks. But our civilization has exactly reversed these priorities. Most people look at the world and only a few look along it. We think of science as basic knowledge and religion and philosophy as private luxuries. But suppose, as religion claims, that "human science is but the backward undoing of the tapestry-web of God's science", that "the idea of God *is* the flower; his idea is not the botany of the flower; its botany is but a thing of ways and means—of canvas and colour and brush in relation to the picture in the painter's brain."[28] In that case we would be missing what it *is* by locking the art of sign reading in the closet of subjectivity.

Let's be different. Let's try the thought-experiment of the child, asking "What's that?" and trying to read the world as a sign, asking deeper questions than merely what it looks like and how it works. Let's take the insanely sane risk of supposing the world means something and ask what.

To read the signs aright, we need some principles of sign reading. These must be realistic, that is, based on what signs really are. What are they? Signs are either natural or conventional. Conventional signs are made by people and could have been different-like the letters of the alphabet or the signals of a baseball team. Natural signs are found in nature, as smoke is a sign of fire or a smile of happiness. We cannot make them different.

Natural signs tell us more than conventional signs about what they signify because in a natural sign the thing signified is in some way really present, really

[28] George MacDonald in C. S. Lewis, *George MacDonald: An Anthology* (New York: Macmillan, 1978), no. 187, p. 81.

there, in the sign itself. Where there is smoke, there *is* fire. There *is* happiness in a smile, as there *is* not a curve ball in the catcher's two fingers signaling it. A natural sign is a living example of what it signifies; it effects what it signifies, like a sacrament. That is, it *works,* like real magic. (In fact, it *is* real magic. The whole world is full of real magic.)

If, as our thought-experiment suggests, the whole world is a sign, it must be a natural sign. Therefore, it has what it signifies; what it points to, beyond itself, is also here, in itself. And if what earth signifies is heaven, heaven is in some way present here and now, *in* the earth, as the sun is in the sunlight or health is in rosy cheeks. That does not mean heaven cannot also be transcendent. The sun is also more than all the sunbeams. What is here and now can also be there and then. The present heavenly seed can be part of the future heavenly flower.

In fact, heaven includes earth as the soul includes the body. My soul includes my body because it is my *me,* my personhood, and part of this is what I call "my" body. The material body cannot contain the immaterial soul (Where is it? In the pineal gland? All over? Do I lose part of my soul when I get a haircut?), but the soul is wide embracing enough to contain the body. Similarly, earth is too small to contain heaven (Where is it? In Disneyland?), but heaven is wide enough to contain earth.

Let's return to our principles of sign reading, our exploration of the relation between signs and things signified by them, to find out what earth tells us about heaven, supposing that it is heaven that earth's hauntings point to. Signs can also be divided into verbal and pictorial signs. Scripture is God's verbal sign, nature his pictorial sign. A principle of sign reading that applies to picture signs, or images, is that images are less than things imaged in three ways. First, things are more substantial than their images, more real. Images are "only" images. We can mistake images for things, as a child might be terrified of a picture of a wild animal, especially a moving picture. Second, things are multi-dimensional, while images usually have fewer dimensions. For instance, a flat, two-dimensional picture is an image of a solid, three-dimensional object; and an unmoving, three-dimensional statue is an image of a moving, four-dimensional person. Third, images are not as clear and detailed as things. No portrait can capture every pore of skin, every hair.

Now if earth is an image of heaven, we know at least three things about heaven. First, it is more real, more substantial than earth. We usually think of it as somehow thin, wispy, and cloudy. But it is earth that is as wispy as a wind, "like grass, that today is and tomorrow is cast into the oven".[29] Scripture's imagery corrects this popular fallacy, if unthinking familiarity has not dulled its instructive shock.

Second, this principle means heaven has more dimensions than earth, not fewer. There are important consequences of this, especially concerning matter and time. It means heaven is not merely spiritual, lacking the four dimensions of matter (three of space and one of time), and eternity includes rather than excludes all of time, as we have already seen.

Third, heaven is clearer, more detailed and specific

[29] Matt. 6:30.

than earth, not vaguer. It is "too definite for language".[30] That's why the mystics and the resuscitated say it is "ineffable".[31] Our *ideas* about heaven may be vague, insubstantial, and one-dimensional; but when we compare the real heaven with earth instead of comparing our ideas of heaven with earth, it is earth that is vague, insubstantial, and one-dimensional.

Not that earth is unreal. In itself it is real in all three of these ways, and *more* real than our thoughts of it. But it is less real than heaven, for it is heaven's image. It is no insult to earth to be told "You are only an image" because it is an image of the supremely real. Its function is the greatest imaginable: it is a prophet continually crying out "there's more" as our thoughts prophetically cry out that there's more, a whole world, beyond them. Good prophets do not point to themselves, nor do healthy thoughts, nor does the world. When we hear the prophet saying (however obscurely), "thus saith the Lord", we should not linger very long counting the prophet's teeth.

Heaven on Earth

The haunter, then, as well as the haunting, is here. The King has come as well as his kingdom. The thing pointed to by all the signs is both here and there, both now and then, both beyond the signs and in the signs. Heaven is incarnate.

To use that word is to suggest the Word himself. We

---

30 C. S. Lewis, *Perelandra* (New York: Macmillan, 1965), p. 33.

31 Raymond Moody, *Life after Life* (New York: Bantam Books, 1975), pp. 25–26.

may as well take our thought-experiment to its end and let the ultimate cat out of the proximate bag: It is Christ. Christ the Haunter, the incarnate divine Mind, the Logos. His dimensions are cosmic; they infinitely exceed those of the epidermis of a first-century Jewish carpenter, though that was the temple in which he resided here, the holy place. The divine Idea perfectly and completely expressed before the world was created, the divine Word that was the instrument creating the universe, the divine design reflected in all created order, finally focuses at this single point: a human individual who says "I am", claiming to be the divine I AM "before Abraham was".[32] All signs lead to him because all signs come from him.

It is only a thought-experiment, a hypothesis, a vision; I offer no proof. But it is an infinitely meaningful picture, either the greatest and deepest truth or the most colossal fake ever perpetrated, and we must look carefully before deciding.

One way of looking is to ask what new light this vision sheds on other things, on the world. We have used the world as a light to look at heaven; now let us use heaven as a light to look at the world. In this vision, what does the world look like? What difference does the Haunter make to the haunted world?

The whole world becomes God's mask, God's performance, God's act, God's pantomime. Like all good art, it both entertains and instructs; it offers both joy and wisdom and perhaps even (how awfully unfashionable!) moral lessons.

The whole world is a love letter. The haunting of

[32] John 8:58.

romantic love is the clue to the central theme of the story; it tells us the kind of story we're in. All artistry reflects the artist; and if God *is* love, then his world is the eternal love made visible in time. It is made of matter, but more fundamentally, it is made of love.

The whole world is a face. That haunting, too, is central. The world is not the impersonal machine it seems to be. Have you ever seen one of those picture puzzles that mask a face as jungle leaves or bushes? "Find the man in the picture." Once you do, the picture never looks the same again: it is not a jungle but a man. Once you see the face of God, the world is forever transformed into his features.

The whole world is a sacrament, an effective sign that makes really present what it signifies. The doctrine of the Real Presence of Christ in the Eucharist does not say too much, but too little; it can be extended to include the whole world. As Teilhard de Chardin says in *The Divine Milieu,* we should be able to hear from everything in the world the words "This is my Body."[33]

The transcendent is immanent, heaven is on earth, the

[33] Teilhard de Chardin, *The Divine Milieu* (New York: Harper & Row, 1965), pp. 123–126: "It is Christ whom we make or whom we undergo in all things. . . . When the priest says the words *Hoc est Corpus meum,* his words fall directly on to the bread and directly transform it into the individual reality of Christ. But the great sacramental operation does not cease at that local and momentary event. . . . As our humanity assimilates the material world, and as the Host assimilates our humanity, the eucharistic transformation goes beyond and completes the transubstantiation of the bread on the altar. . . . In a secondary and generalised sense, but in a true sense, the sacramental Species are formed by the totality of the world, and the duration of the creation is the time needed for its consecration."

beyond is within. What everything points to, what cannot be caught, confined, codified, defined, bottled, or labeled—this is also *in* everything, like light. Light is no particular color; therefore it can be in every color. It can be immanent because it is transcendent. Color itself transcends any particular shape; therefore it can be immanent in any shape. So heaven, because it is no part of the universe (you can never get there in a rocket ship), is present in all parts of the universe. The whole universe is an atom in heaven, or a womb. To ask, "Where is heaven" is like an unborn child asking "Where is the world?" Outside heaven is not earth but hell, no man's land. "All that seems earth is Hell or Heaven."[34]

Earth in Heaven

If earth is a part of heaven, does that mean all earthly things are parts of heaven? Is there dirt in heaven? Cats? Do they eat cat food? Is there sex in heaven? How about beer?

How much earth is in heaven? Well, remember that everything real and valuable on earth came from heaven to begin with. A cat is not merely evolved molecules in motion; it is a divine idea, a work of art, and a sign. It is a natural sign: it has something of what it signifies, and what it signifies is heavenly; so there is something of heaven in the cat. And heaven does not die. God does not throw his artwork into the wastebasket; God doesn't make junk. All his work has eternal value. It passes through time and seems to pass away—"today is

[34] C. S. Lewis, "Wormwood", in *Poems,* ed. Walter Hooper (New York: Harcourt, Brace & World, 1964), p. 87.

and tomorrow is thrown into the fire"—but it *is* in eternity. As the first movement of a symphony passes away to make room for the second but also eternally *is* a part of that symphony, so earth *is* part of heaven; time *is* part of eternity. *Macbeth's* three witches quickly move off the stage after act 1, scene 1; but they *are*, indelibly and unchangeably, part of the eternal reality of the play.

This applies both to humanity and nature, according to the Bible, for humanity is "like grass, which is renewed in the morning; in the evening it fades and withers".[35] In Plato, we are angels imprisoned in bodies, but in the Biblical view, we are part of nature. Our hope for eternity is not *out* of nature but *with* it. If we are eternalized, nature is, too; if nature is not, neither are we. Both have value simply because they are divine *opera*. Remember, God doesn't make junk.

There *is* a junkyard. The Bible calls it Gehenna. Outside Jerusalem, the holy city, there was a valley called Ge Hinnom, which pagan tribes had used for human sacrifice.[36] The Jews thought such a place fit only for burning garbage. It was later used as a biblical image of hell, the spiritual garbage dump of the cosmos. God makes no garbage, but we do; and a good cosmos must eventually purify itself of spiritual garbage like egotism, hate, greed, cowardice, or lust. Hell is the cosmic Roto-Rooter service. We can even rejoice that it exists, for we should want our spiritual garbage burned away, if we do not identify our selves with that garbage. If we do, *we* are burned eternally—not as a punishment but as a

---

[35] Ps. 103:15.
[36] "Gehenna", in John L. McKenzie, *Dictionary of the Bible* (New York: Macmillan, 1965).

psychological necessity. God cannot allow that garbage into heaven; and if we do not want to throw it away, if we clutch our garbage so close that we become garbage, there is only one place for us. Rather than indulging in pointless speculation about comparative population statistics of hell and heaven and rather than morbidly dwelling on the terror of the only ultimate tragedy in all creation, let's just make a mental note, in case we should find ourselves traveling in the wrong direction, that every road has two directions.

As to our curious questions about how much earth is in heaven, let's first be sure our motives in asking that question are not clutchingly childish: "I don't want to go there if I can't take my security blanket with me." If not, C. S. Lewis' answer can serve as a paradigm:

"Yes," my friend said. "I don't see why there shouldn't be books in Heaven. But you will find that your library in Heaven contains only some of the books you had on earth." "Which?" I asked. "The ones you gave away or lent." "I hope the lent ones won't still have all the borrowers' dirty thumb marks," said I. "Oh yes they will," said he. "But just as the wounds of the martyrs will have turned into beauties, so you will find that the thumbmarks have turned into beautiful illuminated capitals or exquisite marginal woodcuts."[37]

Finally, as to the meaning of the haunting, Saint Paul lets the last cat out of the bag. "The whole creation has been groaning in travail together until now."[38] History

[37] C. S. Lewis, *God in the Dock* (Grand Rapids, Mich.: Eerdmans, 1970), p. 216.
[38] Rom. 8:22.

is cosmic pregnancy. Mother Earth was impregnated by Father Heaven some two thousand years ago. The haunting we feel is cosmic birth pangs, contractions. They are coming only a few minutes apart now—is the time at hand, I wonder?

Chapter 4

The End of the Quest: The Joy of Heaven

We've explored our thirst; let's explore our heavenly drink. We've looked at our road; let's look at the golden castle at the end of the road. We've felt our exile and our longing for home; what does home feel like?

A Map of Joy

Let us explore the joy of heaven, its satisfaction of the deepest hunger of our heart. But it is misleading to speak of joy as "satisfaction"; that confuses it with happiness or even with pleasure. The distinction between pleasure, happiness, and joy can be made clear by a map of the self, a psychograph:

Think of the self as a canyon with two sides that meet only at the bottom. The two sides of the self are the cognitive and the conative, knowing and feeling. The Greeks projected these halves of themselves into two gods, Apollo and Dionysus, gods of heaven and earth, sun and vegetation. Nietzsche popularized these images, calling our rational side the "Apollonian" and our irrational side the "Dionysian".[1] The life of the self is a fire

---

[1] Friedrich Nietzsche, *The Birth of Tragedy,* esp. sec. 1, "The Birth of Tragedy, or: Hellenism and Pessimism", in *Basic Writings of Nietzsche,* trans. Walter Kaufmann (New York: Modern Library, 1968).

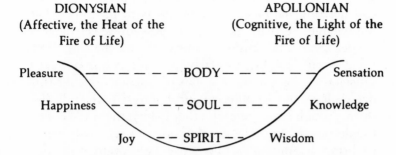

DIONYSIAN	APOLLONIAN
(Affective, the Heat of the Fire of Life)	(Cognitive, the Light of the Fire of Life)

Pleasure — — — — — — BODY — — — — — Sensation

Happiness — — — — — — SOUL — — — — Knowledge

Joy — — SPIRIT — — Wisdom

that gives both light (Apollo) and heat (Dionysus).

There are not only two sides but also three levels to the canyon. (The map has two dimensions, vertical as well as horizontal.) We can explore any of three levels. The most external, surface level is the body, or rather the ensouled body (for the soul is the life of the body, and we are living bodies, not corpses). At this level the Apollonian and Dionysian are quite clearly distinct. They are (1) the senses' power to receive sense data or experience and (2) the instinct to seek pleasure and avoid pain (which Freud, consistent with his philosophical materialism, sees as *the* basic drive in all we do: "the pleasure principle").[2]

On the second level, halfway down, we meet a more inward dimension of ourselves: our soul—that is, our

---

[2] Cf. "Formulations of the Two Principles of Mental Functioning", in *The Standard Edition of the Complete Psychological Works of Sigmund Freud,* vol. 12, trans. James Strachey (London: Hogarth Press, 1958); "Beyond the Pleasure Principle", p. 7 of vol. 18 of the *Complete Works; Civilization and Its Discontents,* trans. James Strachey (New York: Norton, 1961), p. 41: "the motive force of all human activities is a striving towards the two confluent goals of utility and a yield of pleasure."

consciousness, thoughts and feelings, knowing truth and desiring happiness. Happiness is to pleasure what knowledge of truth is to awareness of sense data: a deeper level. The senses are our outsight; the conscious mind is our insight. Similarly, pleasure is our outward satisfaction, happiness, our inward satisfaction. At this deeper level the Apollonian and Dionysian are still distinct, though closer to each other than at the surface. For the deeper the knowledge, the more it necessarily tends to bring happiness, while sense perception does not necessarily bring pleasure.

The deepest level is spirit. The living waters run here at the bottom of the canyon. Many people do not even realize they exist on this level; and some do not even realize the level of soul but see themselves (or, more frequently, others) as mere material organisms, complex animals. Thus there are six possible philosophies of human nature. The first three are mainly Western: (1) that human nature is only body organism (materialism), (2) that it is both body and soul (dualism), and (3) that it is body, soul, and spirit (the biblical view).[3] The other three philosophies are mainly Oriental: (4) the denial of the real existence of the body, (5) the denial of both body and individual soul, and (6) the denial of body, soul, and spirit. The fourth is one interpretation of the Hindu doctrine of *maya,* or illusion. The fifth seems to be the teaching of the Upanishads, that the true self is only spirit *(atman),* which is identical with God *(Brahman): tat tvam asi,* "thou art that".[4] Brahman alone is real *(Brahman salyam jagan mithya,* "Brahman alone is real,

---

[3] 1 Thess. 5:23.
[4] *Chandogya Upanishad* 6. 9. 4.

the rest is illusion"),[5] therefore spirit alone is real. The sixth is Buddhism, with its doctrine of *anatta* or no *atman*. Our map assumes the reality of all three aspects of the self, for philosophies are usually right in what they affirm and wrong in what they deny.

Another map of the same basic structure of the self is the following:

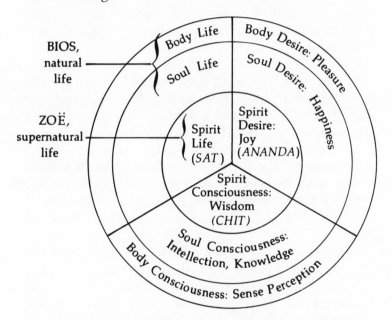

Here we see the same three levels of depth (body, soul, and spirit) but three areas or aspects of each level: what Saint John calls "life", "light", and "love"; what Hinduism calls *sat, chit,* and *ananda* (infinite being, infinite consciousness, and infinite bliss, the three attributes

[5] *Chandogya Upanishad* 6. 2. 2.

of Atman–Brahman); and what Christian theology orig-
inates in the three Persons of the Trinity (the Father,
source of all being, energy, life and power; the Son, the
Logos, Light, Mind or Word of God; and the Holy
Spirit, the beatitude of love between the Father and the
Son). These are our only three absolute needs; life without any one of them is impossible, subhuman, or intolerable. Life without life is impossible; life without light
(understanding) is subhuman; and life without love is
intolerable.

The life of the body and the soul together is the
"life" the New Testament calls *bios,* natural life. The life
of the spirit is more than natural life, or *zoë.* If we
choose it, it is our spirit's participation in God's own
life as Father, source of life. Our spirit's consciousness is
then a participation in the Word of God, the divine
consciousness, the "light that enlightens every man who
comes into the world",[6] the cosmic Christ. And our
spirit's joy is a participation in God's own eternal inner
joy of love between the Father and the Son: the Holy
Spirit.

The body is our relation to what is less than ourselves
(the material world); the soul is our relation to ourselves, or self-consciousness; and the spirit is our relation to what is more than ourselves (God). That is why
we usually discover the real, living God and the reality
of our own spirit at the same time and why we can't find
our own deepest identity until we find God.

It is our spirit that thirsts for God, whether or not our
conscious souls do. We have six thirsts. On the bodily
level, we thirst for pleasure and sense experience (curi-

---

[6] John 1:9 (AV).

osity); on the soul level, for happiness and knowledge; on the spirit level, for joy and wisdom. Pleasure and sense experience come from the world; happiness and knowledge come from ourselves (though many try in vain to find them in the world); joy and wisdom come from God (though many try in vain to find them in themselves or in the world).

Pleasures and sensations are like ripples on our surface; happiness and knowledge are like undercurrents in our inner waters; joy and wisdom are sunken treasure at the very bottom.

Each step deepens the one before it. Knowledge is a kind of depth perception or X-ray of sense perception; it sees forms and structures and essences behind external appearances. In turn wisdom discovers the deepest significance or ultimate meaning and value of what knowledge turns up. Similarly, happiness is a deepening of pleasure; we can see this when we are happy even when in pain. (Yes, it happens; ask any mother in childbirth!) And joy is deeper than happiness, for our joy can remain even when our feelings are upset. There are deeper feelings than the feelings, just as there are deeper reasons than the reason: "The heart has its reasons which the reason cannot know."

Joy *can* be in the spirit without happiness being in the soul, but joy usually flows out into the soul and even the body. A joyful spirit inspires joyful feelings and even a more psychosomatically healthy body. (For example, we need less sleep when we have joy and have more resistance to all kinds of diseases from colds to cancers.) But the home of joy is the spirit. We feel joy in the conscious soul only because the spirit is the life of the soul, as the soul is the life of the body. Joyful feelings are not joy, but joy's overflow, not the wave but the wave's imprint in the sand.

Not everyone knows what the spirit is and how it is distinct from the soul. Does it really make a difference? Only the difference between life and death. The soul makes the difference between life and death to the body, and the spirit makes the difference between life and death to the soul. A body without a soul is not a living body but a corpse. The difference between a living body and a dead body is not a bodily difference. Immediately after death the body has the same weight, shape, and size; but its life has departed. Life is not a *thing,* like the body, but the life *of* that thing. Similarly, a soul without spirit is a dead soul, and the difference between a dead soul and a living soul is not a soul difference. Dead souls think (dead thoughts) and feel (dead feelings) just as living souls do, but they have no life. If you want to see dead souls, or at least dying souls, just walk through certain city streets.

Greek philosophy (or at least Socratic-Platonic philosophy) teaches the immortality of the soul. The Bible does not: The only immortal one is God.[7] We attain immortality not by the unfree passivity of being born but by the act of free choice to be "born again".[8] Without the divine miracle of raising the dead, there is no hope for immortality.[9] That immortality is bodily as

[7] I Tim. 6:15–16: "the King of kings and Lord of lords who alone has immortality and dwells in unapproachable light".

[8] John 3:3: "Unless one is born anew he cannot see the Kingdom of God."

[9] I Cor. 15:17–19: "If Christ has not been raised, your faith is futile and you are still in your sins. Then those also who have fallen asleep in Christ have perished. If for this life only we have hoped in Christ, we are of all men most to be pitied."

well as soul and spirit immortality.[10] Finally, souls are not said to be immortal but mortal, that is, able to die.[11] Hell is precisely that: the death of the soul.

Spirit is unchanged by bodily death, which only clarifies its "fundamental option" for or against God. Souls are purged and perfected by bodily death (if their spirits live). Bodies are killed.

Spirit has only two choices: for or against God, for spirit confronts God, the absolute, the one and only. Here is the only area of absolute either/or: yes or no to God. (That is why conscience, which is the voice of spirit, is so absolutistic: It is the voice of God.) C. S. Lewis is thinking of the spirit when he says, "There are only two kinds of people in the end: those who say to God: 'Thy will be done', and those to whom God says in the end: '*Thy* will be done.'"[12]

Soul has many choices, not just one, for our thoughts and feelings are multicolored, not black or white. And body is the most dispersable of all, for it is part of the world of matter, which is maximally dispersable.

Spirit is where we decide who we are—our identity, our *I*. It is where we are selves, where we are ones. Our Dionysian and Apollonian halves are not selves, not wholes. Where are they one? Or are we only two halves glued together? No, we are wholes, and we find this

[10] 1 Cor. 15:35, 38: "But some one will ask, 'How are the dead raised? With what kind of body do they come?' . . . God gives it a body as he has chosen."

[11] Matt. 10:28: "Do not fear those who kill the body but cannot kill the soul; rather fear him who can destroy both body and soul in hell."

[12] C. S. Lewis, *The Great Divorce* (New York: Macmillan, 1946), p. 72.

wholeness only at the bottom of the bowl where the two sides converge. Just as "everything that rises must converge" in God,[13] everything that descends must also converge at the heart of the self, which is the image of God. The human *I* reflects the divine *I AM*. This is the spirit or "heart" (as Scripture calls it). It is both center and bottom.

Here at the bottom of the canyon the waters of life flow together and mingle; joy and wisdom are one. Deepest joy *is* deepest wisdom; beatitude is "the beatific vision". Happiness is not of itself knowledge, but joy *is* wisdom and wisdom *is* joy. The reason for this unity is that the object of joy and wisdom, unlike that of knowledge and happiness, is not an abstract, partial ingredient in the whole; and it is not known with an abstract aspect or part of ourselves, the intellect. Rather, in joy and wisdom the living God lets himself be touched by the human heart, center to center, heart to heart, spirit to spirit, I to Thou, "deep calling unto deep".[14]

Scripture invites us to "know the Lord" with the heart, not (first of all) the head. The biblical sense of "know" is "to love". The word is even used of physical love: "Now Adam knew Eve his wife, and she conceived."[15] She did not conceive a concept but a conception, a child. On the spiritual level, there is an incredible and wondrous parallel: God wants to be our spirit's husband.[16] Our spirit's love and intercourse with

[13] The Flannery O'Connor title is from Teilhard de Chardin, *The Future of Man* (New York: Harper & Row, 1964).

[14] Ps. 42:7.

[15] Gen. 4:1.

[16] Isa. 54:5.

God conceive ourselves, our new identity, our destiny. We are our own mothers. What we are now is only our womb, our raw material, our potential self. But we cannot be our own fathers, our own gods; that is the Oedipus complex, the dream of getting rid of our father, marrying our mother, and being our own father, that is, our own god. It is our primal sin, "original sin", the refusal of the divine marriage proposal. Its result is death, spiritual barrenness—ultimately, hell, "the outer darkness", the only ultimate alternative to joy.[17]

Some Divine Attributes of Joy

Because joy comes not from the world, through the body (like pleasure) or from ourselves, through the soul (like happiness) but from God, through the spirit, it "smells of divinity"—it has divine attributes. It is a heavenly element falling into an earthly compound, and we can mentally abstract the element and consider it in itself even though it exists in us in mixed form, not pure.

For one thing, joy seems to have a necessity to it, as God does. God not only *is* but could not be otherwise, could not change. We change, so we are not always in joy, nor joy in us; but joy itself is unchangeable, eternal, and necessary. When it comes, though it appears new to us, a surprise, it also seems old, ancient, having existed "before the beginning of time". However late in time it comes, it comes from before the beginning of time: "Late have I loved thee, O Beauty so ancient and so

[17] Matt. 8:12.

new."[18] Pleasure and happiness have nothing of that air
of eternity about them that joy does.

Though joy comes from before time, it always seems
to arrive late ("Late have I loved thee"). For eternity is
always late and always early: always late because all the
past time we spent without it is wasted, always early
because it is a surprise that it shows up in time at all. It is
a shock like the Incarnation—in fact, very suspiciously
like the Incarnation.

Another reason joy, though eternal, comes as a surprise can be seen by referring again to the map of the
self. Joy is in the spirit, not in the soul; and soul is at least
partly under our control. Spirit is not. Spirit rules soul,
but soul does not rule spirit. We can control pleasure and
even happiness to an extent, but never joy; it is a sheer
gift of God. Thinking the conscious soul can control joy
is like thinking the body can control happiness; such
thinking reduces joy to happiness or happiness to pleasure.

Yet the joy in our spirit does not stay there, bottled up
and stagnant. Spirit is essentially dynamic, and its joy
flows out in three directions: back to God in gratitude
and rejoicing, out to others like a watering fountain, and
into our own soul and body as a sort of overspill. Joyful
feelings and thoughts, even pleasure and health, result
from joy; and this is a foretaste of heaven:

> The faint, far-off results of those energies which God's
> creative rapture implanted in matter when he made the
> worlds are what we now call physical pleasures; and even
> thus filtered, they are too much for our present manage-
> ment. What would it be to taste at the fountain-head that

[18] Augustine, *Confessions*, X. 23.

stream of which even these lower reaches prove so intoxicating? Yet that, I believe, is what lies before us. The whole man is to drink joy from the fountain of joy. As St. Augustine said, the rapture of the saved soul will "flow over" into the glorified body . . . *torrens voluptatis.*[19]

The home of joy is God. We are God's colonies, and he visits his colonies. The fire of God descends into the air of our spirit and even into the waters of our soul and the earth of our body. Feelings of joy are like the hot crater made by a meteor that has burst through the atmosphere, parted the seas, and come to rest on the sea bottom.

Another divine attribute of joy seems to be that it has no finite opposite, as God has no opposite. Like Brahman, God is "the One without a second".[20] (Satan is not God's opposite; Satan is not a bad god but a bad angel.) But joy is also "One without a second". Pleasure has a finite opposite: pain. Happiness has a finite opposite: unhappiness or sadness. But joy has no imaginable finite opposite, for joy is of itself infinite.

In ordinary language "joy" is often used to designate merely an intense degree of happiness. Then it has a finite opposite: an intense degree of unhappiness (grief, sorrow, or anguish). But the opposite of true joy is far worse than anguish, as joy is far better than happiness. In fact, its opposite is hell.

Joy is the life of heaven. Hell is not eternal life in pain or unhappiness, but (according to Scripture) eternal

[19] C. S. Lewis, *The Weight of Glory* (New York: Macmillan, 1949), p. 14.
[20] *Brihadaranyaka Upanishad* 4. 5. 15.

death—an emptiness shaped only by the fullness it is empty of, an absence of God's presence and therefore of life and light and love.[21] No light can define hell because hell is precisely the absence of light, the "outer darkness". Whatever is definable is between light and darkness and is lit up by the light. Pure light cannot be lit up by any light; that's why trying to define God is like trying to illuminate the sun with a flashlight. But pure darkness also is not lit by any light. If it were, it would not be pure darkness. Unless we are to call Jesus deluded, hell *is,* but *what* it is cannot be said.

Another divine attribute of joy is that it is not just self-sufficient but more than self-sufficient. Pleasure is less than self-sufficient, seeking satisfaction. Happiness is simply self-sufficient, satisfied and at rest. Joy is more than self-sufficient, bursting out of itself and calling for rejoicing. As God the Father, infinitely perfect, nevertheless dynamically bursts forth from within himself to utter the Logos, the Word, out of no need but out of sheer superfluity and generosity, and as the Trinity express themselves in creating a world for the same reason, so joy, though as self-sufficient as happiness, nevertheless comes out of itself and calls for praise and rejoicing.

Praise and rejoicing and glorifying and exulting sound terribly foreign to the modern sensibility, quite outdated. So much the worse for the date; if egalitarianism means we look up to no one and nothing as superior and worthy of praise, it is spiritual starvation. Praise is a need quite different from any practical need. To praise God is not like "praising" a breakfast cereal or a football

---

[21] Cf. Matt. 10:28, 18:8, 25:41.

team. True praise is our response not to what happens to turn us on subjectively but to what is objectively good in itself, intrinsically valuable, worthy of praise. We praise a beautiful sunset not for the pleasure it gives us but for what it is in itself, but we praise a food only for the pleasure or utility it gives us. We praise God "for his own glory".[22]

We praise not only God but also joy, and this is legitimate as long as it is secondary and not a substitute for praising God. Just as we can love love after we love God, and know something about knowledge after we know God, so we can praise joy. We do not write a great poem entitled "Hail to Corn Flakes" or "Hail to Sex", but we do write "Hail to Joy":

> Freude, schöne Gotterfunken,
> Tochter aus Eylesium,
> Wir betreten, feuer-trunken,
> Himmlische, dein Heiligtum.[23]

Joy Stops the Pendulum: Boredom versus Frustration

Human life is a pendulum swinging between pursuit and peace, contention and contentment, seeking and

---

[22] Cf. the Gloria of the pre-Vatican II Mass: "We give thee thanks for thy great glory".

[23] "Hymn to Joy" ("An die Freude"), trans. as "Hymn to Joy" by Edgar A. Bowring, *The Poems of Schiller* (New York: Worthington Co., 1880), p. 72.

> Joy, thou Goddess, fair, immortal,
>   Offspring of Elysium,
> Mad with rapture, to the portal
>   Of thy holy fane we come!

satisfaction. One of life's most pervasive dilemmas is that of boredom versus frustration. Peace and contentment soon become dull and boring, as retirees and utopians both discover. That's why a leisured and economically secure culture like ours (or late Rome) turns to excitement and pleasure seeking: to relieve the boredom of success. But pleasure seeking becomes frustrating. It is like a leaky cask, says Plato.[24] You get jaded and need stronger and stronger doses of pleasure by a law of diminishing returns. Finally, you reach the point of no return, give it up, and turn to some peace of mind cult (as our culture, like late Rome's, is also doing). Neither gives us the joy we were designed for; that's why the pendulum keeps swinging. It is the restless heart again.

Americans are turning to hundreds of peace of mind techniques today, both mystical and psychological, because they have just come from a generation of excitement seeking, especially by sex and drugs. It is no accident that nearly all the Oriental religions that have so suddenly become popular in America forbid drugs and strictly regulate sexual activity; they sell well in a peace buyer's market. But of course the peace will pall, and the boredom will lead to a new cult of kicks. The Oriental search for peace through mystical experience and a transformation of consciousness is only the inward version of the Western search for peace through social utopianism. Both run aground on the fatal flaw of all utopias: success. While striving for the goal, life has a purpose; but once the goal is reached, purpose, creativity, and interest sag into a limp felicity, and the human

[24] Gorgias 493b ff.

spirit rebels—the pendulum does not stop until the spirit is either dead (in hell) or fully alive (in heaven).

Kierkegaard's famous three "stages on life's way" exemplify this pendulum. The "aesthetic stage" (which is not "aesthetic" in the sense of artistic but in the sense of a pursuit of pleasure and the conquest of boredom) is excitement without peace. It is pleasure seeking that eventuates in emptiness, meaninglessness, and despair. The "ethical stage" (which is not "ethical" in the sense of socially or legally approved, but a good and faithful conscience) is peace without excitement and eventuates in either self-righteous Phariseeism or bourgeois Philistinism. The exemplar of the aesthetic is Don Juan, master of the art of seduction. The exemplar of the ethical is the good judge—solid, secure, and upright but never troubled by the passion for the infinite or by the beautiful terror of the unknown.[25]

The third stage, the "religious" (not a visible, institutional creed, code, or cult but a lived relationship with God), has the passion of the aesthetic because it is concrete and direct, while the ethical is abstract. Ethics loves goodness; religion loves God. Ethics alone brings no joy because God is joy and the giver of joy; therefore only a real relationship with God is joy, and only joy overcomes the dilemma of the peace versus pleasure-seeking pendulum.

The pendulum also casts light on Kierkegaard's opposite number and twin founder of Existentialism,

---

[25] Cf. *Either/Or: a Fragment of Life,* 2 vols., trans. David and Lillian Swenson and Walter Lowrie (Princeton: Princeton University Press, 1944); *Stages on Life's Way,* trans. Walter Lowrie (Princeton: Princeton University Press, 1940).

Nietzsche. Nietzsche diagnoses the same tragic split in modern life: his "Dionysian versus Apollonian" is basically the same as Kierkegaard's "aesthetic versus ethical".[26] Dionysus, god of earth, growth, and grape, represents the dark, fascinating, and dangerous life of the irrational instinctual, and passionate. Apollo, god of sun and light, represents reason and justice: a well-lit and well-ordered world. Dionysus is like thick soup, like black bean soup; it sticks to your bones, but you can't see far into it. Apollo is like thin soup, like consommé; it is clear and light but not very nourishing.

Nietzsche's images of beauty are fascinating but ultimately destructive, like Dionysus himself, who drove his worshippers mad and was himself torn to pieces by the Titans, monstrous enemies of the Olympian gods. Nietzsche was a martyr to his god and shared his tragic fate; by the time of his death, his mind was dismembered by psychosis. On the other hand, Nietzsche's images of ordinary goodness are shallow, sheepish, and dull. Again, the choice is between excitement without peace and peace without excitement.

Can't true goodness, rationality, and peace be interesting? Something happened between Spenser and Milton, for Spenser's images of goodness are still fascinating, even romantic, while Milton cannot portray a God more fascinating than his Satan. Charles Williams, C. S. Lewis, and J. R. R. Tolkien have often been praised as nearly the only modern novelists who can make good more fascinating than evil. (G. K. Chesterton is a fourth, at least in *The Man Who Was Thursday.*) Williams speaks of "a terrible good", Tolkien, of "the peril of light and joy"; and Lewis's Christ figure in the

<hr/>

[26] See note 1.

Chronicles of Narnia is Aslan, the great lion who is "not a tame lion . . . but he's good".[27] Hitler has been seen (by writers such as Hannah Arendt and Max Picard) as teaching modern man the badly needed lesson of the dullness, tawdriness, and banality of evil.[28] Alan Watts has diagnosed the major cause of the unattractiveness of Christian theology in the twentieth century as not an intellectual or moral failure but an aesthetic one: Its images of God are theologically and morally correct but aesthetically dull and powerless.[29] Teilhard de Chardin also sees "the heart of the problem" as an image problem: "Man would seem to have no clear picture of the God he longs to worship."[30] It is because a joyless person can only picture a joyless God.

Perhaps one reason excitements like gambling, violence, alcohol, and promiscuity are often temptations to the ethical and conventionally religious person is that his or her life is full of peace but not of joy. It lacks the ingredient that is in joy but not in peace or happiness: passion. Such a person is rarely tempted by avarice, selfishness, or lust for power, the desire to control one's life. The need is to yield to ecstasy—if not to God, then

[27] Charles Williams, *Descent into Hell* (London: Faber & Faber, 1949), pp. 16, 65; J. R. R. Tolkien, *The Fellowship of the Ring* (New York: Ballantine Books, 1965), p. 490; C. S. Lewis, *The Lion, the Witch and the Wardrobe* (New York: Macmillan, 1950), p. 64.

[28] Hannah Arendt, *Eichmann in Jerusalem: A Report on the Banality of Evil* (New York: Viking Press, 1963); Max Picard, *Hitler in Our Selves,* trans. Heinrich Hauser (Hinsdale, Ill.: H. Regnery Co., 1947).

[29] Alan Watts, *Behold the Spirit* (New York: Vintage Books, 1971), p. 154.

[30] Teilhard de Chardin, "The Heart of the Problem", in *The Future of Man* (New York: Harper & Row, 1964), p. 260.

to an irrational passion; if not to the mystery of light, then to the mystery of darkness. The general principle such a case illustrates is that whenever we lack an aspect of joy (here, passion or excitement), we seek it as water seeks low ground or a magnet seeks metal. And if we do not find it where it is—in a lived love relationship with God—we will likely try to find it where it isn't—in the world.

Pleasure has aliveness but agitation; happiness has peace in place of agitation, but sleepy satisfaction in place of aliveness. Only joy has both peace and aliveness, aliveness without agitation and peace without sleepiness. (I am using "happiness" here in the popular current sense of satisfaction or contentment. Aristotle, however, uses it to mean an *active* state of soul. This would seem more akin to joy.)[31]

Walking or even running is the appropriate posture for agitation, and, in fact, walking around is an effective posture for problem solving or for working out unfulfilled desires. Lying down is the appropriate posture for satisfaction; and it is no accident that this posture is used in psychoanalysis, for the goal there is homeostasis, balance, adjustment, and peace. It is ironic that Freud criticizes Eastern mysticism's "oceanic feeling" as the death-wish, the undoing of birth and alienation between ego and world, yet proposes the same ultimate goal himself in homeostasis.[32]

[31] Artistotle, *Nicomachean Ethics* 1, 7 (1098s 6–16).

[32] Sigmund Freud, *Civilization and Its Discontents,* trans. James Strachey (New York: Norton, 1961), p. 11 ff. Freud usually calls homeostasis the "constancy principle". Cf. Ernest Jones, *The Life and Work of Sigmund Freud* (New York: Basic Books, 1953). W. B. Cannon used the term "homeostasis" first (*Encyclopedia of Psychology,* vol. 2, "homeostasis" [New York: Herder & Herder, 1972]).

Joy is neither homeostasis nor agitation. Its quiet is far more lively than agitation and far more peaceful than the deepest sleep, for it is not deep sleep but deep waking. Agitated waking spills out spiritual energy, wastes it into the future by refusing the present. Joy is pure affirmation of the present; all its waking is concentrated in the only real time there is, not wasted on one of the two times that *are* not (for just as the past *is* no more, the future *is* not yet). This is maximum life. Kierkegaard says, "You believe that only a restless spirit is alive, whereas . . . only a quiet spirit is truly alive."[33]

This state of mind is like light: traveling faster than matter, yet making no sound, no perturbation. Pleasure is the restless mind moving along a line, never reaching the end. Happiness is the mind resting at the end. Joy is the mind eternally moving *at* the end, motion at a point: the cosmic dance. Pleasure is moving; happiness is still; joy is moving while still. Pleasure is like work, happiness is like sleep, joy is like play. Pleasure is like action, happiness is like rest, joy is like contemplation. Pleasure is a river running to the sea; happiness is the full, calm sea; joy is a great and glorious storm on the sea.

Joy and Tears: Ek-stasis

The distinction between joy and happiness explains why joy brings forth tears, why we *weep* for joy. Joy is not just satisfaction, not just full but overfull, like a fountain. Our present vessel is too small to contain it, like old wineskins bursting with new wine. Tears are its

[33] Sören Kierkegaard, *Either/Or;* Robert Bretall, *A Kierkegaard Anthology* (New York: Modern Library, 1936), p. 93.

spillage, its overflow. The new wine of joy is a divine thing, and human vessels break and die under that "weight of glory": "No man can see God and live."[34] It is the blessed death we long for.

The laws of thermodynamics say physical energy naturally tends to diffuse itself. The laws of love say goodness is also "naturally diffusive of itself".[35] And the creative energy is visible in both. God created the world not out of reason or necessity or practicality, but out of sheer joy. It is all gloriously superfluous, like a gargoyle. The world is full of gargoyles—who ever thought all that space and all those stars were *necessary?* The final, unanswerable argument for the divine superfluity is the ostrich. A required exercise for every theologian should be a visit to the zoo to contemplate the proboscis monkey and "Tyger, tyger, burning bright".

Every great human artist, too, creates not out of necessity but out of the joy of superfluity. Not that all creating is happy. It may even be unhappy, like repentance, or painful, like childbirth. But it is a joyful pain, a bittersweetness. In fact, we prefer these tears to all other smiles:

> Have you not seen that in our days
> Of any whose story, song, or art

[34] Sören Kierkegaard, *Philosophical Fragments,* ed. H. V. Hong, trans. David Swenson (New Jersey: Princeton University Press, 1962). Robert Bretall, *A Kierkegaard Anthology* (New York: Modern Library, 1936), p. 168: "There once lived a people who had a profound understanding of the divine; this people thought that no man could see God and live." Cf. Gen. 32:30.

[35] Aquinas, *Summa Theologiae,* I, 44, 4; I, 45, 1, 6–8.

Delights us, our sincerest praise
Means, when all's said, "You break my heart"?[36]

When joy comes, it indeed "breaks our heart", our containing vessel. For like love, joy is a universal solvent; it cannot be contained. Just as love is not in us but we are "in love" ("it's bigger than both of us"), joy is not in us but we in it: "Enter into the joy of thy Lord."[37] Even in paganism, Jove is a god—in fact, a very big god, bigger than the world.

We see this godlike joy bigger than the world in the myths and fairy tales. Bigger than the frame of the story, it pierces the very life-membrane (*hymen*) of the story, as of our soul. Tolkien calls this the *eucatastrophe,* the heartbreaking happy ending:

> The eucatastrophic tale is the true form of fairy-tale, and its highest function . . . giving a fleeting glimpse of Joy, Joy beyond the walls of the world, poignant as grief . . . a catch of the breath, a beat and lifting of the heart, near to (or indeed accompanied by) tears . . . when the sudden "turn" comes we get a piercing glimpse of joy, and heart's desire, that for a moment passes outside the frame, rends indeed the very web of story, and lets a gleam come through.

> Seven long years I served for thee,
> The glassy hill I clamb for thee,
> The bluidy shirt I wrang for thee,

[36] C. S. Lewis, "Epigrams and Epitaphs", 2, *Poems* (New York: Harcourt, Brace & World, 1964), p. 133.
[37] Matt. 25:21.

And wilt thou not wauken and turn to me?
He heard and turned to her.[38]

This heartbreak is an ecstasy, an ek-stasis, a standing outside ourselves, an interior death and resurrection. Though we die (we stand *outside ourselves*), we live (*we stand* outside ourselves). Poets and lovers have always known that joy is a kind of death.

The magic of ek-stasis can come from a great myth or fairy tale, or from a great piece of music, or from a great love. You can lose yourself in it; you become the music or the love or the beauty. You "identify with it", that is, you find your identity in it more than inside your epidermis. You are overjoyed to discover you are not an ego in a bag of skin; you literally *are* the other. When this happens—for example, when you become the music you hear, so if anyone asked you who you were, you would not say you were a person listening to music but you were that music—you may feel both overjoyed and terrified: overjoyed to escape yourself and terrified of not being able to get back into yourself again.

All Reality Is Ek-stasy

In the experience of self-forgetful ek-static joy, as in that of self-forgetful, ek-static love, we are privileged to stand at a unique point of vision, a point where the lines of our subjective sight and the lines of objective reality converge, a window onto the ultimate law of being. Everything, from matter to spirit, from humanity to God, is ek-static. Everything lives outside itself; every-

[38] J. R. R. Tolkien, "On Fairy Stories", in *A Tolkien Reader* (New York: Ballantine Books, 1966), pp. 69–70. The quotation is from *The Black Bull of Norroway*.

thing lives a leap. When the unborn John the Baptist leaped in his mother's womb upon Mary's greeting, he was enacting a cosmic mystery.[39] That leap in the heart was heaven in the heart, heaven at the heart of earth. It is the place in the fairy tale when the sudden "turn" comes.

Christianity is, through and through, a religion of leaps. Others are religions of divine laws and human effort or of divine peace and human happiness, but Christianity is a religion of divine and human leaps. First, God eternally leaps out of himself into himself. Each Person of the Trinity is eternally engaged in the ecstasy of self-giving.

> Even within the Holy One himself it is not sufficient that the Word should *be* God, it must also be *with* God. The Father eternally begets the Son and the Holy Ghost proceeds: deity introduces distinction within itself so that the union of reciprocal loves may transcend mere arithmetical unity or self identity. . . . For in self-giving, if anywhere, we touch a rhythm not only of all creation but of all being. For the Eternal Word also gives himself in sacrifice; and that not only on Calvary. For when he was crucified he "did that in the wild weather of his outlying provinces which he had done at home in glory and gladness." From before the foundation of the world he surrenders begotten Deity back to begetting Deity in obedience.[40]

Second, the creation of the world is a leap—a leap from nonbeing to being. Making one being out of an-

[39] Luke 1:41.
[40] C. S. Lewis, *The Problem of Pain* (New York: Macmillan, 1962), pp. 151-152.

other is like a walk or a slide; creating something out of nothing is a leap. Human creativity knows something of that, too, even though only by remote analogy. The creative idea, however prepared for, does not gradually emerge from its raw material; it is born suddenly and unpredictably.

All birth, slow or fast, is a leap from nonbeing to being. That's why Jesus used birth as the analogy for salvation when he talked to Nicodemus.[41] Entering God's Kingdom, redemption, sanctifying grace, salvation, being born again—all these are different terms for the same real happening, the thing the whole of Christianity is ultimately about: the divinization of humanity by the humanization of divinity, people leaping into God as a result of God leaping into people. More than moral improvement, more than intellectual belief, Christianity is a sharing in divine life, supernatural life, eternal life. As radical as the leap from physical death to physical life, this is the leap from spiritual death to spiritual life.

Fourth, the Incarnation, which brings this eternal life into time, is a leap: "In the stillness of the night, the eternal Word leaped down." How dramatic!—God leaps an infinite distance over the canyon of nothingness from the side of eternity to the side of time.

Fifth, the believer's leap of faith in response to God's leap is like the acceptance of a marriage proposal, which permits the divine bridegroom to impregnate us with his life. What God asks of us is not to try a little harder to obey his laws, or to experiment with mystical stages

---

[41] John 3:3.

of consciousness, but to give ourselves recklessly to him, to leap out of our skins in holy abandon.

Sixth, Scripture is full of dramatic, "leaping" imagery to describe our destiny, heavenly joy. The coming of the Son of Man will be "like lightning".[42] The blessed "will run to and fro like sparks among the reeds".[43] The Divine life is not divine rest but divine dynamism: "My Father is still working, and so am I."[44]

We leap to God because he leaped to us in Christ, and God leaped to us because he is eternally leaping within himself like a flea circus. The whole of reality is ek-static leaping, a cosmic dance, God engaging in a wild acrobatic display with humanity. "From the highest to the lowest, self exists to be abdicated (leaped out of) and, by that abdication, becomes the more truly self, to be thereupon yet the more abdicated, and so forever. This is not a heavenly law which we can escape by remaining earthly, nor an earthly law which we can escape by being saved. What is outside the system of self-giving is not earth, nor nature, nor 'ordinary life', but simply and solely Hell."[45]

In fact, even hell depends on the universal ek-stasy: "That fierce imprisonment in the self is but the obverse of the self-giving which is absolute reality; the negative shape which the outer darkness takes by surrounding . . . the shape of the real."[46] Heaven is a phoenix rising from its own ashes. Hell is a coiling constrictor circling

[42] Matt. 24:27.
[43] Wisdom of Sirach 3:7.
[44] John 5:17.
[45] C. S. Lewis, *The Problem of Pain,* p. 152.
[46] Ibid., pp. 152–153.

round itself in an ever-tightening grasp, crushing itself, even eating itself. Heaven is ek-stasis; hell is in-stastis. Heaven is coinherence; hell is incoherence.[47] Heaven is aspiration; hell is greed. Heaven is love; hell is lust. Heaven is a fountain flowing; hell is a toilet bowl flushing. Heaven is centrifugal; hell is centripetal. Hell grasps after being God; heaven empties itself even of God: "Have this mind among yourselves, which is yours in Christ Jesus, who, though he was in the form of God, did not count equality with God a thing to be grasped, but emptied himself, taking the form of a servant."[48]

Yet even hell borrows what reality it has from heaven. Hell is heaven's ape. Its spiritual death (the death of the spirit) mimics the death to self or death to egoism that is heaven, the ecstasy of dying into God, dying into life. The distinction between these two deaths is the distinction between the suicide and the martyr. Though often confused, they are exact opposites. If you commit suicide, then in killing yourself, you kill your whole world. You hate everything so much that you want to kill it. If you are a martyr, you love something so much that you want to die for it. Martyrdom enacts the mystery of love and death, loving something more than the self, ek-statically identifying with that something more than with the self.

But we must all be martyrs. Like priests and monks,

[47] Cf. Charles Williams, "The Way of Exchange", in *Charles Williams; Selected Writings,* ed. Anne Ridler (London: Oxford University Press, 1961), and its exemplification in Williams, *Descent into Hell.* Cf. also Mary McDermott Shideler, *The Theology of Romantic Love: A Study in the Writings of Charles Williams* (Grand Rapids, Mich.: Eerdmans, 1962).

[48] Phil. 2:5–7.

martyrs are mirrors of something in us, special examples of universal truths. Our deepest destiny is death—not just to the body but to the ego. There are three deaths: of the body (physical death), of the ego (ekstasis, heaven), and of the spirit (hell, spiritual death). The first is the door to either the second or the third. The second (heaven) is spiritual martyrdom; the third (hell) is spiritual suicide.

We are all destined to be martyrs because our destiny is not merely to experience joy while remaining the same person, not merely to fill our existing capacity for joy. Rather, it is to increase that capacity infinitely by a bursting of our seams, a shedding of our snakeskins, a transformation from caterpillars to butterflies. We are not just to imitate Christ but to "put on Christ", to "be in Christ", to "share the divine nature".[49] The New Testament is quite strong about that, however weakly it is preached. Without losing our humanity (indeed, by perfecting it), we are to become gods and goddesses. Incredible, unimaginable, shocking, even blasphemous as it sounds, that is the clear and consistent teaching not of human words but of the word of God:

> But to all who received him, who believed in his name, he gave power to become children of God; who were born not of blood nor of the will of the flesh nor of the will of man but of God.[50]
>
> Truly, truly I say to you, unless one is born anew, he cannot see the kingdom of God. . . . That which is born

[49] Rom. 13:14; 2 Cor. 5:17; 2 Pet. 1:4.
[50] John 1:12.

of the flesh is flesh, and that which is born of the Spirit is
spirit. [51]

For all who are led by the Spirit of God are sons of
God. . . . When we cry "Abba! Father!" it is the Spirit
himself bearing witness with our spirit that we are children of God, and if children, then heirs, heirs of God and
fellow heirs with Christ. [52]

See what love the Father has given us, that we should be
called children of God; and so we are. [53]

He has granted us his precious and very great promises,
that through these you may . . . become partakers of the
divine nature. [54]

This is infinitely more marvelous than if a rebel worm
were given the gift of human nature through a redeemer
worm, who gave up his human dignity to become a
worm and die as a worm (in fact, to be killed by the
rebel worms) in order to win for worms not only forgiveness but even the power to become human. For the
gap between worm and humanity is only finite, but the
gap between humanity and God is infinite. The difference between any two finite quantities is finite; the
difference between any finite quantity and infinity is
infinite. And to bridge this infinite difference is our
ultimate destiny. It requires death and resurrection,
transformation, not just moral improvement:

Morality is indispensable; but the Divine Life, which
gives itself to us and which calls us to be gods, intends
for us something in which morality will be swallowed

[51] John 3:3, 6.
[52] Rom. 8:14–17.
[53] 1 John 3:1.
[54] 2 Pet. 1:4.

up. We are to be re-made. All the rabbit in us is to
disappear—the worried, conscientious ethical rabbit as
well as the cowardly and sensual rabbit. We shall bleed
and squeal as the handfuls of fur come out; and then,
surprisingly, we shall find underneath it all a thing we
have never yet imagined: a real Man, an ageless god, a
son of God, strong, radiant, wise, beautiful, and drenched
in joy.[55]

The crowning glory on our glory is our forgetting
our glory. Heaven's joy is the ek-stasy of self-forgetfulness even of our heavenly self: "Every one there is
filled full with what we should call goodness as a mirror
is filled with light. But they do not call it goodness.
They do not call it anything. They are not thinking of it.
They are too busy looking at the source from which it
comes."[56]

This heavenly secret of self-forgetfulness is the secret
of joy on earth as well as in heaven. All joy is un-self-
conscious; self-consciousness spoils joy. To stop and
turn to see how you're doing spoils whatever you're
doing, whether it's bad or good: lusting, resenting,
fighting, singing, bowling, loving (physically or spiritually), or sharing the divine nature.

You can do incredible things in the state of self-forgetfulness. Frail mothers have lifted four-thousand-pound
automobiles to save their babies pinned underneath.
Inventors have gone without sleep for many days under
the spell of creative work's fascination. Doctors have

[55] C. S. Lewis, "Man or Rabbit", in *God in the Dock* (Grand
Rapids, Mich.: Eerdmans, 1970), p. 112.

[56] C. S. Lewis, *Mere Christianity* (New York: Macmillan, 1960),
pp. 130–131.

worked beyond the limits of physical endurance to save
lives on battlefields. Patients have fooled medical prog-
noses and recovered from "incurable" diseases just because they could forget themselves in laughter.[57]

God created the world in this self-forgetful laughter.
(Remember the ostrich every time you think God takes
himself seriously.) So extroverted that his extroverted
consciousness is another Person, so outside himself that
he is a second self, and then so outside themselves in
love that they are the Third, the Spirit, God is the model
for our heavenly self-forgetfulness and the reason our
supreme joy in heaven will not be our joy but others'.
The question "what will I be in heaven?" will no longer
interest us. This may not sound very joyful to us now—
in fact it may sound positively unattractive—which is
precisely an index of our distance from joy. The saints
know better; Anselm says this about heaven:

> Ask thy inmost mind whether it could contain its joy
> over so great a blessedness of its own. Yet assuredly, if
> any other whom thou didst love altogether as thyself
> possessed the same blessedness, thy joy would be dou-
> bled, because thou wouldst rejoice not less for him than
> for thyself. But if two, or three, or many more, had the
> same joy, thou wouldst rejoice as much for each one as
> for thyself, if thou didst love each as thyself. Hence, in
> that perfect love of innumerable blessed angels and
> sainted men, where none shall love another less than
> himself, every one shall rejoice for each of the others as
> for himself. If, then, the heart of man will scarce contain

[57] Raymond A. Moody, Jr., *Laugh after Laugh: The Healing Power of Humor* (Headwaters Press, 1978).

his joy over his own so great good, how shall it contain
so many and so great joys?[58]

Beyond Joy

In ek-static joy we forget ourselves. But we also forget
joy, for joy points beyond joy to its object, to God. This
precisely *is* its joy, its ek-stasis. Joy can no more be
caught than the wind. We are swept up in joy's heavenly
hurricane. It is not the goal but the vehicle, Elijah's fiery
chariot.[59]

Joy is so fascinating that it is easy to forget this and
make joy itself the goal. C. S. Lewis documents this
popular mistake from his own experience in *Surprised by
Joy:*

> . . . the assumption that what I wanted was a "thrill", a
> state of my own mind. And there lies the deadly error.
> Only when your whole attention and desire are fixed on
> something else . . . does the "thrill" arise. It is a by-
> product. Its very existence presupposes that you desire
> not it but something other and outer. . . . All images
> and sensations, if idolatrously mistaken for Joy itself,
> soon honestly confessed themselves inadequate. All said,
> in the last resort, "It is not I. I am only a reminder. Look!
> Look! What do I remind you of?"
> . . . Inexorably Joy proclaimed, "You want—I myself
> am your want of—something other, outside, not you or
> any state of you". . . . I thus understood that in deepest
> solitude there is a road right out of the self, a commerce
> with something which, by refusing to identify itself with
> any object of the senses, or anything whereof we have

[58] Anselm *Proslogium,* ch. 25.
[59] 2 Kings 2:11.

biological or social need, or anything imagined, or any state of our own minds, proclaims itself sheerly objective. Far more objective than bodies, for it is not, like them, clothed in our senses; the naked Other, imageless (though our imagination salutes it with a hundred images), unknown, undefined, desired.[60]

Joy is the touch of God's finger. The object of our longing is the not the touch but the Toucher. This is true of all good things—they are all God's touch. Whatever we desire, we are really desiring God. But is this true of evil things too?

There are no evil things, only evil desires. All things are created by God and therefore good. All that is desirable in things is an image of the supremely desirable God. Therefore even our evil desires are searchings for God. There is simply nothing else to desire except God or God's images and reflections. Evil is not desiring evil things but desiring lesser goods and desiring in the wrong way (selfishly, not unselfishly).

All the different things we desire are really one; for they are reflections of aspects of God, and God is one—not only in the sense that there is only one of him but also in the sense that there are no divisions in him, not even between himself and his attributes or among his different attributes. What to us is many good things is in itself, in God, one. For instance, in us justice and mercy are different, and head and heart are different. In God justice *is* mercy and mercy *is* justice; knowledge *is* love and love *is* knowledge. Unlike us, God does not *have* attributes that are distinguishable or detachable from his

[60] C. S. Lewis, *Surprised by Joy* (New York: Harcourt, Brace & World, 1955), pp. 168, 220–221.

being. I could still be, and be me, if I were not tall, or white, or young. These are accidental to my essence. But there is nothing accidental in God. All in him is his essence, which is one. All his attributes are one with his essence, therefore are one with each other.

The practical consequence of this difficult and abstract theological truth is that all the many good things we desire, which to us are diverse, are really one in God, like white light splintered into colors by a prism. The infinite oneness of God's goodness is refracted by the prism of time and space into many good things. But there is "only one thing necessary", and God's command to seek it is his love pointing us to the path to our joy. It is a tremendous liberation to "seek ye first the kingdom of God and his goodness", not only because "all these other things will be added unto you"[61] but also because we need have only one care, like consolidating our debts, or (much better) like consolidating our love, like monogamy. We are free of everything else, free of the whole world. There is no greater freedom than this, a freedom bigger than the world. For the only other thing besides the whole world is God, and to be free from him is not to be free but to be dead.

There is still more transcendence of joy. The joy of heaven, our fulfillment, is not primarily our joy but God's, not primarily the fulfillment of human desires, as if we were the seekers and God the sought, but of God's desires, or rather God's desire—his single-minded love of us and our perfecting. (God is very single-minded.)

In heaven (and in heaven on earth, the sanctified soul) our will conforms to God's, not God's to ours. The

[61] Matt. 6:33.

reason the saint's desires are satisfied and he has joy is not that God is a divine dispensing machine and the saint has learned to press the right buttons but that he has learned to desire "the one thing necessary",[62] God's will, and therefore always gets what he desires, for God's will is always done. "Thy will be done" is the infallible road to total joy.

It is testable and provable in daily and hourly experience. Time after time, active willing God's will, "Yes" to God, leads out of meaninglessness, passivity, depression, or sorrow into joy. And time after time the pursuit of joy as if it were mine leads to disappointment, emptiness, and restless boredom. Life teaches us by millions of repetitions, yet we need millions more. *Every* time we truly say, "Thy will be done", we find joy and peace; every time we die, we rise. The saint finds heavenly ecstasy in picking up a pin for God. No lesson is more ubiquitously taught. Yet none is more doubted by unbelievers or disobeyed by believers. We are quite insane.

But God keeps kissing frogs, dispensing joy like rain, patiently teaching us to play his music, to learn the heavenly harmony of wills, training us for our perfect parts in the music of the spheres for which we were created. He is very single-minded. He preaches to us only what he practices himself: "There is only one thing necessary." Yet there is no more complex lesson for us than this simplicity.

We desire many things, and he offers us only one thing. He *can* offer us only one thing—himself. He has nothing else to give. There *is* nothing else to give. "Why callest thou me good? None is good but one, that is

[62] Luke 10:42 (AV).

God."[63] God is the only game in town. If we won't play, there's no winning anywhere else. "That is why it is just no good asking God to make us happy in our own way . . . God cannot give us a happiness and peace apart from himself because it is not there. There is no such thing. . . . If we will not learn to eat the only fruit the universe grows—the only fruit any possible universe can grow—we must starve eternally."[64] MacDonald puts it even more succinctly: "All that is not God is death."[65]

The man who said he was God also said he was our joy. If this claim is not true, it is the most blasphemous, egotistical, and insane thing ever spoken by human lips. If it is true, then God's single gift for all our desires is his Son. He *is* joy, joy alive and wearing a real human face, joy concretely real and not abstract, ephemeral, and uncertain. And we are designed and destined to taste this concrete joy, to "taste and see the goodness of the Lord", to drink eternal life like water, to eat God's will like food, to "put on Christ", not merely to imitate him.[66] Becoming parts of Christ ("members of his body", as Saint Paul says), we become parts of joy, *in* joy:[67] "Enter thou into the joy of thy Lord."[68]

The practical consequence of seeking only the "one thing necessary", the concrete Christ himself rather than joy in the abstract, is in fact perpetual, assured joy. We

[63] Mark 10:18 (AV).

[64] C. S. Lewis, *Mere Christianity*, p. 54.

[65] C. S. Lewis, *George MacDonald, An Anthology* (New York: Macmillan, 1978), no. 146, p. 63.

[66] Ps. 34:8; Rev. 22:17; John 4:32–34; Rom. 13:14.

[67] Eph. 5:30.

[68] Matt. 25:23.

do not always have the experience of joy; but we always have Christ: "Lo! I am with you always!" If Christ *is* our joy, then we always have joy. It is I AM who says, "I am with you always",[69] and that I AM is the absolute, the unchangeable, the utterly reliable. Our *I* is flighty, relative, and unreliable. But our *I* can plug into the I AM, and then it and its joy become as eternally solid as the joy of I AM. Faith is that plug.

Faith is incredibly easy. It means simply believing him. He promises to be with us always—well, then, he is with us. What is hard is *not* believing him, calling him a liar or a fool, for if his promises are not true, he is either a liar (if he knows they are not true) or a fool (if he thinks they are).

There is a Chinese parable about three men walking on a wall; they are Fact, Faith, and Feeling. As long as Faith keeps his eyes on Fact, on divinely revealed and promised Fact, all three walk along the wall. But once Faith turns from Fact to look around to see how Feeling is doing, both Faith and Feeling fall off the wall. The point of the parable, applied to joy, is that joy is not in feeling but in faith and that feelings of joy will come along if and only if faith looks at God, not at itself or at feelings. As Lewis found, "only when your whole attention and desire are fixed on something else . . . does the 'thrill' arise".[70] "We are and remain such creeping Christians because we look at ourselves and not at Christ", says George MacDonald.[71] We are creeping because we are weak; and we are weak because "the joy of the Lord

[69] Matt. 28:20 (AV).

[70] C. S. Lewis, *Surprised by Joy*, p. 168.

[71] C. S. Lewis, *George MacDonald, An Anthology*, no. 35, p. 16.

is your strength" and we lack that joy.[72] We lack that joy
because we look at ourselves and not at Christ. How
utterly simple it is! (That is, how *single,* not how *easy.*)

Joy is one of the "fruits of the Spirit" (the Holy Spirit,
the Spirit of Christ).[73] As every orchard farmer knows,
to get the fruit, you must attend to the tree, not to the
fruit. To have joy, you must fertilize the root of joy, and
the hourly fertilizer is obedience. "Heed not thy feelings; do thy work."[74] Pick up a straw (or a messy room)
for the love of God. And then you will experience
heaven on earth. It is scandalously simple:

> Trust and obey
> For there's no other way.[75]

[72] Neh. 8:10.

[73] Gal. 5:22.

[74] C. S. Lewis, *George MacDonald, An Anthology,* no. 39, p. 19.

[75] "Trust and Obey", hymn words by J. H. Sammis. Copyright
1915 by D. B. Towner, Hope Publishing Co.

Chapter 5

The Results of the Quest:
What Difference Does Heaven
Make to Monday Morning?

"Pie in the sky by and by"—it's an old, old accusation
that the longing for heaven is "escapist". Long before
Marx's "religion is the opium of the people", long before Nietzsche's "remain faithful to the earth", Christians were charged with escapism.[1] Gibbon, in *The
Decline and Fall of the Roman Empire,* rehashed the ancient
Roman claim that Christian otherworldliness was to
blame for abandoning Rome to her fall—a charge to
which Saint Augustine replied by writing the world's
first philosophy of history, *The City of God.*

But the charge has been strengthened by modern
psychology, which tells us how people create a fantasy
world to live in when the real world becomes unlivable.
The real world always fails to come up to our dreams
(unless our dreams are incredibly trivial), and the tension between the two may tear a weak soul apart, forc-
ing it to live in either one without the other. For the
majority, this one is the "real world", and they dully and
stoically abandon their dreams. But others abandon re-

[1] Karl Marx, *Critique of Hegel's Philosophy of Right,* trans. A.
Jolin and J. O'Malley (London: Cambridge University Press, 1970),
p. 131. Friedrich Nietzsche, *Thus Spake Zarathustra,* 1. 3.

ality and live in a dream world. Isn't this the origin of the hope for heaven? Freud thinks so.[2]

Furthermore, whatever the *origin* of the idea of heaven, doesn't the idea actually *function* as escapism? The origin of an idea may be unprovable, lost in the mists of an undocumented past; but we can observe and document the present way an idea functions in our experience. Look at the way smaller hopes tempt us to escapism. As you perform some dull duty like cleaning the house or washing the car, you dream of a movie or a vacation. The real present is something to be endured while you await the hoped-for future, where your heart is. How could heaven fail to function in just that way, making earth into a mere waiting station to be endured until the celestial railroad car arrives? If housecleaning can't rival vacations, how can earth rival heaven?

Teilhard de Chardin puts the problem this way: "How can the man who believes in heaven . . . believe seriously in the value of worldly occupations? . . . The Christian believes that life here below is continued in a life of which the joys, the sufferings, the reality, are quite incommensurable with the present. . . . This contrast and disproportion are enough, by themselves, to rob us of our taste for the world and our interest in it; but to them must be added a positive doctrine of judgment upon, even disdain for, a fallen and vitiated world."[3] In other words, why work seriously on a sinking ship?

[2] Sigmund Freud, *The Future of an Illusion* (New York: 1928).
[3] Teilhard de Chardin, *The Divine Milieu* (New York: Harper & Row, 1957), p. 51.

Is It True?

The first and simplest answer to the charge that belief in heaven is escapism is that the first question is not whether it is escapist but whether it is true. We cannot find out whether it is true simply by finding out whether it is escapist. "There is a tunnel under this prison" may be an escapist idea, but it may also be true.

If an idea is true, we want to believe it simply because it is true, whether it is escapist or not. If it is false, we want to reject it simply because it is false, whether it is escapist or not. The only honest reason for anyone ever accepting any idea is its truth. To say, "I don't care if it's true or false, I accept it because . . ." is simply deliberate dishonesty, no matter what reasons follow the "because".

This is so even if the reason is happiness. Suppose the truth would make you unhappy and believing a lie would make you happy (or you think it would), is it so bad to believe the lie? Yes. Truth is prior to happiness because a happiness without truth is not true happiness. George MacDonald says, "I would not favor a fiction to keep a whole world out of hell. The hell that a lie would keep any man out of is doubtless the very best place for him to go. It is truth . . . that saves the world."[4] It is better to be an honest atheist than a dishonest theist, for honesty seeks truth and when the honest atheist sees that God is the truth, the atheist will embrace him and be embraced. But deliberate dishonesty is the locking of the soul's door against the light, the refusal of reality. It

---

[4] C. S. Lewis, *George MacDonald: An Anthology* (New York: Macmillan, 1978), no. 273, p. 113.

is better to reject God than to reject truth; for the truth sought by honestly though mistakenly rejecting God is in fact a divine attribute ("When me they fly, I am the wings"[5]), but the God sought by rejecting truth is not the true God.

Judged by this standard, dishonesty is frightfully popular. Seldom do you hear the naive question, "But is it *true?*" Ideas are accepted because they are relevant, dynamic, viable, radical, traditional, nontraditional, useful, comforting, challenging, or for a hundred other reasons or rejected because they are abstract, unfashionable, unworkable, irrelevant, upsetting, traditional, nontraditional, and the like.[6] Our civilization seems to echo Pilate's indifference: "Truth? What's that?"[7]

To care for truth is especially crucial in religion, where we seek the divine Other, the true God (unless we

[5] Ralph Waldo Emerson, "Brahman", in *Poems,* 1886.

[6] Mortimer Adler, *How to Read a Book* (New York: Simon & Schuster, 1972), p. 165: "No higher commendation can be given any work of the human mind than to praise it for the measure of truth it has achieved; by the same token, to criticize it adversely for its failure in this respect is to treat it with the seriousness that a serious work deserves. Yet, strangely enough, in recent years, for the first time in Western history, there is a dwindling concern with this criterion of excellence. Books win the plaudits of critics and gain widespread popular attention almost to the extent that they flout the truth—the more outrageously they do so, the better. Many readers, and most particularly those who review current publications, employ other standards for judging, and praising or condemning, the books they read—their novelty, their sensationalism, their seductiveness, their force, and even their power to bemuse or befuddle the mind, but not their truth."

[7] John 18:38 (JB).

are those who call on the mountains to fall on us and hide us from his presence).[8] It is especially crucial in regard to heaven: "We are very shy nowadays of even mentioning heaven. We are afraid of the jeer about 'pie in the sky' and of being told that we are trying to 'escape' from the duty of making a happy world here and now into dreams of a happy world elsewhere. But either there is 'pie in the sky' or there is not. If there is not, then Christianity is false, for this doctrine is woven into its whole fabric. If there is, then this truth, like any other, must be faced, whether it is useful at political meetings or not."[9]

Do not think I am trying to "sell" heaven by wheedling you into believing it because it is useful or because it will make you happy to believe it. Whether it makes us happy or not, we must believe only what is true. We are not shopping for religious beliefs like clothes, picking faiths to suit our fancy. We must be clear about this because we are about to embark on a survey of many psychological advantages of belief in heaven, in answer to the charge of escapism; none of these is a valid reason for believing it. (The reasons for believing it are philosophical arguments, intuitive wisdom, faith in divine revelation in the Bible and the Church, and above all the resurrection of Jesus.)

Although the question "Is it true?" is the first and inescapable question if we are honest, the question "What difference does it make?" is legitimate, too. If the only difference heaven makes is future, not present, or if

[8] Luke 23:30.

[9] C. S. Lewis, *The Problem of Pain* (New York: Macmillan, 1962), pp. 144–145.

the only difference it makes to the present is escapism from it, then even if heaven is true, we do not want to pay much attention to it—it is true but unimportant or harmful and distracting. So we must answer the objection: Why isn't heaven escapist? What difference does it make to Monday morning? "True" does not *mean* "true to me", but I want to know what this truth means to me.

What Does Heaven Mean to Me?

There was once a race of people who lived in tiny cottages (though they did not feel them to be tiny because they knew nothing to compare them with). Some were ugly; some were cozy; some were a little bigger; some a little smaller. There was a tale told throughout the land, widely but not unanimously believed, very ancient and supported by most of the sages—a tale of a great and glorious castle, with a king and minstrels and feasts and tournaments and gold and tapestries, and a horrible dungeon in the cellar. The tale further had it that everyone in the cottages was eventually going to the castle to live there forever, either in the great hall in joy or in the dungeon in misery.

We are the people, of course, and the tale is Christianity. It may be true or it may be false, but it is at least important. Mere honesty demands it be investigated, for if it is true, it is not escapism but reality, and it is realistic to think about it. Anyone more interested in the size and cost of the cottage next door than in the great castle is simply a clod. And an escapist, because if the tale is true, the castle is his destiny, too.

To change the story a little, suppose you have just

moved out of a dingy little hut into a great new mansion. Would you stay on the front porch looking back at your hut rather than exploring your new home? Well, the mansion is one of the "many mansions"[10] in the Body of Christ, and the Christian is already there. According to the New Testament, "eternal life" begins now.[11] Exploring the deeper reaches of the mansion whose porch we already inhabit is not escapism from our real condition. Unless Christianity is simply false, the mansion *is* our real condition; it is escapism to ignore it.

One more parable. There was a rumor among the caterpillars that they were destined to become butterflies. Some caterpillars believed it; others disbelieved; and still others doubted. Now what would be the reasonable attitude of each of the three groups of caterpillars toward this rumor? Which could reasonably call it escapist? Would not even the uncertain want to explore it further? For if it is true (and "uncertain" means "iffy"), it is not escapism. The charge of escapism therefore logically boils down to the charge of falsehood; only those who are certain the rumor is false can reasonably call it escapist. Otherworldliness is escapism only if there is no other world. If there is, it is worldliness that is escapism.

It is unreasonable (and in fact escapist) not to plan for a trip to Australia before you go, especially if it is a one-way trip. But the trip to heaven or hell is surer, longer, and more certainly one-way than a trip to Australia. For every earthly trip, you at least make some inquiries at

[10] John 14:2.
[11] I John 5:13; John 17:1-4, 19:30.

the travel bureau. The Church claims to be the heavenly travel bureau as well as the ship, the Noah's ark, in which we go. Simply to ignore this claim as escapism is the sheerest escapism.

The escapism of worldliness is compounded by the fact that we are already embarked on our journey to the other world. As soon as we are born, we begin to die. This world is like a rocket ship; we are already launched into the beyond. Life is an escalator, and there is no way off except at the end. The only choice is between directions: up or down.

Death does not come to me as an accident from without, though its occasions do (such as a speeding car); it is written into my genes. My very being is a "being-toward-death", as Heidegger says.[12] So my concern for life after death is innate to my human condition, not escapist from it. "The beyond" is not beyond *me;* it is "the beyond within". My end is not just my *finis* but my *telos,* not just my finish but my destiny.

Unlike animals, we live by destiny, out of our future, not only out of our past; by planning and free choice, not by blind instinct and causal determinism; by history, not by nature. Animals live by nature, not history; their lives are only the outworking of their genetic programming and environmental conditioning—except perhaps for some of the higher animals that seem to tremble on the brink of human personality. A mere animal is like an unfolding flower: "physical". The word comes from the Greek *physis,* which originally meant "emergence . . . that which arises . . . opening up and inward jutting

[12] Martin Heidegger, *Being and Time* (New York: Harper & Row, 1962), p. 296.

beyond itself" (*in-sich-aus-sich-hinaus-stehen,* in Heideggerian German).¹³ But we are determined from without and from above, not only from within and from below; by final causes, not only by efficient causes. "The shape of Man's life is not a growth and unfolding from within, culminating in a return upon itself; its figure or symbol is not the self-enclosed circle, but an arch that reaches out toward something."¹⁴ That something is, finally, heaven. Thinking about heaven is not escapism because it determines my essence. My destiny determines my essence; animals' essence determines their destiny. I am a flying arrow, determined by the target because I have been launched by the mind of a divine archer, a mind with a purpose. Finding my purpose is the exact opposite of escapism; it is finding my essence.

Concern for heaven is as escapist as looking through the windshield rather than in the rearview mirror as you are locked in a speeding car lurching over foggy, rocky terrain with the road maps gone. We should do *some* looking back, for looking back is an aid to looking ahead; "those who do not know history are condemned to repeat it." But "Where are you going?" is the first question for the traveler, and we are travelers.

"We are embarked."¹⁵ That is the passionate point of Pascal's "wager". "You *must* wager. It is not optional." We can think agnosticism, but we cannot live it. The winds of time are blowing the ship of self along the

¹³ Martin Heidegger, *Introduction to Metaphysics* (New York: Doubleday Anchor Books, 1961), p. 12.

¹⁴ Romano Guardini, *The Last Things* (New York: Pantheon Books, 1954), p.18.

¹⁵ Pascal, *Pensées,* 418, trans. A. J. Krailsheimer (New York: Penguin Books, 1966), p. 150.

waters of life past the port of God, past the harbor entrance of faith. Every moment we do not turn the ship toward the harbor, we move farther away. There comes a point of no return. Not to choose this harbor is itself a choice: "He that is not for me is against me."[16] Not to choose at all is an option only for observers, not for participants; for the audience, not for the players. Birth has made us participants. God has proposed spiritual marriage to us; to say nothing in reply is to say no. If we are not pregnant with God, we are barren; no one is half pregnant. If we are not on the road to heaven, we are on the road to hell; there simply are no other options. Earth is only the castle's drawbridge, the road to the great hall or to the dungeon, upstairs or downstairs. "All that seems earth is Hell or Heaven."[17]

The Hereness of Heaven

According to the New Testament, everyone is a member of one of two kingdoms (the "two cities", Augustine calls them), two invisible organisms, (the Body of Christ or the body of sin, as Saint Paul calls them), fallen and redeemed humanity or fallen and unredeemed humanity.[18] Through these two bodies flow two totally different spirits, animating principles, life-bloods, which the New Testament calls *bios* (natural life) and *zoë* (supernatural life). The law governing *bios* is natural law:

[16] Matt. 12:30.

[17] C. S. Lewis, "Wormwood", in *Poems* (New York: Harcourt, Brace & World, 1964), p. 87.

[18] Augustine, *The City of God,* esp. 14. 28; Rom. 6:6, 7:24, 8:10; 1 Cor. 12:20, 27.

the cause and effect determinism of physics and chemistry, the sociological determinism of heredity and environment, and the psychological determinism of selfishness, survival, the primal natural instinct. *Zoë* transforms these forces as a digestive system transforms food. The law governing the whole body whose life is *zoë* is God's love. Romans 8:28, perhaps the most spectacularly astonishing verse in the Bible, is literally true for every cell in the Body of Christ: "*All* things work together for good for those who love God, for those who are the called according to his purpose." Every atom in the quadrillion-mile universe and every "chance" event in its trillion-year history is deliberately and perfectly planned and controlled by God for the ultimate end of our good, our heavenly joy. Galaxies revolve and dinosaurs breed and rain falls and people fall in love and uncles smoke cheap cigars and people lose their jobs and we all die—all (that's what it says, "*all*") for our good, the finished product, God's work of art, the Kingdom of heaven. There's nothing outside heaven except hell. Earth is not outside heaven; it is heaven's workshop, heaven's womb.

What about evil and suffering? If they are not merely illusions, as Buddhism and Christian Science teach, they, too, though not created by God, become part of Providence's perfect plan for our ultimate good. Augustine says, "God would not allow any evil to exist in his works unless his omnipotence and goodness were such as to bring good even out of evil."[19] The solution to the "problem of evil" is time. It's a fairy tale; and all God's lovers live happily ever after.

[19] Augustine, *Enchiridion,* 11.

This is not fantasy or mysticism or extravaganza; it's the plain bare bones of Christianity. It's not a philosophy, a piece of human speculation; it's not even a theology, a human interpretation of divine revelation. It's a divinely declared fact. To deny that everything, even evil, works for good is to deny at least one of three rock-bottom fundamentals that, when combined, make this conclusion inescapable: (1) God is all good, willing only our good; (2) God is all powerful, able to do whatever he wills; and (3) God is present now, doing his thing in all times and places. To deny any one of these is to deny that God is God. But to affirm all three is to affirm total providence, total heaven, total joy in the last analysis. Those are the only options. Once again, "all that seems earth is hell or heaven."

More, this long-run, after-death heavenly joy is also present now, even if we don't see it or believe it or take advantage of it. Listen to Dostoevsky say it:

> "Mother, don't weep, darling," he would say, "I've long to live yet, long to rejoice with you, and life is glad and joyful."
>
> "Ah, dear boy, how can you talk of joy when you lie feverish at night, coughing as though you would tear yourself to pieces?"
>
> "Don't cry, mother," he would answer, "life is paradise, and we are all in paradise, but we won't see it, if we would, we should have heaven on earth the next day."
>
> Every one wondered at his words, he spoke so strangely and positively; we were all touched and wept.[20]

[20] Fyodor Dostoyevsky, *The Brothers Karamazov*, trans. Constance Garnett (New York: Modern Library, 1950), p. 343.

We are in heaven now. The Kingdom has come, for the Kingdom is Christ, and Christ has come, and God has put us into Christ.

Yet we are also not yet there: "Not that I have already obtained this or am already perfect; but I press on to make it my own, because Christ Jesus has made me his own . . . I press on toward the goal for the prize of the upward call of God in Christ Jesus."[21] The Kingdom has come, yet it is still coming. "It is finished", yet we finish it: "In my flesh I complete what is lacking in Christ's afflictions for the sake of his body, that is the Church."[22] The plant has been planted, but it is still only a seedling. The inconceivable has been conceived—heaven has come into the womb of the world—yet it is only a fetus.

This is why heaven is not escapist: earth is heaven's womb. Would it be escapism for a fetus to think about birth? Does life after birth make life in the womb any less important? Doesn't it make it infinitely *more* important? If a mother knew her fetus would be stillborn, would she not care for it far less?

Heaven is not escapist because we are already there, just as the fetus in the womb is already in the world because the womb is in the world and subject to its laws, such as the laws of gravity and genetics. We are not yet born from the world-womb, but we are already part of the heavenly Body.

The matter of this womb shields our unprotected eyes from the light of heaven as the womb shields the fetus from the light of this world. If we stood face to face

21 Phil. 3:12–14.
22 Col. 1:24.

with the light streaming from the face of God right now, we would be blinded, dazzled, and squashed. "No man can see my face and live." God is like the sun; the most ecstatic joy available in our present experience is like a sunbeam. If we were able to run up the sunbeam into the sun, we would be volatized. Our business here is a process of thickening, becoming more real, learning to endure more light.

Heaven is present, which means three connected things: (1) It is a present, a gift. (2) It is (or begins) in the present, not in the future. (3) It is present rather than absent; it is "here". Let's look at this third meaning for a minute.

A *thing* cannot be present; it can only be. Only a person can be present. Things are just "there"; persons are "here". When your name is called, you can say "Present!" A stone can't. Heaven is not a thing or even a place; it is a Person; that's why it (he) is present. Heaven is where God is—God defines heaven, not heaven, God—and God is present in every place. Therefore heaven is present in every place as well as every time. No place or time contains God; he contains them.

Even our human consciousness is present to many times and places without being contained by them as physical bodies are. I can be present in my consciousness to Chicago while my body remains in Boston. "Through space the universe grasps me and swallows me up like a speck; through thought I grasp it."[23]

God is present to us because he is presence itself. He is eternally present to himself; that is his essence. The three Persons of the Trinity are subsisting relationships

[23] Pascal, *Pensées*, 113, p. 59.

to each other, present to each other. In the beginning was presence. God's presence to himself by self-knowledge is the Word; his presence by love is the Holy Spirit. Heaven is present because God is present, and God is present because presence is his very essence.

What Difference Does It Make?

The only thing whose presence can make an all-encompassing difference, a difference to everything in my life, is something not contained by but containing my life. That's me. I am the constant amid millions of variables that make up my life. All my experiences are not X or Y or Z, but all my experiences are mine. Each experience is "I experiencing X and Y in way Z". X, Y, and Z are the variables; I am the constant. The only way everything can become green is if green is in our eyes or our eyeglasses. Heaven makes a total difference because it is not an ingredient; it is not a new object seen but a new see-er. Heaven is my new identity, my true identity. "Your life is hid with Christ in God."[24] Only the One who designed you and is even at this moment providentially sculpting you in a thousand unrecognized ways into the masterpiece he always had in mind for you to be knows the secret of your identity. The artist knows the form; the work of art knows only the half-finished raw material it presently is.

If this earth is "all there is", then this is all I am: my earthly identity, my ego and what it possesses, me and mine. But death removes all I possess, even my body. If that's all I am, I'm not much. If I'm not stronger than

[24] Col. 3:3.

death, then I'm not much before death either. If I have no heavenly identity, I don't have much of an earthly identity either.

This is the fundamental question about my identity: How much am I? Am I "from the earth, earthly" or from heaven?[25] From dust or from spirit? G. B. Shaw says somewhere that the ancients were proud to think themselves to be bastard offspring of the gods, while we moderns are humbled to think ourselves to be legitimate offspring of the apes. Am I made in the image of King Kong or in the image of King God? Am I a potential god or a rational rabbit? It makes an infinite difference.

Finding My Identity by Ecstasy

If heaven makes a difference to my identity, how do I find that difference? Human identity, unlike the identity of things in nature, is a problem, not a given. How do I find out who I am?

By the oldest and profoundest paradox of them all: "He who loses his self will find it."[26] The most complete self-loss and self-finding is ecstasy, standing outside yourself. And the complete moment of standing outside yourself is the moment of death. Death is the "golden key" to my identity.[27] Death is the door not only to life but also to selfhood.

At death, God's love ravishes us right out of ourselves, sweeps us off our feet, off the ground, out of the

---

[25] I Cor. 15:47 (AV).

[26] Matthew 10:39.

[27] Death is one interpretation of the central symbol in George MacDonald's wonderful little fairy tale, *The Golden Key*.

earth, and out of the body. After death we are ravished even further: not only out of our bodies but out of our souls, our selves. Heaven is so self-forgetful that mystics who have experienced foretastes of it here often say they were absorbed into God, annihilated, or seen through as illusory.

This can't be literally true for the simple reason that only a self can be self-forgetful. Only one who exists can say, "I do not exist." No, the self God loved enough to create and redeem is not annihilated or illusory. It has found itself by completely forgetting itself; it has become a transparent window to God's light. Its mind thinks only God's thoughts and its will wills only God's will; so it can say like Christ: "I and the Father are one."[28] Yet they are also two: "The Father is greater than I."[29] "The two become one"—fleshly marriage dimly symbolizes our destiny, spiritual marriage to God.[30] Life is learning to prepare for that destiny. That's what the Christian love ethic is all about. Ethics is practicing scales for the heavenly symphony.

Love (*agapē*) is the deepest of three kinds of ecstatic foretastes of heaven. The first and most obvious kind is the bittersweet experience of beauty, the thing the Romantic poets see, "the many-splendored thing", the angel in the flower: "turn but a leaf and stir a wing". Whether it comes through nature, art, music, or the human face, it is a breeze that blows a grace from a far country. It whispers a tale of joy that makes us painfully aware of our joylessness, yet that very pain is an incom-

[28] John 10:30.
[29] John 14:28.
[30] Eph. 5:31.

parable joy. This is the bittersweetness we have already explored just a tiny bit.

The second kind of earthly ecstasy that lifts us a few inches off the earth into heaven is the passionate, self-forgetful devotion to Truth, Truth with a capital T, Truth as an absolute. Pascal typifies this when he says, "My whole heart strains to know what the true good is in order to pursue it. No price would be too high to pay for eternity."[31]

The third and deepest foretaste of heaven is love. "The true, the good (love) and the beautiful"—but "the greatest of these is love."[32] For love, unlike beauty or truth, is *our* work; it comes from us as well as to us. We create not only things lovable, but love itself. We create things beautiful and things true, but not beauty or truth themselves.

Love is not quite our creation; it is our co-creation. It comes through us (if we let it); we are its tubes, its channels. God, who *is* love, is its source. It comes to us with an invitation to ecstasy. We are invited to take it and pass it on, to swim in the divine circulatory system, to be both veins and arteries. We receive God's love by faith and give it back by passing it on in the form of works ("the works of love").[33] Faith and works are one thing, one reality: the divine life itself, *zoë,* which *is*

---

[31] Pascal, *Pensées,* 429, p. 163.

[32] 1 Cor. 13:13.

[33] Cf. Sören Kierkegaard, *Works of Love* (Princeton: Princeton University Press, 1946). "To the Christian love is the works of love. To say that love is a feeling or anything of the kind is an unchristian conception of love." Robert Bretall, *A Kierkegaard Anthology* (New York: Modern Library, 1936), p. 281.

love. So much for the false problem of the Reformation, the problem of faith "versus" works.

The ecstasy of love is our training for heaven because it constructs the self that lives outside itself, which is the only kind of self that can live in heaven. Beauty experiences something of heavenly ecstasy, but love creates it. (In fact, love even creates beauty, for to be loved is to become newly beautiful.) Beauty is the aroma of heavenly food; love is the eating of it. Beauty is God's silhouette; love is his life blood. Beauty is the shadow of heaven; love is its substance.

So earthly beauty gives us moving hints of the shape of heaven, but *agapē* on earth is the very substance of heaven. Therefore if our early life is made of *agapē,* heaven and earth are made of the same stuff for us, and heaven is no more an escape from earth than the sun is an escape from sunlight. Sunlight says "Made in the sun", as a Ford says "Made in USA". Love says "Made in heaven". Just as there are Ford factories abroad, there are love factories in heaven's colonies. We are heaven's colonies.

"All that seems earth is hell or heaven"—every bit of love and beauty and truth that anyone ever experiences on earth is made in heaven and is a participation in heaven. For heaven is God's presence; and God is present in all goodness, all truth, and all beauty. God is not a truth, a good, or a beauty, but Goodness Itself and Truth Itself and Beauty Itself. He is neither a particular thing nor an abstract, universal quality, like "goodness in general". He is a concrete universal. In God all goodness, truth, and beauty exist, coexist, meet, and are perfected, like the generatrices of a cone meeting at its point. God is the point of it all. "It all" is heaven; earth is only heaven's outer border, the arc of the cone. "All that seems earth is hell or heaven."

Fearlessness

Faith in heaven's presence produces the greatest psychological revolution imaginable. If we don't observe this revolution taking place in ourselves, it can be for only one reason: Our faith is much smaller than a grain of mustard seed.

Faith and faith's fruit, love, cast out fear. Jesus keeps telling His disciples, "Fear not, only believe . . . why are you afraid, O you of little faith?"[34] Christian faith is faith in heaven having come. If faith were merely hope for the future, we could still fear the present. But faith is in God's present (gift) of his present (now) presence (here).

Surface appearances are fearsome: poverty, disease, pain, war, betrayal, death. But faith sees them as appearances of the universal sacrament, faith-testing and deceptive appearances. That looks like bread, but it's really the Body of Christ. That looks like failure, but it's really Providence. As the author of Job Socratically says, what do we know, anyway? (He says it more gracefully than that, but that's what God's answer comes down to.) We are like flies crawling along a fingernail on the tenth angel from the left in the sixth row of angels in a Michelangelo fresco. We see a few loose threads on the back side of life's tapestry, and unless we are told by the Weaver, we can only guess at the shape of the picture.

But we have been told. Faith is simply believing what

[34] Mark 5:36; Matt. 8:26.

we have been told, believing the unbelievable: that God has the ace up his sleeve; that the worst the devil can do is to contribute unwillingly to the best God does; that even deicide worked out for our salvation; and that when we feel like saying with Hamlet, "How weary, stale, flat and unprofitable seem to me all the uses of this world. Fie on it!" or feel like reading Ecclesiastes, we can also read the rest of the story, from Genesis to Revelation.[35] "All authority has been given to me, in heaven and on earth", said the Author's Son.[36] Chance is not a word in God's vocabulary. Our providences may be merely general; God's extends to every hair on our head, every war, every hemorrhoid.

That is what we have been told, what faith believes. The logical consequence of believing what we have been told is utter fearlessness. Nothing in the universe can separate us from our joy, from our God. Nothing can harm us. We are impervious. We are redeemed, inde-structible souls guaranteed new, indestructible bodies. We can even rejoice in all the sufferings of our earthly bodies (that's what it says, not "endure" but "rejoice in"; don't argue with me, argue with the Bible) because they are "working out an eternal weight of glory".[37] Not *despite* all these things but "*in* all these things we are more than conquerors through him who loves us, for I am sure that neither death, nor life, nor angels, nor principalities, nor things present, nor things to come, nor powers, nor height, nor depth, nor anything else in all creation, will be able to separate us from the love of

[35] Shakespeare, *Hamlet*, act 1, scene 2.
[36] Matt. 28:18.
[37] 2 Cor. 4:17.

God in Christ Jesus our Lord."[38] Simple biblical realism. Inescapable logic.

Anyone who knows even a little psychology knows that repressed fears still kick around. We may bury them, but we bury them alive. The fear of death is the primary fear, as the desire for life is the primary desire, nature's first instinct. For death means the loss of everything. It may also mean getting it all back again, or getting in exchange something incomparably better, but it does mean losing everything first; and that is fearsome, losing *everything*. But the fear of physical death is not the worst fear, if we are not merely physical. Fear of spiritual death is worse—fear of losing our very self, spirit, soul, identity. "What does it profit a man if he gain the whole world and lose his own soul?"[39]

Spiritual death means hell. Now suppose both death and hell were utterly defeated. Suppose the fight was fixed. Suppose God took you on a crystal ball trip into your future and you saw with indubitable certainty that despite everything—your sin, your smallness, your stupidity—you could have free for the asking your whole crazy heart's deepest desire: heaven, eternal joy. Would you not return fearless and singing? What can earth do to you if you are guaranteed heaven? To fear the worst earthly loss would be like a millionaire fearing the loss of a penny—less, a scratch on a penny.

But this *is* our true state, according to God's own word. This is the Gospel, the scandalously good news: that we are guaranteed heaven by sheer gift. "Let him who is thirsty come, let him who desires take the water

[38] Rom. 8:37–39.
[39] Matt. 16:26.

of life without price."⁴⁰ The only qualification is thirst, desire; "all who seek, find". To this day millions of Christians simply can't believe it. They persist in thinking of God as a stern judge and of their road to heaven as the onerous piling up of good deeds for the day. They've read the New Testament a dozen times and missed the whole point. If they hadn't missed it, how could they go around with long faces and worried consciences all the time? It wasn't worrywarts who won the world. Nor was it iron wills. It was doubting Thomases and foot-in-mouth-disease Peters and persecuting Pauls who became little Christs by believing the good news of the big Christ: "It is finished." The lamb has kayoed the dragon.⁴¹ The Athenians have beaten the Persians. A bunch of American college kids have beaten the world champion Russian Olympic hockey team for the gold medal. The impossible has happened.

The Joy of Failure

If we are already in heaven, we cannot fear even failures. For we are already in heaven *together with our failures.* They are transfigured by heaven's light. They contribute to the Kingdom of heaven as the darkness in a painting contributes to its light. To the painter, the darkness is part of the light: "If I say, 'Let only darkness cover me, and the light about me be night', even the darkness is not dark to thee, the night is bright as the day. For darkness is as light with thee."⁴² This is why we can not

⁴⁰ Rev. 22:17.
⁴¹ Rev. 12:3, 14:1, 19:20.
⁴² Ps. 139:11–12.

only *endure* but *"glory* in our weaknesses", like Saint Paul: because God's "strength is made perfect in weakness".[43] Our weak earthly bottles contain heavenly wine. Of course they burst; that's what they're intended to do.

Failures are real, not illusions. We fail to pass a test or get a job; we fail to love or be loved; we fail to be wise enough, or strong enough, or good enough. Not all things are successes; not everything works for our earthly good. Therefore either Scripture lies when it says all things work together for our good, or it is our heavenly good that is being made out of our earthly failures.

Even moral failures, through the door of repentance, are admitted into heaven. As a dramatist uses villains as well as heroes, the divine dramatist uses even our sins, our lives' villains, the enemies within. He's like a French cook: he uses everything in the kitchen, even leftovers, to make a great new sauce.

There is simply nothing left to fear. Fear presupposes faith in the reality of its object. Someone who does not believe in ghosts does not fear ghosts. But ultimate failures, heavenly failures, are ghosts: unreal, only appearances.

And even if we do fear, if we are so foolish as to fear the nonexistent, that's part of the plot too. Our very fears, our very foolishness in fearing nonexistent final failure, is also part of God's all-inclusive providential plan for our final success. The Christian vision goes a step beyond "There is nothing to fear but fear itself." There is not even fear to fear! And even if we do fear fear

---

[43] 2 Cor. 12:9.

16   *Heaven: The Heart's Deepest Longing*

itself, that's part of the plot too—as is the fear that it isn't part of the plot. There is no escape. Heaven's success always has the last word, enclosing and transforming our earthly fears and failures.

Why Not Go Ahead and Sin Then?

If even moral failures, even sins, are part of the plan and if we believe this, why not sin? Why doesn't this vision of an all-inclusive heaven produce amoralism and make nonsense of (1) the serious duty to resist temptation, (2) the real, objective distinction between good and evil, (3) ultimately, the distinction between heaven and hell, and (4) the character of God as righteous, just, and holy? On all four issues, isn't this vision pantheism rather than theism, Oriental rather than Western, Hindu rather than Christian? If not, why not?

It is not because in order to be included in heaven's Kingdom, sins must be honestly repented. Every sin meets its necessary fate: expulsion from the Kingdom. And if we cling to this spiritual garbage, we will find ourselves in the universe's spiritual garbage dump. God does not forgive sins; he forgives sinners and destroys sins.[44] If the sinner does not identify himself with his sins, he is not destroyed. This not-identifying, this refusal, is repentance.

Only past sins can contribute to heavenly perfection through repentance, not those being committed or planned. There is a story about Tetzel, the Dominican monk who went around sixteenth-century Germany selling indulgences and scandalizing Martin Luther. He

[44] C. S. Lewis, *George MacDonald: An Anthology*, no. 13, p. 7.

used to sing a little ditty: "Sobald das Geld im Kasten klingt, Die Seele aus dem Fegfeur springt." ("As soon as your money falls into my casket, your soul leaps free from the fires of Purgatory!") A thief came up to him and asked how much it would cost for an indulgence to forgive all his past sins. "A thousand gold pieces." "And how much for one to forgive all my future sins as well?" "Two thousand more." "All right, here's three thousand. Give me the indulgence." "Here it is. Thank you." "And now here's one of those future sins. See this sword? Hand back the three thousand."

The point is that sin and repentance are opposites: sin casts out repentance, and repentance casts out sin. You can't repent of present or presently planned sins because you can't sin and repent at the same time.

Saint Paul (who teaches the vision of fearlessness) gives an even better answer to the objection of amoralism in Romans 5 and 6. Watch the following three points emerge in this passage (5:20–6:18): (1) the vision of God's grace as triumphing over even sin, (2) the objection of amoralism it naturally gives rise to, and (3) Paul's answer to this objection:

(1) Where sin abounded, grace did much more abound. So that, as sin reigned in death, grace also might reign through righteousness to eternal life through Christ Jesus our Lord. (5:20–21)

(2) What shall we say then? Are we to continue in sin that grace may abound? (6:1)

(3) God forbid! How can we who died to sin still live in it? Do you not know that all of us who have been baptized into Christ Jesus were baptized into his death? . . . For he who has died is freed from

> sin. . . . So you also must consider yourselves dead
> to sin and alive to God in Christ Jesus. (6:2, 3, 7, 11)

The same three points come up a few verses later: (1)
"You are not under the law but under grace" (6:14). (2)
"What then? Are we to sin because we are not under the
law but under grace?" (6:15). (3) "By no means!. . . .
thanks be to God that you who were once slaves of sin
have become obedient from the heart . . . and having
been set free from sin have become slaves of righteousness" (6:15, 17, 18).

Paul's answer to the question "Why not sin if everything is under heavenly grace?" is: Remember who you
are. Remember your identity and then you will not sin.
Believe in your heavenly life and then you will live that
life. Believe you are a heavenly tree and you will grow
heavenly fruit. If you see yourself as a part of Christ,
you will act like Christ; if you see yourself as fallen
Adam, you will act like fallen Adam. We act out our
perceived identities. Tell a kid he's a beast and he'll act
beastly; tell him he's lovable and he'll act lovable. *Me-
mento mori,* said the medieval maxim: Remember death,
and then you will not sin.[45] But the biblical meaning of
this is not: Remember that if you sin you will be
punished after death. It is: Remember that you have
already died to sin, to old self, to Adam; remember who
you are, and you will not sin.

Resentment and Performance Anxiety

The life of heaven on earth is free from two psychological traps that spoil the spiritual life for the worrisome

---

[45] Wisdom of Sirach 7:36. Cf. Saint Thomas More's sermon on
this verse (1522), "The Four Last Things: Death", in *The Wisdom of
Catholicism*, ed. Anton Pegis (New York: Modern Library, 1949).

rabbit. One is resentment: We often live an inner no while performing an outer yes to goodness and live an inner yes to evil while outwardly rejecting it. We see its attractions as real, not as the fakes they are because we think of ourselves as animals required to perform unnaturally as gods instead of gods performing unnaturally as animals. C. S. Lewis voices our inner resentment to God this way: "Sometimes, Lord, one is tempted to say that if you wanted us to behave like the lilies of the field you might have given us an organisation more like theirs. . . . To take a poor primate, a beast with nerve-endings all over it, a creature with a stomach that wants to be filled, a breeding animal that wants its mate, and say, 'Now get on with it. Become a god.' "[46]

The other trap is "performance anxiety" for God. No one performs well when he feels anxiety to please the one for whom he is performing, whether the performance is a play for an audience, the sex act for a mate, a child's obedience to parents or teachers, or moral virtue for God. When we feel "under the eye", fear of failure and rejection constricts us. We feel we are loved only conditionally, only if we perform well. But Christian love (*agapē*), the love that comes from God, is unconditional and thus casts out fear.

Most people do not believe in unconditional love; that God sends his Son as well as his sun on both the just and the unjust; that he loves the sinner in his sin (because that's where he is!)—indeed, that he loves him more

[46] C. S. Lewis, *A Grief Observed* (New York: Seabury/Bantam, 1976), pp. 84–85.

simply because of his greater need.[47] The Good Shepherd in the parable leaves the ninety-nine to seek and save the lamb that was lost, and "there is more rejoicing in heaven over one sinner that repents than over ninety-nine righteous men that need no repentance."[48]

Most people are more certain of justice than of unconditional love. But we don't love justice; we fear it. For we know we are sinners (unless we are fools), and we know that justice demands punishment, and we fear punishment.[49] Thus Chesterton says somewhere that young children like fairy tales unbowdlerized, with the villains killed rather than forgiven because children are innocent and prefer justice, while adults are guilty and prefer mercy. Unless God is more than just, God is a terrible God. Would you like to meet him right now, face to face? If you shrink back, you do not really believe he is unconditional love. If you long for that meeting, you are either a fool or a believer.

Performance anxiety often leads to atheism. For atheism is not merely a belief; it is a choice, an act, in fact an act of deicide. When we can't stand the pressure of living up to his expectations, we kill the Expecter. When the mirror mercilessly shows up all your warts, you want to break the mirror. That is the real point of the Oedipus complex; the primal parricide is not against our human father but God, not the image but the archetype.

[47] Matt. 5:45.
[48] Luke 15:7.
[49] 1 John 4:18: "There is no fear in love, but perfect love casts out fear. For fear has to do with punishment, and he who fears is not perfected in love."

Sartre is a case in point. In his autobiography, *The Words,* he tells how he became an atheist: "Only once did I have the feeling that he existed. I had been playing with matches and burned a small rug. I was in the process of covering up my crime when suddenly God saw me. I felt his gaze inside my head and on my hands. I whirled about in the bathroom, horribly visible, a live target. Indignation saved me. I flew into a rage . . . I blasphemed, I muttered like my grandfather: 'God damn it, God damn it, God damn it.' He never looked at me again."[50]

But God is not Sartre's baleful eye. He doesn't say "Look at your pimples" (except to unrepentant fools who think they have none) but "Look at me in Christ" and then "Look at yourself in Christ". God in Christ is not condemner but Redeemer ("God sent his Son into the world not to condemn the world but that the world might be saved through him"[51]). We in Christ are not the condemned but the redeemed, not pimply Adam but "all fair" bride. That's the Gospel, the good news that's too good to be true yet is true. Not to believe it is to believe the even more unbelievable bad news that God is a liar. God is either a lover or a liar. The Gospel is a sign blocking the commonsensical middle road of justice. The sign says, "Road closed because of flood"—the flood of God's unconditional love. There are only two roads. If God loves us even in our sin, earth is heaven. If he's a liar, earth is hell. "All that seems earth is hell or heaven."

[50] Jean-Paul Sartre, *The Words,* trans. B. Frechtman (New York: G. Braziller, 1964), p. 102.

[51] John 3:17.

To Care and Not to Care

An objection similar to the charge of amoralism but broader is that this faith in heaven's presence produces passivity and apathy. Why struggle against any kind of evil—suffering, weakness, disease, or failure—if there is no failure? If earth is already heaven, let's just sit back and enjoy it. There's no need to do anything, to change anything. That sounds right for a Hindu but hardly for a Christian.

There are three answers to that charge. First, being in heaven is no occasion for passivity because heaven is activity, not passivity. Scripture, saints and mystics, and resuscitated patients always use images of activity, such as singing, and images of waking, such as light, rather than images of rest or sleep to describe heaven. The more heaven is present, the *less* sleepy we are.

Second, fearlessness does not weaken our struggle but strengthens it, as a soldier's fearlessness lets him fight more freely, while fear constricts him or produces passivity. It was David the warrior king who said, "The Lord is my light and my salvation; whom then should I fear?"[52]

Fearlessness comes from heavenly joy: "The joy of the Lord is your strength."[53] Joyless people are weak, weary and apathetic, bowled over by little things, especially personal relationships. They interpret teasing as insult, play as irresponsibility, and disagreement as personal attack. Joyful people are strong, open and eager for action. Their joy gives them an energy and a power. We

[52] Ps. 27:1.
[53] Neh. 8:10.

all know this from experience, but not all of us know where that joy comes from. It comes from heaven.

A third reason heaven does not make us passive to earthly struggle is that heaven is made of the earthly struggle. We are characters in God's drama, and our role is to fight. The fight is like a Zen *koan;* unless the student struggles with it—in fact, unless he fails to conquer it—it does not trigger enlightenment. Unless he beats his brains out against the unbudgeable wall, his brains remain unchanged. Morality is the Judaeo-Christian *koan;* and the necessary stages of the drama are (1) our struggle, (2) our failure and repentance, and (3) God's success, forgiveness, and redemption. All three are our role, our inheritance, our authored essence. Unless we fight, we do not fail. Unless we fail, we do not know our need. Unless we know our need, we're not in the market for God's grace.

We fight, we struggle, we care because earth is a stage—"all the world's a stage"—and heaven is the theatre.[54] Heaven encloses earth. Good actors are both inside and outside their roles, involved in them yet detached from them. They take their roleplaying seriously, yet they know it is a role, framed by a stage. In a serious play, the play/seriousness distinction is overcome. Olivier is Olivier playing Hamlet, *and* Olivier is Hamlet.

Like the incarnate Christ, we have two identities, earthly and heavenly. Of course there is a difference: He came from heaven to earth; we go from earth to heaven. He came from outside to inside; we go from inside to outside. But both of us have double identities, inside

[54] William Shakespeare, *As You Like It,* act 2, scene 7.

and outside the earthly frame, the play. It's not that the play is unreal; real blood is spilt on this stage. Yet it's not "all there is", and we should not live as if it is.

How should we live then? "Teach us to care and not to care", prays Eliot.[55] Life is like a game: on the one hand, to play it well, we must play it with care, with passion. Life is not only a play but a passion play. On the other hand, it's only a game, framed and enclosed by a larger world; and we are to learn detachment before death detaches us willy-nilly. Even if we lose a game, we need not be losers in the world outside the game. Earthly success is not the absolute good for the same reason winning at chess is not the absolute good. Winners inside can be losers outside, and losers inside can be winners outside: "Many of the first shall be last and the last shall be first."[56]

There are only three options: (1) "to care and not to care", (2) simply to care, and (3) simply not to care. Simply to care means idolizing the world as "all there is": Western secularism. Simply not to care means rejecting the world as illusory: Eastern mysticism. "To care and not to care" means taking the world game as real but not as Reality itself. Creation is somewhere between God and nothingness, between absolute reality and absolute illusion.

We should be able to say to everything in the world, following Charles Williams's epigram, "This also is Thou, neither is this Thou", perceiving both God's immanence ("this also is Thou") and transcendence

55 T. S. Eliot, "Ash Wednesday".
56 Matt. 19:30.

("neither is this Thou").[57] "To care and not to care" means loving without greed, respecting without grasping, for "a man is in bondage to whatever he cannot part with that is less than himself".[58]

But the greedy grasping of the secularist, like all errors, is based on a half truth. It is the truth that we must care absolutely about something. It feels passion and rightly demands an object for it but does not know the true object, God; so it absolutizes something relative, something in the world. It could be anything— communism, anticommunism, nationalism, internationalism, sexism, antisexism, sex, man, woman, superman, the Yankees, hating the Yankees, ecclesiolatry, antiecclesiolatry, or even stamp collecting. "I feel very religious; do you have a God I could worship?"

It's common to reject fanaticism and idolatry, but it's less common to understand its cause, its need. It is a desperate reaction against the dullness of relativism, which is the more popular form of secularism. If there is no God, no heaven, and no hell, if this is all there is, then there is nothing absolute, no real object for our infinite passion. And if we refuse to idolatrously invest infinite passion in finite objects, we will simply suppress and starve our infinite passion. The world used to be full of fanatics; now it is full of dull relativists, laid back and mellow, or apathetic like Camus' *Stranger* or Feiffer's,

[57] Mary McDermott Shideler says, in *The Theology of Romantic Love: A Study in the Writings of Charles Williams* (Grand Rapids, Mich.: Eerdmans, 1962), pp. 213–214, that "Williams believed this to be a quotation, but neither he nor—so far as I know—any of his students has ever been able to locate the source."

[58] C. S. Lewis, *George MacDonald: An Anthology* (New York: Macmillan, 1978), no. 57, p. 26.

Trudeau's, and the *New Yorker's* jaded cartoon characters. This world has no blacks or whites, only grays. Fie
on it!

Heavenly Humor: The Last Laugh

"To care and not to care" means both seriousness and
humor. On the one hand "it is a serious thing to live in a
society of possible gods and goddesses".[59] But on the
other hand it means the comedy of "those who deal
with the world as though they had no dealings with
it".[60] It means the levity that lets the saint play with his
life and become a martyr, that lets Saint Thomas More
crack jokes about his beard on the executioner's block.[61]

The world separates humor and seriousness; heaven
joins them. The world can't be serious and joyful at the
same time; if this is all there is, it's pretty grim, and joy
is mere comic relief. But heavenly joy is not comic relief;
it is a laughter "too good to waste on jokes".[62] It is not
an outlet of tension, a vacation from dull, onerous
everydayness. It is the everyday work of heaven;
heaven's work is play!

[59] C. S. Lewis, *The Weight of Glory* (New York: Macmillan, 1949),
pp. 14–15.

[60] 1 Cor. 7:31.

[61] C. Whibley, *Henry VIII*, vol. 2 (1904), pp. 265–266. Quoted in
E. E. Reynolds, *The Field Is Won: The Life and Death of St. Thomas
More* (Milwaukee: Bruce Publishing Co., 1968). "Also even when he
should lay down his beard on the block, he having a great gray
beard, striked out his beard and said to the hangman, 'I pray you let
me lay my beard over the block lest ye should cut it'; thus with a
mock he ended his life."

[62] C. S. Lewis, *The Last Battle* (New York: Macmillan, 1956), p.
161.

I know that my tendency to use images like play and dance for the highest things is a stumbling-block to you. You . . . call it "heartless." You feel it a brutal mockery of every martyr and every slave. . . . Dance and game *are* frivolous, unimportant down here; for "down here" is not their natural place. Here, they are a moment's rest from the life we were placed here to live. But in this world everything is upside down. That which, if it could be prolonged here, would be a truancy, is likest that which in a better country is the End of ends. Joy is the serious business of heaven.[63]

The saint and the clown share a great secret. It is the union of the two meanings of the word "light": (1) truth and (2) levity, the opposite of darkness and the opposite of heaviness. Clowns leap and saints levitate because their bodies follow their spirits.

One of the delightful surprises experienced by the resuscitated patients we hear so much about lately is that the "being of light" (either God or a divine messenger) takes repented sin lightly. He laughs at past sins, and they laugh with him. They do not condemn themselves because God does not condemn them. This is a scandal only to those who have not yet met Jesus: "Woman, where are your accusers? Has no one condemned you?" "No one, Lord." "Then neither do I condemn you. Go and sin no more."[64]

God forgives. That simple point sticks in the craw of the Pharisee, ancient or modern. Jesus scandalized them by showing his Father's solution to sin: to love the sinner, to forgive, and thus to cast out fear. Let's go

[63] C. S. Lewis, *Letters to Malcolm: Chiefly on Prayer* (New York: Harcourt, Brace & World, 1963), pp. 92–93.
[64] John 8:11.

through that again, because it's the heart of the Gospel: "Perfect love casts out fear (love forgives), For fear has to do with punishment, And one who fears is not perfected in love."[65] God loves. Love forgives. Forgiveness cancels punishment and thus the fear of punishment. The debt is canceled, though at a fearsome price: the cross. But "the Christian is asked not to swoon in the shadow, but to climb in the light, of the cross."[66] We're free!

This is not "another gospel", as many sincere but worrisome Christians fear. Unbending, unforgiving justice is another gospel. In fact, it is precisely the "other gospel" Saint Paul so roundly condemns in Galatians.[67] The only new thing in the resuscitated patients' account is the imagery: God forgives with a laughing face instead of a stern face. The laughter tells us that he doesn't condemn, the sternness that he doesn't condone. Both are truths. Forgiveness neither condemns nor condones: "Neither do I condemn you. Go and sin no more." That's why the resuscitated who experience God's forgiveness not only laugh at past sins but also "go and sin no more".

All Christians are the resuscitated. "You have died, and your life is hid with Christ in God", says Saint Paul to us, the living. We have also met the "being of light", the Light of the World, and been forgiven.[68] With our feet on the earth, we breathe the air of heavenly joy. It's

[65] 1 John 4:18.

[66] Teilhard de Chardin, *The Divine Milieu* (New York: Harper & Row, 1957), p. 104.

[67] Gal. 1:6; cf. 2 Cor. 11:4.

[68] John 8:12, 9:5.

not something we work up or read a book about; it's something we've been given. The present of heaven is presented to us in the present, and there's no time like the present. In fact, there's no time *but* the present. It's *here,* and the only thing we can add, the only thing God wants from us, is our desire for it, our yes to it. The "it" is a him; his name is Jesus.

What do we want? Infinite joy. Very well, here he is. Now what? Just say yes. Is that all? Yes. Keep on saying yes, like Molly Bloom at the end of *Ulysses.* Yes yes yes yes yes yes yes.

C. S. Lewis'
Argument from Desire

This essay is about a single argument. Next to Anselm's famous "ontological argument", I think it is the single most intriguing argument in the history of human thought. For one thing, it not only argues for the existence of God, but at the same time it argues for the existence of heaven and for something of the essential nature of heaven and of God—four conclusions, not just one. For another thing, it is far more moving, arresting, and apologetically effective than any other argument for God or for heaven. At least it is that in my experience with students. Finally, it is more than an argument. Like Anselm's argument, it is also a meditation, an illumination, an experience, an invitation to an experiment with yourself, a pilgrimage.

I shall first state the argument as succinctly as possible. Second, I shall show how C. S. Lewis, who more than anyone else is associated with it, uses it in three different ways (autobiographical, practical-pastoral, and logical). Third, I shall trace contributions to it back into four lines of historical influence (experiential, historical, epistemological, and practical). Fourth, I shall try to answer the main objections against it.

I

The major premise of the argument is that every natural or innate desire in us bespeaks a corresponding real object that can satisfy the desire.

The minor premise is that there exists in us a desire which nothing in time, nothing on earth, no creature, can satisfy.

The conclusion is that there exists something outside of time, earth, and creatures which *can* satisfy this desire.

This something is what people call God and heaven. Thus the argument seeks to prove the existence of God and heaven via this one aspect of them, desirableness, just as Aquinas' five "ways" seek to prove the existence of God under five aspects, and concludes with: "And this is what people call 'God'."

A word about each premise.

The major premise implicitly distinguishes desires into two kinds: innate and conditioned, natural and artificial. We naturally desire things like food, drink, sex, knowledge, friendship, and beauty, and we naturally turn away from things like starvation, ignorance, loneliness, and ugliness. We also desire things like Rolls Royces, political offices, flying through the air like Superman, a Red Sox world championship, and lands like Oz. But there are two differences between the two lists. First, we do not always recognize corresponding states of deprivation of the second, as we do with the first. And, most important, the first list of desires all come from within, from our nature, while the second come from without, from society, or advertising, or fiction. The first come from our spiritual heredity; the second come from our material environment.

The existence of desires of the second class does not necessarily mean that the objects desired exist. Rolls Royces do, Oz does not. But the existence of desires of the first class, in every discoverable case, does mean that the objects desired exist. No case has ever been found of an innate desire for a nonexistent object.

You may regard the argument as an argument from analogy: by analogy with all our other innate desires, which have real objects, the desire for God and heaven must have a real object. Or you may regard the argument as one whose major premise is established inductively, by generalization. But it is better to regard the argument as a deductive syllogism and the major premise as known in the same way that "all men are mortal" is known: by abstraction of a universal form or principle from individual material instances, by an insight into the universal form or principle that is met in the different instances or instantiations. As we shall see later, this apparently technically nitpicking point is essential to meet the most important objection to the argument.

The minor premise of the argument is an empirical observation, if "empirical" is extended to cover inner experience as well as outer, introspection as well as extrospection. The argument then depends on a personal appeal to introspective experience. Just as we cannot argue effectively about color with a blind man because he has no data, so we cannot argue about this desire with someone who cannot find the desire in question in himself, or who refuses to look for it, or who refuses to admit its presence once it is found. But, then, such a person cannot argue against us either. In a sense (a non-fallacious sense) the argument is an *ad hominem,* like Aristotle's argument against Protagoras' skeptical denial of the law of non-contradiction: if only the skeptic will make some simple admission, he can be refuted, for he contradicts himself by claiming to know something when he says he cannot know anything. But he cannot be compelled to make that admission—in Aristotle's case, to utter a putatively meaningful sentence, in our case to recognize the existence of a desire for a perfect object, or for perfect joy, that no earthly object and no earthly pleasure can fulfill. If someone blandly says, "I am perfectly happy playing with mud pies, or fast cars, or money, or political power", we can query, "Are you, really?" but we can only try to inveigle him out of his childishness; we cannot compel him by logical force.

In a sense, the minor premise of the argument is more interesting than the argument itself. The phenomenon the Germans call *Sehnsucht* is psychologically fascinating, and when it occurs as subject rather than object— i.e., when we experience the desire rather than thinking about it—it is obsessive and imperious—in fact, even more imperious than erotic desire at its height. Faced with a choice between the perfect earthly beloved and the fulfillment of *Sehnsucht,* we choose *Sehnsucht;* for the object of *Sehnsucht* is the perfect heavenly beloved, whether we know it or not. As Lewis says, "Joy is not a substitute for sex; sex is very often a substitute for Joy."

The conclusion of the argument is not that all that is meant by God or heaven in the Bible or in the popular imagination must exist. What the argument proves to exist is unidentifiable with any image or representation. Lewis describes it thus in *Surprised by Joy:*

> . . . something which, by refusing to identify itself with any object of the senses or anything whereof we have biological or social need, or anything imagined, or any state of our own minds, proclaims itself sheerly objective. Far more objective than bodies, for it is not, like them, clothed in our senses: the naked Other, imageless

(though our imagination salutes it with a hundred images), unknown, undefined, desired.

It is the concept of an unknown *x,* but an unknown whose *direction* is known, so to speak. God is *more*—more beauty, more desirability, more awesomeness. God is to great beauty what great beauty is to small beauty or to a mixture of beauty and ugliness. And the same with other perfections. But the "more" is *infinitely* more; thus the analogy is not proportionate. Twenty is to ten what ten is to five, but infinity is not to twenty what twenty is to ten, or five, or one. But it *is* "in that direction", so to speak. The argument is like a parable: it points down an infinite corridor in a finite direction. Its object is not "God" as conceived and defined already, but a movingly mysterious *x* which is always more than any image, notion, or concept. It does not presuppose but supplies a definition of God, and one which reverses the normal positive notion of definition *(de-fino)* by asserting that God is the one *not* captureable in any finite terms. The definition of its "God" is "that which is more than any definition", the God whom "eye has not seen, ear has not heard, neither has it entered into the heart of man". In other words, this is the real God.

II

There are especially three passages in C. S. Lewis where the argument from desire is stated at length, though *Sehnsucht* itself seeps out from many a page of Lewis, most perfectly in "The Weight of Glory", the best sermon I have ever read. (Have you ever read a better one?) But the three passages in which Lewis *argues* for God from *Sehnsucht* are in *Surprised by Joy, Mere Christianity,* and the introduction to *The Pilgrim's Regress*. The *Surprised by Joy* passages are not primarily intended to argue but to reveal. The book is not philosophy but autobiography. Yet an argument is hinted at. The passage in *Mere Christianity* is more argumentative than *Surprised by Joy*, but is is primarily practical, a matter of pastoral guidance. Only in the early work, *The Pilgrim's Regress,* did Lewis use it as an explicit argument. I do not know why this is so. There is no reason to think it was because Lewis thought the argument a bad one, for there is no passage in Lewis' later works that even remotely suggests that.

The passage in *Surprised by Joy* first defines the desire by contradistinction from other desires as follows: "an unsatisifed desire which is itself more desirable than any other satisfaction". Lewis then implicitly argues for the existence of the object of this desire when he discovers the fact that the desire is essentially intentional, or reaching out and pointing beyond itself to its object. He confesses and turns from his earlier subjectivist error:

> I had smuggled in the assumption that what I wanted was a "thrill", a state of my own mind. And there lies the deadly error. Only when your whole attention and desire are fixed on something else . . . does the "thrill" arise. It is a by-product. Its very existence presupposes that you desire not it but something other and outer. . . .
>
> Images or sensations . . . were merely the mental track left by the passage . . . not the wave but the wave's imprint in the sand. The inherent dialectic of desire itself had in a way already shown me this, for all images and sensations, if idolatrously mistaken for Joy itself, soon confessed themselves inadequate. All said, in the last resort, "It is not I. I am only a reminder. Look! Look! What do I remind you of?"

> Inexorably Joy proclaimed, "You want—I myself am your want of—something other, outside, not you or any state of you."

Like Augustine, ending the autobiographical part of his *Confessions* in Book X, Lewis, on the last page of the book, confesses his present state of soul with regard to *Sehnsucht*:

> I now know that the experience, considered as a state of my own mind, had never had the kind of importance I once gave it. It was valuable only as a pointer to something other and outer. While that other was in doubt, the pointer naturally loomed large in my thoughts. When we are lost in the woods the sight of a signpost is a great matter. . . . But when we have found the road . . . we shall not stop and stare, or not much; not on this road . . . We would be at Jerusalem.

These passages describe the desire and head us off from the subjectivist error about it, but they do not so much argue from it to the existence of its object as immediately look along the desire at its mysterious object, or look at its intentionality and see immediately that it must have an object, simply because it is thus essentially intentional. But Lewis does not (1) distinguish natural or innate desires from others or (2) argue from the principle that all natural desires have objects, yet, in this book.

The passage in *Mere Christianity* is also essentially practical, meant to head the reader off from two popular mistakes. Lewis first calls our attention to the desire, then to two mistakes about it, then comes the argument:

> Most people, if they had really learned to look into their own hearts, would know that they do want, and want acutely, something that cannot be had in this world.

There are all sorts of things in this world that offer to give it to you, but they never quite keep their promise. . . . Now there are two wrong ways of dealing with this fact, and one right way.

(1) The Fool's Way—he puts the blame on the things themselves. He goes on all his life thinking that if only he tried another woman, or holiday, or whatever, then this time he would really catch the mysterious something. . . .

(2) The Way of the Disillusioned "Sensible" Man—He soon decides that the whole thing was moonshine. And so he represses the part of himself which used to cry for the moon. . . .

(3) The Christian way. The Christian says [and here is the argument]: Creatures are not born with desires unless satisfaction for these desires exists. A baby feels hunger; well, there is such a thing as food. A duckling wants to swim; well, there is such a thing as water. Men feel sexual desire; well, there is such a thing as sex. If I find in myself a desire which no experience in this world can satisfy, the most probable explanation is that I was made for another world.

Note that Lewis does not claim certainty for the conclusion here, just probability. For the conclusion here is only a hypothesis that explains the data better than any other, but this fact does not prove with certainty that this hypothesis is true.

Yet it does show the practical necessity of taking this desire seriously: "I must keep alive in myself the desire for my true country." Like Pascal's "Wager", the argument here shows that you are a fool if you turn your back on this strong clue, this strong probability that infinite happiness exists and that you are designed to enjoy it.

In the introduction to *The Pilgrim's Regress,* Lewis does two things more clearly than he does anywhere else. First, he defines exactly how this desire differs from all others. Second, he argues from the principle that nature makes nothing in vain to the conclusion that the one who can satisfy this desire must exist.

> The experience is one of intense longing. It is distinguished from other longings by two things. In the first place, though the sense of want is acute and even painful, yet the mere wanting is felt to be somehow a delight. . . . This hunger is better than any other fullness; this poverty better than all other wealth. . . . In the second place, there is a peculiar mystery about the *object* of this desire. . . . Every one of these supposed objects for the desire is inadequate to it. . . . It appeared to me therefore that if a man diligently followed this desire, pursuing the false objects until their falsity appeared and then resolutely abandoning them, he must come out at last into the clear knowledge that the human soul was made to enjoy some object that is never fully given—nay, cannot even be imagined as given—in our present mode of subjective and spatio-temporal experience. This desire was, in the soul, as in the Siege Perilous in Arthur's castle—the chair in which only one could sit. And if nature makes nothing in vain, the One who can sit in this chair must exist.

Here the conclusion is not called "the most probable explanation" but something that "must exist". *If* nature makes nothing in vain, if you admit the premise, the conclusion necessarily follows. Of course, one who wants to refuse to admit the conclusion at all costs will deny the premise—but at the cost of a meaningful universe, a universe in which desires and satisfactions match.

In other words, God can be avoided. All we need to is embrace "vanity of vanities" instead. It is a fool's bargain, of course: Everything is exchanged for Nothing—a trade even the Boston Red Sox are not fool enough to make.

III

I believe C. S. Lewis is the best apologist for the Christian Faith in the twentieth century. Many virtues grace his work, but the one that lifts him above any other writer who has ever written, I believe, is how powerfully he writes about Joy, or *Sehnsucht,* the desire we are speaking of here. Many other writers excel him in originality. He did not mean to be original. ("Our Lord never tried to be original", he noted.) Perhaps a few modern writers excel him in clarity (though offhand I cannot name one) or grace, or beauty, or accuracy, or popular appeal. But no one has written better of Joy.

Yet he never wrote a whole book about this thing, though he admitted in his autobiography that it was the leitmotif of his whole life: "The central story of my life is about nothing else." Lewis says somewhere that he wrote the books he wanted to read, the books he wished someone else would write, but they didn't, so he did. That is why I originally wrote *Heaven: the Heart's Deepest Longing:* because, incredibly, no one had ever written a whole book about the deepest longing in human life. This essay differs from the rest of the book in three ways. It is, first of all, about the argument, not just the experience. Second, it pretends to scholarliness. Third, it tries to relate this experience more to the history of philosophy. We turn to the historical aspect now.

From a historical point of view I think one of Lewis'

chief claims to fame is that he pulled together, co-alesced, and sharpened to a fine point a number of important strands in the history of Western religious and philosophical thought around this argument. The argument does not just float loose on the surface; it flowers from immense, deep tangles of growing things. Some of the most important names in our history are involved in this tangle: Moses, Solomon, Plato, Christ, Paul, Augustine, Bonaventure, Jung. I discern four distinct aspects of the argument, four strands of influence. One name that crops up in all four strands is Pascal, whom Lewis evidently read and admired, though he quoted him only sparsely. But lack of extensive quotation from Pascal is no proof of a lack of deep influence; such is the case with Kierkegaard, who fleshes out many of the *Pensées* but almost never mentions Pascal's name.

The first influence-strand is psychological, or experiential. It is a double experience, a negative and a positive. The negative experience is unhappiness, rest-lessness. The positive experience is longing, *Sehnsucht* itself. Let's look at the negative side first.

Solomon, or whoever wrote Ecclesiastes, knew the emptiness, vanity, and wretchedness of human life even at its best as well as anyone ever did. Pascal says,

> Solomon and Job have known and spoken best about man's wretchedness, one the most fortunate, the other the most unfortunate of men; one knowing by experi-ence the vanity of pleasure, the other the reality of afflic-tions.

Herman Melville, in *Moby Dick,* and Thomas Wolfe, in *You Can't Go Home Again,* have both called Ecclesiastes the single greatest and truest book ever written about human life under the sun. Its conclusion is that life is "vanity of vanities". Why? Why call life "vanity"? I do not mean by that question: What evidence does Solomon use to prove his conclusion? That is painfully obvious: the oppressions of the poor, the endless cycles of time, the inevitability of death, the strength of evil over good, the indifference of nature to justice, the uncertainty of all our works, the near-impossibility of being both wise and content at the same time, and above all the mystery, remoteness, and invisibility of a God whose ways are past finding out. No, I mean a more mysterious "Why?" Why do we call this "vanity"? Why do we rail against these things? Why do we not obey the reasonable advice of nine out of ten of our psychologists, who in book after book tell us to accept ourselves as we are, become well-adjusted citizens of the Kingdom of This World, and even accept death as a friend, not an enemy? (Freud called it "making friends with the necessity of dying".) No one but a sheep or a scholar is fool enough to believe such inhuman nonsense. Instead, something in us thrills to the gloriously irrational passion of the poet Dylan Thomas when he says, "Do not go gentle into that good-night / Rage, rage against the dying of the light."

What is that thing in us that gloriously disobeys the advice of our comfort-mongering modern sages and rises to the dignity of despair? Death is the most natural thing in the world; why do we find it unnatural? "Do fish complain of the sea for being wet?" asks Lewis, in a letter to Sheldon Vanauken. "Or if they did, would that not indicate that they had not always been, or were not destined always to be, sea creatures?" But we complain about death and time. As Lewis says, "Time is just another name for death." There is never enough time. Time makes being into non-being. Time is a river that takes away everything it brings: nations, civilizations, art, science, culture, plants, animals, our own bodies, the very stars—nothing stands outside this cosmic stream rushing headlong into the sea of death. Or does it? Something in us seems to stand outside it, for something in us protests this "nature" and asks: Is that all there is? We find this natural situation "vanity": empty, frustrating, wretched, unhappy. Our nature contradicts nature.

Thus there is a double datum: (1) the objective datum of death and time and all the other things in nature that make us unhappy; and (2) the subjective datum that they make us unhappy. The objective datum can be explained scientifically, but what of the subjective datum? That needs to be explained too.

There is a clue in Ecclesiastes 3:11, the one verse in the book that rings with hope like a bell in a swamp. Solomon says to God, "You have made everything fitting for its time, but you have also put eternity into man's heart." Time does not satisfy the restless heart. We cry out for eternity because God has put this desire into our hearts. Our hearts are restless until they rest in him because they were designed by him to rest in him alone. Resting in nature is unnatural for us. Our nature is to demand supernature.

The wretchedness and dissatisfaction and restlessness of the heart, the spirit, the image of God, the God-child in us alienated from Home and the Father, is the negative side of the coin. The positive side is the hopeful longing, the energy and the homing pigeon's instinct that moves Augustine through the pages of the *Con-*

fessions. It is the poignancy of E. T. looking for that magic place "Home". Pascal says, "an infinite abyss can be filled only with an infinite object, i.e., God himself." We spend our lives trying to fill the Grand Canyon with marbles.

Even the pagan at his best knew this. Plato in the *Symposium* let the cat out of the bag. Eros, love, desire, climbs the steps of a hierarchy and will not rest with lesser, lower, particular, limited and material loves, beautiful as they are. Only Beauty Itself, absolute, pure, unmixed, perfect and eternal, will satisfy the soul. Lewis says somewhere that no one should be allowed to die without having read Plato's *Symposium*. And he surely speaks for himself in the Narnia books when he has Professor Digory Kirke exclaim, "Why it's all in Plato! All in Plato! What *do* they teach them in the schools nowadays?" Plato is eminently convertible, Christianizeable. Paganism at its best is a virgin, Christianity a wife, modernity a divorcée. I love Chesterton's three-sentence summary of the history of Western thought: "Paganism was the biggest thing in the world, and Christianity was bigger, and everything since has been comparatively small."

A second ingredient in the background of our argument is the historical account of the Fall, recorded in Genesis 3. Our present wretchedness and restless search is a historical fact, not just a myth. Therefore the origin or cause of this fact cannot be a mere myth either, but must be a real event. The only two candidates are Creation or Fall. Either God or Man created our wretchedness. Did God push us, or did we fall? The story of a Fall, a Paradise Lost, a Primordial Tragedy, is a nearly universal theme in the world's myths. For our myths are infinitely wiser than our science, which knows nothing of such archaic and spiritual events. Our science comes from our conscious mind, but our myths come from our unconscious, which is much deeper and wiser. The unconscious remembers things the conscious mind has forgotten. The Priest of Glome is wiser than the Fox, the Greek philosopher, in Lewis' novel *Till We Have Faces*.

Myths are even prophetic, pointing to the truth from afar, as Greek philosophy is prophetic. For God has not left himself without witnesses even outside Israel, though none of these other witnesses is divinely guaranteed and infallible. The human soul has intellect, will, and emotions; some knowledge of the true, the good, and the beautiful. And God sent prophets to all three areas of the soul: philosophers to enlighten the intellect, prophets to straighten out the will, and myth-makers to tease and touch the emotions with a desire for himself. The philosophers have an analogue in the soul, a philosopher within: our understanding. The prophets have an analogue in the soul too, a divine mouthpiece called conscience. And the myth-makers too have an analogue in the soul, a dreamer and poet and myth-maker within.

But the truths of the myths got terribly distorted, like the message in the party game whispered around a large circle. That's why Lewis calls myths "gleams of celestial strength and beauty falling on a jungle of filth and imbecility"—because "they are based on a reality far more solid than we think, but they are at an almost infinite distance from their base."

The Biblical story of the Fall explains our present experience as a scientific hypothesis explains observed data. The data here are very strange: that we alone do not fit the world of time and death, we alone do not obey the advice of our own psychologists to accept ourselves as we are. The explanation must be equally strange. The human lock is weirdly shaped. The Biblical key is also weirdly shaped: a story of a radical tragedy at our very roots. There are all sorts of difficulties with the story. But it fits—the key fits the lock. What happened in Eden may be hard to understand but it makes everything else understandable.

Eden explains, e.g., the strange coimplication of our greatness and wretchedness. As Pascal says, "All these examples of wretchedness prove his greatness. It is the wretchedness of a great lord, the wretchedness of a dispossessed king." And: "Man's greatness can be deduced from his wretchedness, for what is nature in animals [e.g., pain and death] we call wretchedness in man, thus recognizing that he must have fallen from some better state which was once his own. Who indeed would think himself unhappy not to be the king except one who had been dispossessed? . . . Who would think himself unhappy if he had only one mouth and who would not if he had only one eye? It has probably never occurred to anyone to be distressed at not having three eyes, but those who have none are inconsolable."

Eden even explains why music moves us. As Charles Williams wrote, "A voice went out from Eden. All music was the fallen echo of that sound."

Our longing for a home and a happiness that we do not ever experience in this world is a great mystery. And the story of the Fall is a great solution to it.

A third, epistemological strand of historical influence for our arguments stems from Plato and his famous doctrine of Anamnesis, or Recollection. According to this doctrine, when we discover an eternal truth, we are really remembering a knowledge that is innate to us but which our conscious mind had forgotten. In light of what we have just said about the historical events in Eden being an explanation of our present unhappy state, in light of the Christian doctrine of the Fall, Plato's doctrine of Anamnesis makes acceptable sense. It also makes sense in light of our present experience of learning the truth. For whenever we discover an eternal truth, we experience an "aha!"—a moment of recognition (re-cognition, knowing-again). It is like the aha! experience of remembering an empirical object like a lost wallet when we meet it in a Lost and Found Department. If we had never known the wallet in the past, we would not be able to pick it out in the present. We recognize it only because there is a memory image in us, which came from our past experience of it. Similarly, when, like Meno's slave boy, we discover an eternal truth of mathematics like the Pythagorean Theorem, or an eternal truth of ethics such as the fundamental conclusion of Plato's *Republic,* that justice is always more profitable than injustice, or the definition of justice as health of soul—when we discover such eternal truths in the Lost and Found Department of ideas that is the history of Western thought, we experience a shock of recognition (re-cognition), a *déjà vu,* an aha! The innate truth-detector in us buzzes like a Geiger counter—not infallibly, but nonetheless really. Knowledge need not be infallible to be knowledge. Meno's slave boy's truth-detector went off too soon. He made a mistake before he found the truth. But then, on the second attempt, he corrected his mistake. We too often aha! too soon and seize on a falsehood as a truth; or too late, and miss a truth that is under our nose. But we do aha! We do recognize.

From this aha! experience two possible lines of explanation of it lead out. Reductionism explains it away, debunks it (or tries to) as only empirical generalization, or projection of subjective expectation, or habit, or even by the wires of experience and memory being crossed in the brain, as the *déjà vu* experience can be explained as a new experience being misfiled into the brain's memory category.

But suppose we do not explain it away, but explain it. Two dimensions of non-reductionistic explanation present themselves: the ontological, as in Augustine's theory of Divine Illumination, or the psychological, as in Jung's theory of the Collective Unconscious.

Augustine's idea of Divine Illumination as the source of a priori knowledge uses the image of *light* for truth and in so doing reveals something extremely important and usually forgotten in debates between Platonists like Augustine and Lewis and empiricists or positivists or analytic philosophers who criticize them. As I shall try to show in the last section of this paper, a Platonist always puts the truth of *seeing* the *light* above the truth of calculation; *intellectus* above *ratio;* the fourth quarter of the Divided Line in the *Republic* over the third quarter; the First Act of the Mind, or Simple Apprehension of an essence, above or prior to the Second and Third Acts of the Mind, judgment of a proposition as true or false, and reasoning or inference. Here is a more primordial notion of truth than the relational truth of a judgment, relating predicate to subject or proposition to fact. It is the absolute truth of an essence, or Platonic Form, and this is something like light, something almost substantial. Thus Lewis speaks of edible and drinkable truth in *The Great Divorce* (chap. 5), and Christ claims to *be* the truth, not just to *speak* it (John 6:14).

An alternative non-reductionistic explanation of the aha! epistemological experience is Jung's theory of the Collective Unconscious. It may be used either as a substitute for or as a supplement to the ontological explanation of Augustine. It may also be used either as a substitute for or as a supplement to the historical explanation of Eden. It presupposes first that there *is* an Unconscious, as nearly every philosophical psychologist except Sartre and Behaviorists do, and second that Christopher Columbus Freud only landed on its beach. Freud's mistake was not to overestimate its depth and complexity and innate power to inform and direct the conscious self, but to underestimate it, in reducing it all to the sex drive. Scott Peck has shown in a very practical, popular, and effective way in the first half of his bestseller *The Road Less Travelled* how incredibly wise our unconscious is. So impressive is this wisdom to him, in fact, that in the second half of the book he voyages far beyond the shores of scientific psychology into the hypothesis, apparently shared by Jung, that the unconscious is God. It is a heresy, of course, but every heresy is based on a truth that is bent. The heretic is mistaken, but some truth must be taken before it can be mis-taken. The truth the Jungian takes is, I believe, precisely the truth of the Augustinian Divine Illumination—which, by the way, St. Thomas also teaches. But he clarifies it so that only *in* God's light do we see light. Divine Illumination is not an object of consciousness; it is the sun shining behind us rather than in front of us. As Chesterton says, God is like the sun: only in the light of the One who cannot be seen (because he is too light, not too dark) can everything else be seen. Let one thing be mystical and everything else becomes rational. Let one thing be not a knowable object, and everything else becomes a knowable object. Let one thing be an *x* and everything else becomes a why.

The Platonic epistemology of a priori knowledge is not as intellectually silly as its current reputation. It is based on data, evidence: the fact that we function like homing pigeons, we know what is not our home, like E. T., and we also know what things are closer to Home, to heaven, to God, than other things, though we do not know this infallibly and we can and do make many, many mistakes about it, even eternal mistakes. But we can and do judge that *y* is farther and *z* nearer to *x*, to Home, even though we have never been Home, never experienced God or heaven as we have experienced *y* and *z*. In order to judge truly whether *y* is more or less perfect than *z*, we must use a standard, *x*. Even if we do not know *x* as an explicit, defined, experienced or even experienceable object, we still *use x*, and thus *implicitly* know *x*. Knowledge of what is better implies knowledge of what is best. Knowledge of imperfection implies knowledge of perfection. Progress implies an unchanging goal—how can you make progress toward a moving goal line? How can a baserunner score a run if home plate keeps moving?

The program is in our computer because our Creator has designed and programmed us. *Because* "Thou hast made us for thyself", therefore "our hearts are restless until they rest in thee." It is not a program that appears on our computer screen as data, as information to store and recall. Rather, it is an operational program, a procedural rule, a practical command and direction we follow. It is a program of the heart, not of the head, or conscious mind.

But "heart" does not mean sentiment, emotion, or feeling in Scripture, as it does in modern parlance. It means our center, our I. Pascal is quite correct to say "the heart has its reasons which the reason does not know." The heart has *reasons*. The heart has eyes. Love is not blind. How could love be blind? God is love. Is God blind? One of those three propositions must be false: that love is blind, that God is not blind, and that God is love.

This "heart" that we have spoken of is the central concept of the fourth strand of influence, the practical or pastoral. It is the heart that is the organ of the unconscious knowledge of the way home that we have just explored. The heart is our guide, our homing pigeon. Though it is fallen and in need of correction by divine revelation, though it is "desperately wicked", according to Scripture, yet its very wretchedness shows its greatness, as the height from which we have fallen measures the depths of our fall. We are not simply bad, but a good thing gone bad, a sacred thing profaned.

Jesus appealed to the heart constantly, e.g., when he said, "Seek and you shall find." It is the heart that seeks. Pascal comments, with this promise of Jesus in mind,

> There are three kinds of people: those who have sought God and found him, and these are reasonable and happy; those who seek God and have not yet found him, and these are reasonable and unhappy; and those who neither

seek God nor find him, and these are unreasonable and unhappy.

There is no fourth class, those who find without seeking. Christ's promise that all who seek, find, is simultaneously reassuring and threatening: reassuring in that everyone in Pascal's second class eventually graduates into his first class (all seekers find, all who are reasonable and honest and intend God, intend repentance and faith, will find him and become happy); but threatening in that no one who does not seek will find. It is the seeking heart that determines our eternal destiny. In the heart heaven or hell are decided.

Christ presupposed the primacy of the heart in John 7:17 when he answered his critics' hermeneutical question, "How can we know your teaching, whether it is from God?" with scandalous simplicity: "If your will [or heart] were to do the will of my Father, you would know my teaching, that it is from him." When it comes to knowing persons rather than things or concepts, the heart rightly leads the head. Who understands you best, a brilliant psychologist who has spent ten thousand hours interviewing you as a case study for his doctoral dissertation but who does not care about you personally, or your best friend, who is not terribly bright but who loves you very much?

William Law, one of Lewis' favorite writers, is as embarrassingly simple as Jesus because he too sees that the heart decides all, when he says, in *A Serious Call to the Devout Life,* "If you will honestly consult your own heart you will see that there is one and only one reason why you are not even now a saint: because you do not wholly want to be." Augustine says the same thing in the *Confessions:* that it is the divided will, the divided heart, that accounts for sin in us, that accounts for the astonishing introspective discovery of Paul in Romans 7 that "I do not understand my own behavior. For the good that I would do, I do not, and the evil that I would not, that I do."

Heart, will, and desire are essentially one. The Argument from Desire is the Argument from the Heart. Even in the heart whose "fundamental option", as Rahner puts it, is to run from God, to reject God, there is still, until death, a spark of the fire of desire for God, thus hope for repentance, for turning. It is to such an unbeliever that Pascal addresses *his* argument from desire, the famous "Wager".

The Wager presupposes the same heart-desire for happiness that Lewis' argument presupposes, but moves in a different direction: the practical calculation of winning or losing God rather than the theoretical insight that there must be a God. It is as if Lewis played with the blue chips of the truth sought by metaphysical argument while Pascal played with the red chips of the passion to possess God, to attain happiness. Lewis tries to prove God exists; Pascal, skeptical of all argument for God's existence, does instead what Scripture does: inveigles us to make a leap of faith, a wager. "It is a remarkable fact", Pascal writes, "that no canonical writer ever tries to prove the existence of God. Rather, they all strive to make us believe in him." The Wager appeals to our desire for God, our love of God, though on a very low and selfish level. Lewis begins with the implicit desire for God, the desire to leap into his arms, and concludes that therefore God must exist. Pascal begins with "You can't be certain God exists, but you can't be certain he doesn't, either" and concludes that we should leap into his arms.

The Wager works like Martin Buber's story about an atheist who came to a rabbi demanding that the rabbi prove to him God's existence or else he would never believe. When the rabbi refused, the atheist rose to leave, angrily. The rabbi's parting words were: "But can you be *sure* God does not exist?" Forty years later, that atheist told that story, and added that he was still an atheist, but that the rabbi's words continue to haunt him every day. If that man is honest and continues to seek and to let himself be haunted, he will one day leap and find.

Augustine uses a little thought-experiment to the same effect in his sermon "On the Pure Love of God". He says: Imagine God appeared to you and said he would make a deal with you, that he would give you everything you wished, everything your heart desired, except one. You could have anything you imagine, nothing would be impossible for you, and nothing would be sinful or forbidden. "But," God concluded, "you shall never see my face." Why, Augustine asks, did a terrible chill creep over your heart at those last words unless there is in your heart the love of God, the desire for God? In fact, if you wouldn't accept that deal, you really love God above all things, for look what you just did: you gave up the whole world, and more, for God.

Augustine's experiment can help you prove to yourself that the minor premise of Lewis' argument is true, that the strange desire exists, and that it is a desire for nothing less than God. Once again, the heart has led the head. Love has instructed understanding. The fear of the Lord has proved to be the beginning of wisdom.

IV

Finally, I want to defend the argument against five objections that have been made or could be made against it.

First, one may simply deny the minor premise, saying, "I simply do not observe any such desire for God, or heaven, or infinite joy, or some mysterious *x* which is more than any earthly happiness." This denial can take two forms. First, one may say, "I am not perfectly content now, but I can imagine myself to be perfectly content if only I had a million dollars, a Lear jet, an immortality pill and a new mistress every week." The reply to this, of course, is: "Try it. You won't like it." Billions of people have performed trillions of "if only" experiments with life, and they all had the same result: failure. The "if only" faith is the most foolish faith in the world, the stupidest wager in the world, for it has never paid off. It is like the game of predicting the end of the world: every batter who has ever approached that plate has struck out. There is very little reason to hope that the present ones will not do the same.

A second form of the denial of the minor premise is not "I would be perfectly content if only . . ." but "I am perfectly content now." This, I suggest, verges on culpable dishonesty, the sin against the Holy Spirit, and requires something more like exorcism than refutation. This is Merseult in Camus' *The Stranger.* This is subhuman, this is vegetation, this is pop psychology. Even the hedonist utilitarian John Stuart Mill, one of the shallowest minds in the history of human thought, said that it is better to be Socrates dissatisfied than a pig satisfied.

A second objection concerns the major premise. How can anyone know the truth that every natural desire has a real object without first knowing that this natural desire too has a real object? John Beversluis offers this objection in his book *C. S. Lewis and the Search for Rational Religion,* one of those rare books that is even worse than its title. Beversluis seems to believe that every single argument Lewis ever concocted is not only fallacious but downright foolish. In other words, we have in Lewis something like a negative pope speaking ex cathedra: always infallibly wrong rather than infallibly right. Beversluis formulates his objection to this particular argument as follows:

> How could Lewis have known that every natural desire has a real object *before* knowing that Joy *(Sehnsucht)* has one? I can legitimately claim that every student in the class has failed the test *only* if I *first* know that *each* of them has individually failed it. The same is true of natural desires.

This argument is very foolish and very easy to refute. It amounts to saying that only through sense experience and induction is any knowledge possible, that there is only a posteriori knowledge, no a priori knowledge. This is Positivism, or at least Empiricism. The classical Empiricists and Positivists objected to all deductive reasoning as fake, as never really proving what the reasoning appeared to prove and claimed to prove, because there is no way, they contended, to know the truth of the major premise, the general principle, except by enumerative induction, i.e., by first knowing every example of it, including the conclusion. Thus knowledge really always works, according to them, in the opposite order from the way a syllogism claims to work: never from the universal to the particular but always only from the particular to the universal.

But surely this is simply not so. We can and do come to a knowledge of universals through abstraction, not only by induction. We know that all men must be mortal, or capable of speech, or laughter, or prayer, not in the same way that we know that all men have non-green skin, by mere sense observation, but by understanding something of human nature, which we meet in, and abstract from, the individuals we experience. The objector denies the fourth quarter of Plato's Divided Line, Wisdom or Reason as distinct from reasoning, hypothetical deduction, "if . . . then" calculation, inference. He denies what Plato called *epistēmē* as distinct from *dianoia,* or, what the medieval scholastics called *intellectus* as distinct from *ratio.* Descartes did this at the beginning of the *Discourse on Method* to insure agreement among all men, for all have the same "reason" or "good sense" in the sense of logic—there is, e.g., no Protestant or Catholic logic, no French or English logic. But there *are* differences in reason in the sense of wisdom. All men are *not* equal here, and Descartes simply denies or ignores this.

The issue between ancients like Plato, Aristotle, Aquinas, and Lewis, and moderns like Descartes, Hume, the Logical Positivists, and Beversluis can be put this way: Is there a third way of knowing in addition to sense perception and logical calculation? Is there a third kind of meaningful proposition in addition to empirically verifiable propositions and logical tautologies, Hume's "matters of fact" and "relations of ideas", Kant's "synthetic a posteriori judgments" and "analytic a priori judgments"? Are synthetic a priori judgments of objective truths possible?

The answer, surely, is: of course they are! In empirical propositions the predicate is accidental to the subject. In tautologies, the predicate is essential to the subject. But in metaphysical propositions, in synthetic a priori propositions, in propositions which express acts of understanding, the predicate is a *property* of the subject in Aristotle's technical sense: not the explicitly defined essence of the subject, as in "all effects need causes" or "red things are red", nor accidental to the subject, as in "some effects are red", but, as in "all men are mortal", understood as contained in and "flowing from" the essence of the subject, formally caused by the essence of the subject. (Formal casuality is the one of Aristotle's four causes which drops out of the sight of the Empiricist.) *Because* man is a rational animal, he must be mortal (caused by his animality), loquacious (caused by his rationality), humorous (caused by the combination) and prayerful (caused by his rationality's awareness of God).

Thus the proposition "every natural, innate desire has a real object" is understood to be true because we understand what a natural desire is and what nature is. Nature is meaningful, teleological, full of design and purpose. It is ecological, arranging a fit between organism and environment, between desire and satisfaction, between appetite and food. "Nature makes nothing in vain."

All reasoning begins with some understanding of this type, some seeing. Seeing is not just sensory, but also intellectual. Some people just don't see things as well as others. All important disagreements in the history of philosophy come from this fact. That's why they are practically irresolvable, and why the history of philosophy does not lead to eventual general worldwide agreement as the history of science does.

A third objection against Lewis' argument from desire, also from Beversluis, is that its major premise, like all metaphysical propositions, confuses grammar with reality and reads grammar into reality. This is a typical Logical Positivist objection. "Lewis was correct, of course, in claiming that every desire is a desire *for* something. But from this purely conceptual observation nothing follows about what really exists. All desires must have *grammatical* objects, but they need not have *real* ones. People desire all sorts of imaginary things."

This is simply a misunderstanding, and quite inexcusable. Lewis' argument does not begin with a purely grammatical observation but with a metaphysical observation: that real desires really do have real objects. But he does not say that *all* desires do, only that all natural, innate, instinctive desires do. Desires for imaginary things, like Oz, are not innate. Desire for God is.

A fourth argument is that the major premise that an innate hunger proves a real food is simply untrue. Beversluis says, "the phenomenon of hunger simply does not prove that man inhabits a world in which food exists. . . . What proves that we inhabit a world in which food exists is the discovery that certain things are in fact eatable."

This is simply Empiricism blinding itself to the signnature, the significance, of desire, as Empiricists tend to do to everything. Thus Beversluis says, "The Desire in and of itself proves nothing, points to nothing." But surely it does! My finger points to my dog's food. My dog, a true Empiricist, comes and sniffs my finger. Dr.

Beversluis is doggedly Empiricistic. To this mentality nothing has a built-in, real, metaphysical significance. Only words are signs, things are not, to the Empiricist. In other words, the world is not full of the grandeur of God, and Paul must have been philosophically wrong (perhaps *mythically* right?) in saying, in effect, that the world is a sign and that we should be able to read it, that "the invisible things of God are known *through* the things that are made."

A fifth objection from Beversluis: "If Joy's object really is God, and if all desire is really desire for him, why when he was brought face to face with him did Lewis *cease* to desire him and search for a way of escape?" Lewis himself admits he did this. He was brought in "kicking and struggling, the most reluctant convert in all England". For God was "a transcendental Interferer", and "no word was more distasteful to me than the word *Interference*". Beversluis says, "Either God is the ultimate object of desire or he is not. If he is, then it makes no sense to talk about shrinking from him the moment he is found."

I think this is just about the silliest and shallowest objection I have ever read. It shows an outstandingly immature understanding of human nature, fit perhaps for a merely logical mind but not for a human mind that exercises even a little of that non-empirical and non-tautological kind of knowing called understanding or insight or wisdom or mental seeing. By this way of knowing, everyone knows that we often love and hate, desire and fear, the same object at different times or even at the same time, especially if that object is a person. How did a virgin feel about her wedding night in the days before the sexual revolution? Was there not often a fear of the great, the mysterious, the unknown, the "bigger than both of us", as well as a deep desire for it? Did Beversluis never have a hero, even a sports hero, when he was a child, whom he both desired and feared to approach? Did he never have a *parent?* Has he never met God in prayer?

Lewis has. The deep self-knowledge that lies behind his argument from desire comes from that experience, an experience no mere Positivist or Empiricist can understand. The argument from desire cuts to our heart. Its critics try to head Lewis off at the pass between the empirical and the logical walls of the canyon. But not only do they fail to head him off, they head themselves off, for their positivistic assumption is self-contradictory, being itself neither empirical nor tautological. Lewis' head feeds off his heart. Therefore his thought pulsates with real blood. Their bloodless formal critiques proceed from the ghostlike head already cut off from the heart. But any organ cut off from the heart atrophies and dies. Thus the critiques perish, but the argument from desire goes on beating, like Augustine's restless heart, until it rests in God.

Postscript

I began by referring to Anselm's "ontological argument". Let me end there too by asking whether the Argument from Desire is similar to Anselm's argument, as its objectors usually maintain.

It seems so, for (1) *Sehnsucht* is a privileged, unusual desire, as the idea of God is a privileged idea; (2) it is the most moving desire, as the idea of God is the most moving idea; (3) and it seems that the very fact of the psychological occurrence of this desire in consciousness is claimed to prove the real, objective existence of its object, just as the idea of God is claimed to prove the real God.

But there are significant differences, so that objections to Anselm's argument are not valid against Lewis'. For one thing, unlike the ontological argument, the argument from desire begins with data, facts, rather than simply the meaning of a word or concept. For another thing, Lewis does not begin with God, or a definition of God, as Anselm does, but ends with God, as Aquinas does ("and this [this thing we have proved] is what people call 'God'."). For a third thing, there is a major premise in the argument from desire, a general principle about all natural desires. Thus desires follow a general rule. But the idea of God in the ontological argument is the exception to the rule, the rule that no idea includes or proves existence.

Most importantly, the argument does not derive existence from the desire alone, as the ontological argument derives existence from the idea alone. Rather, the argument from desire first derives a major premise from the world (that nature makes no desire in vain) and then applies that principle about the nature of the world to this desire. Thus the argument is based on observed facts, both outer (about the world) and inner (about desires).

Appendix B

The Weight of Glory and the Weightlessness of Glory: A Dialog between C. S. Lewis And the Mystics

1. The Experience of Glory

We all know what the *weight* of glory is, whether or not we have read Lewis' golden sermon. We know it from the magic words of the poets; or we know it from the wordless word of great music, work of the Muses, not of man; or we know it from the word spoken by human love, the moment when the world's most prosaic word suddenly becomes the most wonder-full word in the world, the word "we"; or we know it in high liturgy, in the solemn joy of adoration before the astonishing mystery of God-with-us, when we are side by side with Mary, hailed by the angelic annunciation of the heavenly glory, visited from another world, another dimension; or we meet the glory in great art, when a picture becomes no longer an object *in* this world but a magic window opening up onto another world for us, a hole in our world, as the stars were to the ancient Greeks and as the painting of *The Dawn Treader* was to the Pevensie children; or we know it in the electrical shock of an absolutely perfect flower, or in the high, clear, crystal glass of a winter night, or in the seagull's haunting, harking call to return to Mother Sea. For some, the glory is not so much in the far country as in the magic word "home", the fairest place on earth, attained after Ulyssean adventures, Herculean labors, or prodigal wanderings aplenty. All of us *will* know it flat in the face when we die; we shall be hailed by the Angel of Death with the same lightsome glory with which Mary was hailed by the Angel of Life, because Christ has made Death into life's golden chariot, sent to fetch his Cinderella bride out of the cinders of this fireplace of a world, through a far midnight ride, to his very own castle and bedchamber, where Glory will beget glory upon us forever.

Suppose you reply that you have never felt this "weight of glory". That is too bad, but here are two things that are much worse, two dangerous conclusions you may be tempted to draw from your not feeling the "weight of glory". One: Since I have missed out on this most precious secret, I must be worthless and may as well despair. *It* is worth much, therefore *I* am worth little. Two: Since I have never experienced this thing, those who do are foolish dreamers of foolish dreams. I am worth much, therefore it is worth little.

Both conclusions are not only logically fallacious but spiritually destructive. They amount to a sigh and a sneer, despair and pride—the two things we can most profitably exorcise from our lives, especially the sneer, the lowest thing in the world.

But *no* one is devoid of the invitation to glory. Hide as we may, we are all hailed by the angel. Ah, but we hear the hailing only on the "hailing frequency": that spiritual ear that is buried at the very bottom of our being, buried under the louder shouts and bellows of a hundred hungry, howling animals, the this-worldly desires. So you may never seem to hear the heartbreakingly sweet voice of the nightingale that sings every night in our heart. But it is there whether we hear it or not. Be sure of that. If you are a human being, made in the image of God, then you too are a potential god or goddess, creature of the Creator, glory reflecting Glory, deep calling unto deep. All are weighted by the Glory. But not all feel the weight.

There is no escape from the glory, for the glory is the glory of God, and there is no escape from God. But there is an escape from knowing it, like the dwarfs in *The Last Battle*. We cannot turn the universe inside out, but we can turn our own minds inside out: we can believe we are mere mortals dreaming the dream of immortality, while in fact we are immortals dreaming the terrible dream of mere mortality. We can dream that we are only dreaming the glory, while in fact we are never so wide awake as when we open our eyes to the glory. We can follow Freud the Fraud and call it all illusion, soporific, and wishful thinking, while in fact it calls us to waken to Ultimate Reality. We can think of it as airy and insubstantial, like the creatures in *The Tempest,* while in fact it is the "enormous bliss of Eden", bigger than a twenty-billion-light-year universe of a trillion trillion suns and heavier than death. And stronger too.

2. The Definition of Glory

Two features of the glory stand out. First, the wonder, the numinous, the *mysterium tremendum,* the awe. Glory is greater than we can contain, comprehend, or control. It ravishes us right out of our skins, out of our selves, into an *ek-stasy*, a standing-outside-the self, an out-of-the-body-experience; and we tremble in fear and delight. *It* is not in *us, we* are in *it,* like being "*in* love": "it's bigger than both of us". Thus it does not enter into us, we enter into it: "Enter into the joy of thy Lord." St. Anselm says:

> When heart and mind and soul are full of that joy,
> Joy beyond measure will remain.
> Hence, not all of that joy shall enter into those who rejoice
> But they who rejoice shall wholly enter into that joy.

Second, it is *Sehnsucht*—longing, desire beyond desire. Lewis has written so deeply and truly about this that summarizing would be superfluous. In fact, I think no writer has *ever* written better of this than Lewis. (Can you name one?) I predict it will be his chief claim to fame a thousand years from now, if men still live and read on this precious, perilous little globe.

So I shall not put my snow on his bells, to dull their sound, but only remind you of the bells in *Surprised by Joy,* in the "Heaven" chapter of *The Problem of Pain,* in the introduction to *The Pilgrim's Regress,* in numerous passages in the Narnia books, and of course in "The Weight of Glory".

3. The "Weight" of Glory

But why does Lewis use the metaphor of "weight?"? Rather, why did St. Paul, from whom Lewis quoted?

We are going to explore the *weightlessness* of glory, as the other side of glory's coin, but we should first review the more familiar side: just what is glory's *weight?*

Physical weight, of course, symbolizes spiritual weight. But "spiritual weight" does not mean a heavy, depressed spirit or a nose-to-the-grindstone worldliness, a kind of spiritual down-drag or gravity, a spiritual Black Hole. No; "weight" here means profundity, significance, importance, greatness, enormousness, something immeasurably bigger than we have ever met, something that catches us *up* into it rather than down. Charles Williams describes it this way when Pauline first encounters its possibility in *Descent into Hell:*

> There arose gigantic before her the edge of a world of such incredible dimensions that she was breathless at the faint hint. . . . She felt . . . as in a low but immense arc rising above the horizon of her world, or perhaps of the earth itself, the hint of a new organisation of all things: a shape, of incredible difficulty in the finding, of incredible simplicity found, an infinitely alien arrangement of infinitely familiar things. . . .

4. The Weightlessness of Glory

Yet paradoxically (as befits infinity), Glory has an opposite side too, and I would like to complement (not correct) Lewis' account of it by calling our attention to the weightlessness of glory.

Glory seems weightless in at least two distinct but related ways. We could call them levity and levitation, or light-heartedness and light-weightedness. The East calls them *lila* and *sunyata*, "play" and "emptiness".

First, play, levity, the laughter of glory. Lewis knew this well. Here is one of his most glorious passages, from his last book, *Letters to Malcolm: Chiefly on Prayer:*

> Surely we must suppose the life of the blessed to be an end in itself, indeed The End: to be utterly spontaneous; to be the complete reconciliation of boundless freedom with order—with the most delicately adjusted, supple, intricate, and beautiful order? How can you find any image of this in the "serious" activities either of our natural or of our (present) spiritual life? Either in our precarious and heart-broken affections or in the Way which is always, in some degree, a *via crucis?* No, Malcolm. It is only in our "hours off", only in our moments of permitted festivity, that we find an analogy. Dance and game *are* frivolous, unimportant, down here; *for "down here" is not their natural place.* Here, they are a moment's rest from the life we were placed here to live. But in this world everything is upside down. That which, if it could be prolonged here, would be a truancy, is likest that which in a better country is the End of ends. Joy is the serious business of heaven.

Play is more ultimate than seriousness—or rather, in the end, the very distinction between the two collapses. Thus Scripture speaks of divine Wisdom "playing" eternally before the face of God. Thus the martyrs play with their lives. Roasted on a barbecue spit, one says, "I think I'm not well done on this side yet." Another, beheaded for alleged treason, tells the axeman to spare his beard, for *it* has not committed treason. Some of my more serious and worldly students get very angry at that. I understand. The child who plays with toys and knows something greater than toys is threatening to the adult who takes his grown-up toys with ultimate seriousness because he does not know of anything greater.

Chesterton, who was, I believe, the second greatest Christian apologist of our century, ends his magnum opus, *Orthodoxy,* with this profound guess about the divinity of levity and the levity of divinity:

> The tremendous figure which fills the Gospels . . . never concealed His tears. He showed them plainly on His open face at any daily sight, such as the far sight of His native city. Yet He concealed something. . . . He never restrained His anger. He flung furniture down the front steps of the Temple and asked men how they expected to escape the damnation of Hell. Yet He restrained something. I say it with reverence: there was in that shattering personality a thread that must be called shyness. There was something that He hid from all men when He went up a mountain to pray. . . . There was some one thing that was too great for God to show us when He walked upon our earth; and I have sometimes fancied that it was His mirth.

I cannot resist one more longish and Lewisish quotation, from Robert Farrar Capon: a vision of God's creating of the universe as play:

> Let me tell you why God made the world.
>
> One afternoon, before anything was made, God the Father, God the Son and God the Holy Ghost sat around in the unity of their Godhead discussing one of the Father's fixations. From all eternity, it seems he had this *thing* about being. He would keep thinking up all kinds of unnecessary things—new ways of being and new kinds of beings to be. And as they talked, God the Son suddenly said, "Really, this is absolutely great stuff. Why

don't I go out and mix us up a batch?" And God the Holy Ghost said, "Terrific, I'll help you." So they all pitched in, and after supper that night, the Son and the Holy Ghost put on this tremendous show of being for the Father. It was full of water and light and frogs; pine cones kept dropping all over the place and crazy fish swam around in the wine glasses. There were mushrooms and grapes, horseradishes and tigers—and men and women everywhere to taste them, to juggle them, to join them and to love them. And God the Father looked at the whole wild party and he said, "Wonderful! Just what I had in mind! Tov! Tov! Tov!" And all God the Son and the Holy Ghost could think of to say was the same thing. "Tov! Tov! Tov!" So they shouted together "Tov meod!" and they laughed for ages and ages, saying things like how great it was for beings to be, and how clever of the Father to think of the idea, and how kind of the Son to go to all that trouble putting it together, and how considerate of the Spirit to spend so much time directing and choreographing. And forever and ever they told old jokes, and the Father and the Son drank their wine in unitate Spiritus Sancti, and they all threw ripe olives and pickled mushrooms at each other per omnia saecula saeculorum. Amen.

It is, I grant you, a crass analogy; but crass analogies are the safest. Everybody knows that God is not three old men throwing olives at each other. Not everyone, I'm afraid, is equally clear that God is not a cosmic force or a principle of being or any other dish of celestial blancmange we might choose to call him. Accordingly, I give you the central truth that creation is the result of a Trinitarian bash, and leave the details of the analogy to sort themselves out as best they can.

Since life as a whole takes its nature from its maker, not from its parts, we must conclude that life as a whole is play—in fact, a Good Joke. Not like our jokes, like jokes *in* life, comic relief from seriousness. That is Low Jokes. Life itself is a High Joke. For instance: Why are there armadillos? Proximately, because of the environment, natural selection, whatever—the cosmic rays bombarded the primitive slime pools at just the right angle to evolve amoebas into armadillos. But that's like saying that Macbeth exists because Shakespeare read Holinshed's *Chronicles*. The real reason for the armadillo is, as Huston Smith puts it,

> the divine play, sheer protean exuberance. Being as being is so good that God cannot resist any of its possibilities. Wishing with part of herself to be a mother, a child dons apron and suckles her doll. Dolphins and whales are—the archetypal mammal wondering what it would be like to be a fish. Armadillos are the result of its thinking, "Wouldn't it be interesting to dress up in scales and play reptile?"

No one can look at an ostrich, a platypus, or a ferret and wonder whether God is a comedian. But *we* are part of the comedy of nature just as much as the animals are. Indeed, we are the biggest joke of all.

It is immensely healing to laugh at ourselves, especially when the laughter is a sharing in God's laughter, the all-encompassing laughter that is his great secret. One reason it is all-encompassing is that nothing but God is necessary and inevitable and (in that sense) rational. All of creation is overplus, free, extra, superfluous. *Everything is an armadillo.*

A second meaning of "weightlessness" is more difficult and controversial. It is the "emptiness" of the mystics, Western and Eastern alike. The mystical *experience* is strikingly uniform throughout time and place, though the religious, theological, moral, and personal *interpretations* of it are different, especially between Eastern and Western religions.

In this mystical experience—the experience apparently closest to the heavenly vision itself—all the world is seen to be not just *lila,* play (our first meaning of "weightlessness"), but also *sunyata,* "emptiness", nothingness, insubstantial, unheavy. The human self is also often seen to be light and insubstantial, like a bubble, or a sunbeam from the divine sun. Finally, even God is often seen not as a sort of super-*thing* but as "everything *and nothing*", *todo y nada,* in the words of the primary mystical Doctor of the Church, St. John of the Cross.

The closer the mystics come to the glory of God in mystical experience, the more they tend to use the language of emptiness rather than the language of things, substances, or essences. Unless the mystics, including the saints and Doctors of the Church, are simply in error, unless the mystical experience is systematically and universally deceptive, we must account for this weightlessness of heavenly glory somehow, and not just dismiss mysticism as beginning in mist, centering in I, and ending in schism.

5. *The Statement of the Problem: Is it the same glory?*

It may seem stretching the point to ask the question, like comparing apples with oranges; but both experiences, *Sehnsucht* and mysticism, claim to be experiences of the Absolute, in fact Absolute Joy. And there can be only one absolutely absolute absolute.

But there seem to be extreme and insuperable contradictions between the two experiences. In the experience of the *weight* of glory, both the human and the divine self appear as substantial selves, I's. Both selves have a deep desire, or love, or yearning, that is fulfilled by relationship and union with the other self. Both selves are weighted with glory. But in the mystical experience, the joy and glory appears in the opposite form of weightlessness or emptiness, both of the human self and the divine self, and the self and its desire seem to be abolished rather than ratified.

We meet here a problem right at the center of "Comparative Religions": "weighty" Western religions (Judaism, Christianity, and Islam) in their orthodox form versus "weightless" mystical Eastern religions (Hinduism, Buddhism, and Taoism) in their deepest experiences.

6. *The Principles of a Solution.*

To find a solution, we need some principles. Five, to be exact.

1. The first comes from Aristotle. It is the principle that our method must be determined by our content, or subject matter. Since reality is diverse, subject matters are diverse, and therefore our methods must be diverse. There is no one universal method, as Descartes thought. One should not use a mathematical method in ethics, or expect mathematical precision there; nor should we try to use our moral conscience to solve a mathematical equation. A problem of how to write a good novel can't be solved by mathematics *or* ethics, nor can ethics or mathematics be solved by the principles of literary aesthetics.

244 Heaven: The Heart's Deepest Longing

The deeper philosophical reason for Aristotle's principle of method following content is the principle that
being determines knowing rather than vice versa—true
knowledge conforms to reality, not reality to knowledge—and since being is diverse, therefore our methods
of knowing must be diverse too.

For pre-modern philosophy, epistemology, the science of knowledge, must follow metaphysics, the science of being. But for modern philosophy, it is usually
the other way round, for the typically modern mind
agrees with Kant that knowing determines being, and
we cannot know things as they really are in themselves.
I have never ceased to be utterly appalled at this idea and
to consider it the Unforgivable Sin of philosophy.

Following Aristotle's commonsensical and realistic
doctrine, our method must be a religious method because our subject matter is religious. The method of
every religion is some kind of faith. Therefore we must
begin with faith, and then use reason and experience and
imagination to explore that faith. The study of comparative religions can no more be successfuly carried out
by a fundamentally nonreligious and unbelieving
method, such as statistical sociology or empirical an-
thropology, or even analytic philosophy, than a poem
can be successfully understood by a computer or a
human being by astronomy.

Let me put the point in another way. It is not true, as
Alexander Pope wrote, that "the proper study of mankind is man." The proper study of mankind, as C. S.
Lewis replied, is everything. But it *is* true that the
proper *studier* of mankind is man. Similarly, the proper
studier of religious man is religious man, not irreligious
man.

2. A second principle comes partly from Aquinas and partly from Augustine. It addresses the problem: How can we express the experience of the infinite in finite terms? How do we stretch words that have natural meanings to do supernatural duty? In simple terms, how can man speak about God?

In three ways. First, we say not what God *is,* and not what our experience of his glory *is,* but only what it is *not.* Thus we will find many negative, or "emptiness" words. Second, we use analogy: we say what God is *like* and what our experience of the divine glory is *like.* Thus we will find many positive words, which are symbols or metaphors or pointers rather than definitions. Third, we use paradox. We say things like "Joy is the serious business of heaven." Thus we speak both of the weight and the weightlessness of glory.

If we forget any one of these, we are in trouble. For instance, it may be right to describe the experience of God as *not* dualistic, *not* the ordinary duality of human subject confronting natural object. God is not a super-thing. But if we express this point positively rather than negatively, we get the heresy of monism or pantheism. Perhaps this is the origin of the Hindu doctrine that *tat tvam asi,* Atman *is* Brahman, I *am* God.

Or, secondly, we might say that the experience is *like* aesthetic experience; but if we say that it *is* aesthetic experience or is even of the same genus, then we get Romanticism rather than religion.

Or, third, if we take only one half of the paradox without the other half, we are in trouble. Accepting free will but not divine sovereignty makes us Arminians or Modernists; accepting divine sovereignty without free will makes us Calvinists or Determinists. So here: accepting the weight of glory but not the weightlessness makes us anthropomorphic pagans, accepting the weightlessness of glory but not the weight makes us negative mystics, pantheists. To say simply "God is what we long for" brings God down to our level. But to say simply "God is *not* the object of our longing" removes God from our heart and life. We must learn to say, with Charles Williams, to everything in the world, two things: *"This too is thou; neither is this thou."* God is everywhere *and* nowhere, being and not a being, weighty and weightless.

3. A third principle, from Plato, could be called anti-reductionism, or levelling up rather than levelling down. It could also be called remythologizing rather than demythologizing. Hamlet sums it up perfectly when he says to Horatio, who is reluctant to believe in the ghost he has just seen: "There are more things in heaven and earth, Horatio, than are dreamt of in your philosophy."

There are in the long run only three philosophies: that there are more things, fewer things, or the same number of things in heaven and earth, that is, in objective reality, as in our philosophies and dreams, that is, in our subjective consciousness.

If the same number, we have absolute rationalism: all that is real is rational and all that is rational is real; all that is in reality is in consciousness and all that is in consciousness is in reality. You have to be pretty arrogant to say that, though apparently great philosophers like Parmenides, Spinoza, and Hegel have apparently said it. For most of us, the choice is between the remaining two: moreness or lessness.

Lessness means reductionism, debunking, thinking that most of our beliefs about reality are overdone, overblown, naive, idealistic, mythic. Reality is less than we think, "not what it's cracked up to be", as in the old song:

> I joined the Navy
> To see the world
> And what did I see?
> I saw the sea.
> I saw the Atlantic
> And the Pacific,
> And the Pacific
> Isn't terrific
> And the Atlantic
> Ain't what it's cracked up to be.

Thus the reductionistic mind reduces values to personal feelings, beauty to pleasure, love to lust, religious experience to wish-fulfillment, soul to brain, mystery to confusion, thinking to computing, etc.

The remaining option is that reality is more than we know—reality is like Uncle Frankie, who always wore those big old coats with the enormous pockets: you never knew what strange surprises he would pull out of them.

To apply the principle to our issue: If reality is like Uncle Frankie, more than we know, then the solution to most great "either/or" problems is going to be some sort of a "both/and". Weight *and* weightlessness, desire *and* desirelessness, ego-fulfillment *and* ego-loss—and perhaps also both literal, historical, traditional, orthodox, dogmatic, creedal Christianity *and* ineffable, transhistorical, trans-denominational mystical experience. Perhaps. Perhaps Buddha was not a fake, a heretic, or plain confused; perhaps he saw something of God. Let us at least keep the option open one thought longer than we expect. Especially since reality is usually more than our expectations.

4. A fourth principle, from Martin Buber, could be called the logic of personal relations. The I-Thou experience has its own logical principles, foremost among them being the necessity of faith, trust. "Unless you believe, you will not understand" is not only a formula for theologians, as affirmed and practiced in the Middle Ages; it is also a formula for all personal knowledge, human as well as divine, all knowing of a Thou as distinct from an It.

This is not the scientific method. The scientific method wants to assume nothing. It begins with systematic doubt, or distrust, like Descartes' philosophy. Ideas are presumed guilty until proven innocent. No belief is accepted until proved. But the personal method treats the Thou as innocent until proven guilty. It "hopes all things, believes all things, endures all things". It begins with methodic faith or trust rather than methodic doubt.

Let us apply this to God. Let us trust God's natural as well as supernatural leadings, for he surely leads us not only through infallible divine revelation but also through our fallible natural proclivities. If our soul naturally sinks to bliss under the weight of glory and also rises to bliss under its weightlessness, let us begin by trusting both experiences. Without abandoning either Reason or Revelation, let us trust the Unknown to lead us into the unknown, into the wilderness of spirit as he led Abraham and as Jesus led his disciples. We should *expect* problems, puzzles, paradoxes. We must learn to live with mystery. More, we must learn to live *in* mystery. The only way to the Promised Land is through the wilderness.

5. A fifth and last principle of method comes from Augustine and defines the next 1,000 years of medieval Christian philosophy. It is that faith and reason are allies, not enemies, not even separate but equal strangers. They are marriable.

Reason is faith's instrument. Philosophy is the handmaiden to theology. Reason is also God's teaching tool. All truth is God's truth. Reason, properly used, can never contradict faith, properly understood, because God is the teacher in both, and God never contradicts himself.

Reason may crawl like an ant while faith flies like an eagle. But we *are* rational *animals,* and it is proper for us to crawl. Even if we are given a temporary ride on eagle's wings, a moment of glory, we must bring it back to our anthill and explore it with ant eyes too, though not reduce it to ant stature (that would be reductionism). There should be no danger of that unless we are utter fools; when the ant is looking at the eagle, rather than theorizing about it, the ant does not think the eagle is only a flying ant.

Faith is our response to divine revelation, i.e., divinely revealed Fact. If we keep our eyes on Fact, our reasonings will follow Fact, follow the truth. Even our mystical feelings and our rational interpretations of them will follow, because God is no deceiver. Principle 5 follows from Principle 4: we can trust Reason following Faith *because* we can trust God.

7. Transition from Principles to Application.

We are now finally in a position to address our problem, the relationship between the weight of glory and the weightlessness of glory, or, to be brief, Romanticism (in Lewis' sense) and Mysticism. There are at least two different aspects to our problem: the problem of desire and the problem of the desiring ego.

First, concerning desire: Romanticism stimulates the deepest of desires, *Sehnsucht,* while Mysticism seems to attain joy by a total detachment from all desire. Christianity, like Romanticism, tells us to purify our desire (from selfish to unselfish) and attach it to the right object (God, not idols); but not to kill it off. As Lewis says in "The Weight of Glory", our Lord finds our desires not too strong but too weak. Buddhism, however, typical of mysticism, especially Eastern mysticism, tells us that desire is the cause of all our suffering and ignorance, and the supreme obstacle to joy and enlightenment. Can any two ways be farther apart than these, like fire and water, firing desire and drowning it?

A second and even deeper aspect of the problem concerns the desiring ego itself. The weight of glory bespeaks the infinite and eternal reality and preciousness of the individual soul. It is the "secret thread" Lewis speaks of so movingly in the "Heaven" chapter of *The Problem of Pain*. It is the "white stone" with the new name on it, known only to the one who receives it (Rev. 2:17). It is our private mansion in the Father's house with many mansions (John 14:2). Our *I* is eternally real and infinitely precious because it is the image of God, whose name is I Am; we are images of ultimate reality in our individual souls.

But according to the mystics, the I, ego, self, or individual is the great illusion. Can any two claims about the nature of ultimate reality be farther apart? Paradoxically reversing our previous metaphor, Romanticism waters the growth of the I while Mysticism burns it up.

Can our principles help us to sort out the truth in both glories, weighty and weightless? Let us see.

8. *The Problem of Desire.*

First, let us look at desire itself. If we listen to the mystics, must we simply abandon the weight of glory, the greatest joy we non-mystics have ever experienced, those patches of godlight we call *Sehnsucht?* And if we listen to *Sehnsucht,* must we dismiss the mystics as false prophets?

Like most problems, this one is solvable by a distinction. The "desire" the mystics disparage is not *Sehnsucht,* but *tanha,* "selfish craving", the desire to possess and enjoy some object less than ourselves. That includes even our earthly lives and time. Concerning this desire, Lewis agrees with the mystics when he quotes George MacDonald's saying, "We are slaves to whatever we cannot part with that is less than ourselves." Jesus taught nothing more insistently and repeatedly than detachment from earthly riches.

But *Sehnsucht* is a very different desire from all others in at least two ways, as Lewis clearly points out in the preface to *The Pilgrim's Regress.* First, the desire itself, even in the absence of its satisfaction or even any expectation of it, is felt to be infinitely precious, more precious than any other satisfaction. Secondly, and more important here, its object cannot be possessed or even defined. We do not know what we want in *Sehnsucht*. For *Sehnsucht* is not a desire to possess at all, but to be possessed, to be united with what is greater than the self, to lose the self's independence (though not the self's reality) in union with God, whether consciously or unconsciously known.

The distinction between the two kinds of desire is brilliantly set out in an important but little-known passage from Lewis' *Out of the Silent Planet*. Ransom, the earthman, is questioning Hyoi, one of the hrossa of Malacandra, or Mars, about sexual pleasure. The distinction Hyoi draws between *wondelone* and *hluntheline* is precisely the distinction between *Sehnsucht* and selfishness, hoping and having, love and lust, aspiration and perspiration, wonder and wilfulness, goodness and greed, centrifugal desire and centripetal desire:

"Is the begetting of young not a pleasure among the hrossa?"

"It is a very great one, *Hman*. This is what we call love."

"If a thing is a pleasure, a *hman* wants it again. He might want the pleasure more often than the number of young that could be fed."

It took Hyoi a long time to get the point.

"You mean", he said slowly, "that he might do it not only in one or two years of his life but again?"

"Yes."

"But why? Why would he want his dinner all day or want to sleep after he had slept? I do not understand."

"But a dinner comes every day. This love, you say, comes only once while the *hross* lives?"

"But it takes his whole life. When he is young he has

to look for his mate; and then he has to court her; then he begets young; then he rears them; then he remembers all this, and boils it inside him and makes it into poems and wisdom."

"But the pleasure he must be content only to remember?"

"That is like saying 'My food I must be content to eat.'"

"I do not understand."

"A pleasure is full grown only when it is remembered. You are speaking, *Hman,* as if the pleasure were one thing and the memory another. It is all one thing. The *seroni* could say it better than I say it now. Not better than I could say it in a poem. What you call remembering is the last part of the pleasure, as the *crah* is the last part of a poem. When you and I met, the meeting was over very shortly, it was nothing. Now it is growing something as we remember it. But still we know very little about it. What it will be when I remember it as I lie down to die, what it makes in me all my days till then— that is the real meeting. The other is only the beginning of it. You say you have poets in your world. Do they not teach you this?"

"Perhaps some of them do", said Ransom. "But even in a poem does a *hross* never long to hear one splendid line over again?"

Hyoi's reply unfortunately turned on one of those points in their language which Ransom had not mastered. There were two verbs which both, as far as he could see, meant to *long* or *yearn;* but the *hrossa* drew a sharp distinction, even an opposition, between them. Hyoi seemed to him merely to be saying that every one would long for it *(wondelone)* but no one in his senses could long for it *(hluntheline).*

"And indeed", he continued, "the poem is a good

example. For the most splendid line becomes fully
splendid only by means of all the lines after it; if
you went back to it you would find it less splendid
than you thought. You would kill it. I mean in a good
poem."

"But in a bent poem, Hyoi?"

"A bent poem is not listened to, *Hman*."

"And how of love in a bent life?"

"How could the life of a *hnau* be bent?"

. . . At last it dawned upon him that it was not they,
but his own species, that were the puzzle.

Ransom has found, and failed to understand, desire in
its unfallen state among the unfallen *hrossa* of Malacandra. In this state, *wondelone* (joy, hope, *Sehnsucht*) is
clearly distinguished from *hluntheline* (egotism, lust,
tanha); in *Hman's* fallen earthly state, it is not.

Here is another instance, from *Perelandra*: Ransom's
first taste of the Perelandrian fruit. No one has ever
forgotten this fruit who has ever read *Perelandra*.

It was like the discovery of a totally new genus of pleasures, something unheard of among men, out of all
reckoning, beyond all covenant. For one draught of this
on earth wars would be fought and nations betrayed. It
could not be classified. . . . As he let the empty gourd
fall from his hand and was about to pluck a second one,
it came into his head that he was now neither hungry nor
thirsty. And yet to repeat a pleasure so intense and almost so spiritual seemed an obvious thing to do. . . .
Yet something seemed opposed to this 'reason'. It is
difficult to suppose that this opposition came from desire, for what desire would turn from so much deli-
ciousness? But for whatever cause, it appeared to him
better not to taste again. Perhaps the experience had been
so complete that repetition would be a vulgarity. . . .

Ransom, like the mystics, refuses the temptations of *tanha*. Eve's forbidden fruit was not an apple, it was *tanha, grasping* the apple.

9. *The Problem of the Ego.*

A deeper issue than desire is the desirer, the "I" in "I desire". This is the issue behind the issue. The mystical experience seems to reveal the unreality of this desiring ego, while the Romantic experience seems to reveal that it is more real, and its satisfaction more wonderful, than we ever suspected. Must we abandon one of these two precious experiences? If not, how can they be reconciled?

A distinction is in order again, but to see it we must first step back and get the issue into a larger perspective. There are three possible beliefs about how real and valuable the human ego is. Let us call them humanism, pantheism, and theism. For humanism, the human ego is the most real and valuable thing there is. It is independently real, not created, and it is the source of all value and meaning, not subject to divine law and divine providence. For pantheism, the human ego is an illusion, indeed the supreme illusion that blocks the Enlightenment experience of absolute oneness. But for theism, the human ego is derivatively real and valuable as image of God, the human *I am* imaging the divine *I Am*.

From this point of view, we can make the following distinction. The ego's value *is* absolute, as humanism contends, in relation to and in comparison with the things in this world. Compared with economic efficiency, or production, or social utility, or pleasure, or the so-called "quality of life", each and every individual human soul is infinitely valuable. "For what does it profit a man if he gains the whole world and loses his own soul?"

But compared with God, the value of the creature is only finite and is totally relative to its Creator. Our very existence is sheer gift; nothing we have is ours, everything is on loan. We are thus everything compared to the world, nothing compared to God. We are everything and nothing, *todo y nada*. We are like God to the world and like a world to God. We are the world's God and God's world.

There is no contradiction in the same thing being both finite and infinite if it is finite in one relationship and infinite in another. Think of a mirror. It is infinite in its potentiality to reflect images of any other things, but finite in relation to other mirrors and in relation to the mirror-maker. The human soul is like a mirror, reflecting the whole world (thus Aristotle's remark that "the human soul is in a way all things") but it is finite in relation to other human souls and in relation to its Creator.

In light of this distinction, how shall we explain the mystics' experience of the unreality of the ego? It is true not in relation to other people, but in relation to the world and (in another way) in relation to God. In relation to the world, the ego is not a *thing in* the world; as the mirror is not one of many objects it reflects. That is the way the Eastern mystic sees the nothingness, or weightlessness, of the soul. The human soul is also nothing in relation to God. It has no rights, no claims, and no independence, for its very existence is totally dependent on its Creator. That is the way the Western mystic sees the nothingness of the soul. The soul is both infinitely more than the world (thus *not*-a-thing-in-the-world) and infinitely less than God (thus *nothing* compared to God).

A third kind of nothingness of the soul is common to both the Eastern and the Western mystic: utter self-forgetfulness. So ravished by God or by Nirvana that they are unwilling or even unable to turn to look at themselves, the mystics become totally self-forgetful, as if they were not there at all. They are totally transparent, like air to the light. They do not see themselves; they see through themselves. Thus they say they *are* not, for they *see* no self any more. They have died—not biologically, nor ontologically (they still *exist*) but psychologically. And this is bliss and glory. In fact, every great bliss and glory is self-forgetful. All ecstasy is ek-static, standing-outside-yourself. Once you turn around and look at yourself, you spoil it. Supreme happiness is absentmindedness.

But the mistake is to confuse this subjective experience of no-self-*consciousness* with the objective pseudo-fact of no self-*reality;* to confuse the subjective point of view, in which the self is indeed not *seen,* with the objective point of view, in which it is mistakenly concluded that the self is not *real.* Of course it's real! Who's having the experience, anyway? Who's writing the books? It takes a self to deny a self. *Cogito ergo sum.* Or even *non cogito ergo sum:* I cease thinking, therefore I am. For there must be a ceaser to do the ceasing.

The theistic point of view alone accounts for the truth seen in the other two, even in humanism. For there *is* an autonomy, though a created and relative one, to the human ego. In fact, the human self is so autonomous de facto that it can decide to pretend to be its own God, and this is precisely hell. The pantheistic point of view is also understandable from the theistic one, for there must indeed be the death to self-consciousness that is centrally prized among the Eastern mystics. The path to joy which *Sehnsucht* desires is death—not only physical but psychological, the death of self-consciousness and the death of selfish desire, *hluntheline*. Everything that can be possessed must be unpossessed, let go; everything that can be gained must be lost. That is one function of death: to provide us with the liberating release we need but do not want, the release from all that can be *had*, including our own bodies, our lives, and our times, our lifetimes.

For we can take nothing with us in death, and this well-known fact helps us to learn the not-at-all-well-known fact that we can't take anything with us in life either, that only the *I* lives, not its possessions. I suspect that we can't even take our objectifiable personality traits with us when we die. For these came from the world, through heredity and environment, and they must be let go when the world is let go. Only the naked *I* lives through death, and rises again in a new body, a new world, and new heredity and environment. Only the image of God, the I, is immortal.

After death God graciously reclothes this I with a new and true body and world, even new personality traits. The lustful, conscientious, and cowardly rabbit becomes a free, laughing, fearless saint, a veritable god or goddess. And a new body: immortal, powerful, and perfectly obedient instrument of the newly purified soul. And a new world, preternaturally obedient to the new body, "new heavens and a new earth". The three are in harmony, not disharmony: innocence, immortality, and joy instead of sin, death, and suffering, because God, the soul, the body, and the world now sing a common music instead of a cacophonic rivalry.

The soul is harmonized with God; the concertmaster follows the conductor; innocence is restored and sin abolished.

The body is harmonized with this soul; the violins play the melody line the concertmaster receives from the divine conductor; death, the separation and rivalry of soul and body, is abolished and immortality restored.

The world is harmonized with this body; the rest of the instruments follow the melody line of man; suffering, the disharmony between man and nature, body and things, is abolished and the joy of Eden restored.

But to attain this, to get to There from Here, we must die to our present selves; we must learn detachment not only from our present world and body and desires but even from our present self, our personalities (especially the modern "cult of personality"), and objectifiable, knowable patterns of feeling and thinking and behaving. Everything a psychologist could know in us as object is lost in death and in mystical experience, which is a rehearsal for death. The subject, the I, alone cannot die.

But death is rehearsal for resurrection. The indefineable consummation longed for by *Sehnsucht* comes, but not by the direct road, not by desire and fulfillment but by failure and death. It does not come through *hluntheline,* but through the death of *hluntheline.* It does not even come through *wondelone* alone, but *wondelone* is its prophet. Even *wondelone* must die to be resurrected. Lewis found this out in *Surprised by Joy.* It is the very last point he makes, on the very last page; and it never ceases to surprise and often to scandalize readers. How dare

Lewis say the subject of *Sehnsucht* has lost all interest for him since he became a Christian? Easily. *Sehnsucht* is John the Baptist, and when the Messiah comes, John withdraws, his task completed. "He must increase, I must decrease." That is why Jesus calls John the greatest of all the prophets (Mt. 11:11): because he was the least, the one who disappeared. He is like the human self. When the Son rises, the fog disappears to view, filled wholly with light.

There is a beautiful Sufi tale about this, the narrow way to resurrection through death. Moslems and Jews have longings and prophecies about resurrection too, though only Christians know it as news, as "the good news", not just as hope. The story is called "The Tale of the Sands", and when you read it you must remember that you are the stream, the desert is death, the sea is heaven, your longing to cross the desert and reach the sea is *Sehnsucht,* and the wind is the weightlessness of glory, self-forgetful mysticism.

> A stream, from its source in far-off mountains, passing through every kind of countryside, at last reached the sands of the desert. Just as it had crossed every other barrier, the stream tried to cross this one, but it found that as fast as it ran into the sand, its waters disappeared.
>
> It was convinced, however, that its destiny was to cross this desert. And yet there was no way. Now a hidden voice, coming from the desert itself, whispered: "The Wind crosses the desert, and so can the stream."
>
> The stream objected that it was dashing itself against the sand and only getting absorbed; that the wind could fly, and this was why it could cross a desert.
>
> "By hurtling in your own accustomed way you can-not get across. You will either disappear or become a

marsh. You must allow the wind to carry you over, to your destination."

But how could this happen? "By allowing yourself to be absorbed by the wind."

This idea was not acceptable to the stream. After all, it had never been absorbed before. It did not want to lose its individuality. And once having lost it, how was one to know that it could ever be regained?

"The wind", said the sand, "performs this function. It takes up water, carries it over the desert, and then lets it fall again. Falling as rain, the water again becomes a river."

"How can I know that this is true?"

"It is so, and if you do not believe it, you cannot become more than a quagmire, and even that could take many, many years, and it is certainly not the same thing as a stream."

"But can I not remain the same stream that I am today?"

"You cannot in either case remain so", the whisper said. "Your essential part is carried away and forms a stream again. You are called what you are even today because you do not know which part of you is the essential one."

When he heard this, certain echoes began to arise in the thoughts of the stream. Dimly, he remembered a state in which he—or some part of him, was it?—seemed to have been held in the arms of a wind. He also remembered—or did he?—that this was the real thing, not necessarily the obvious thing, to do.

So the stream raised his vapour into the welcoming arms of the wind, which gently and easily bore it upwards and along, letting it fall softly as soon as they reached the roof of a mountain many, many miles away. And the stream reflected, "Yes, now I have learned my true identity."

And thus it is said that the way in which the Stream of Life is to continue its journey is written in the Sands.

10. Practical Conclusions.

Finally, what difference does all of this make to us here and now? What should we *do* about it?

This is certainly a legitimate question, for if an idea makes no difference, especially no doing-difference, to our lives, then it is for all practical purposes meaningless. William James' Pragmatism is surely right about *that*. The practical question, What should we *do?* is even more important and demanding than the theoretical question, How should we *think?*

When Cicero addressed the Roman Senate, everyone said, "How beautifully he speaks!" But they remained in their seats. When Demosthenes addressed the Greek army, they arose, clashed their swords onto their shields, and said, "Let us march!" When Peter—the new Peter, empowered by the Holy Spirit after Pentecost— preached his first sermon, his hearers, touched to the heart, said, not "What should we think?" but "What should we do?" Peter's answer summed up the whole Christian religion in three steps: Repent (to the Father) and believe (in the Son) and receive (the Spirit).

So my final and most important question of all is: What should we do about the weight and weightlessness of glory?

For one thing, we must obey our methodological principles by using a religious method to answer this religious question. Now religion is like science and unlike philosophy in one way: its proofs are experiments, not just arguments. The philosophical way to find out whether there is a God is to argue; the religious way is to pray. Our question of the relation between the weight and weightlessness of glory is answerable more readily in practice, in lived experiment, than in thought. The two experiences are more readily synthesizeable in practice than in theory.

One way this synthesis happens is that the word of the weight of glory is set off with great effect by the background silence of the weightlessness of glory. The word of power springs from the living silence, not just from other words. Perhaps *only* from the silence. Kierkegaard wrote,

> If I were a doctor and I had to prescribe one remedy for all the ills of the modern world, I would say: "Create silence." For even if the Word of God were proclaimed in all its splendor, it would not be heard among all the panoply of noise in the modern world. Therefore, create silence.

But our first concern must not be to *synthesize* these two experiences, nor even to *have* either or both of them. For our goal is not *experiences* but the God that both of these experiences point to in different ways; and our essential task in this life is not to be romantics or to be mystics but to be saints. Our God has not commanded us, "Be ye wonderful, for I the Lord your God am wonderful", nor "Be ye mystical, for I the Lord your God am mystical", but "Be ye holy, for I the Lord your God am holy."

The concentration on sanctity above even mysticism most clearly distinguishes the religions of the Bible (Judaism, Christianity and Islam) from Eastern religions. For our God is not just an It, not Being in the abstract, and not just a state of consciousness, an experience, but he is a Person with a will—a good, holy, and loving will. We always imitate our gods. Wily Ulysses is like wily Apollo; the tranquilly passionless Brahmin is like the tranquilly passionless Brahman; and the Christian saint is like the Saintly Christ.

Sanctity is work. As George MacDonald put it, the only advice for one haunted by the scent of unseen roses is—work. As C. S. Lewis says, the fire of *Sehnsucht* goes out if you try to fuel it with itself, but if you bank it with the unlikely fuel of dogma and ethics, that is, faith and works, the works of love, then it springs up unforeseen. "The door to life usually opens behind us." We are *"surprised* by Joy". That is the practical conclusion concerning the weight of glory.

And concerning the weightlessness of glory? An anecdote answers that question. When I first discovered the magnificent mystical writings of St. John of the Cross back at Yale Graduate School (of all places!), I tried to share some of the fire of my new enthusiasm with a very practical, very simple, and very holy priest, who is now closer to God than St. John of the Cross ever was on earth because he is no longer on earth but in his heavenly home with God. He gave me this advice: "Learn to walk before you dance. Practice the virtues."

How mundane! How disappointing! But how perfectly right!

According to the most practical of all religious authorities, Jesus Christ, only the virtuous, only the pure of heart, can see God. For the instrument with which we see God is ourselves, our hearts, our wills, our loves. By loving, we keep the instrument clear, the mirror bright, the temple ready for the Lord who has promised to come suddenly and visit his temple with the weight of his glory. His yoke is so easy, his burden so light, that the thing that weighs infinitely more than the whole world, namely, the weight of glory, the glory of God, is so totally weightless that we do not even carry it, it carries us, like the wind carrying the stream. All we have to do is to say Yes.

Appendix C

The Man Who Found Heaven in the Bronx

Frodo Grubb had always hated both halves of his name, even though, like his mother who chose the first half, he loved his namesake in *The Lord of the Rings*. Perhaps he hated his name because he missed his dead mother so terribly and took revenge on her for leaving him for a happier land by hating the thing he carried with him every second that spoke of her and kept his aching wound open with the memory. He thought the pain would lessen with time; but, unexpectedly, it didn't. He missed her as much now, at thirty, as he had at ten, when she died.

Since that day, she had always seemed to Frodo to be something in his present, not his past: an unseen presence in his life. Perhaps this is why he had always felt haunted by the unseen and quite convinced that it was as real as the seen. His mother was the only other person he had ever known who took fantasy seriously and who could be whimsical and serious at the same time. (His father had died when he was two, and he had no memories of his essence, only his existence—rather like God, he thought.)

His mother's choice of the name Frodo had been part of her whimsey, and Frodo envied that. He had wanted to be a happy, carefree creature like her (she seemed so strangely free of care in the middle of cares); but her death seemed to put a spell upon him. He felt earthbound, not free to fly, to be the spirit and sprite she was (he could not think: "had been", only "was"). Perhaps this was because he secretly feared to suffer her fate, as if the caterpillar were more secure than the butterfly.

Frodo's friends continually teased him about his name. He felt like a grub much of the time, and when he felt like a hobbit, it was only because he was short, dumpy and hairy: all very well for a hobbit, but pretty ugly for a human. He had once had a fat gerbil and had to give it away because he had the sinking feeling whenever he looked at it that he was looking into a mirror.

Frodo obviously did not have a great self-image. He constantly felt what his friends called "out of it"; but he could never understand just what that meant, what "it" was—and that was precisely why he was "out of it"! He was mordant, eccentric, but in a small, not in a grand, way. He failed to understand things that everyone else understood and understood things no one else understood (or cared to). He could not read between the lines everyone read between, but he read between lines no one else did. But this eccentricity was nothing spectacular; it did not make him a creative genius. Rather, it felt like living in a just slightly tilted world, as if he saw everything at an angle, "off" a few degrees. It was a sense, a different coloration to everything, or (most of all) like a smell. One reason he had never married, besides thinking of himself as ugly, was this: He knew a man and his wife could not be happy if they lived in different worlds, and he had never met anyone who lived in his world.

That sounds arrogant; but arrogance was unimaginable to Frodo. Yet he could not help seeing everyone he met as a small image of the great city he lived in: large and impressive looking from outside and from a distance but very small and dull and ordinary seen close up and from inside. Like many others, Frodo saw the city as ugly; but unlike the others, it continually bothered him that he never understood why the city had to be ugly and its people mirror images of it, tawdry offspring of the great tawdry mother. Because it seemed so to everyone else, it seemed also to him a necessity, a heavy, inevitable thing. But he had never understood this necessity, either in the city or in himself. For he saw himself not as a superior being above all this ugliness but as the ugliest and grubbiest of them all. He classified people as Plastic People and Bug People. He was clearly a Bug Person, a Grubb; but the Plastic People too were Bug People inside and underneath. They only covered their inner life's grubbiness with glamor, glitter, and glaze. He saw through the glaze and saw the grub; but this insight into universal grubbiness did not comfort him for his own; it increased it. It seemed to say, There is no escape.

In order to save his sanity in such a world, Frodo's inner life developed in compensation for his outer grubbiness. It was not the inner life of the great creative artist or of the saint; but neither was it that of the schizophrenic. He was too weak for either extreme, perhaps, and also too weak to travel the road so many of his friends traveled, the road of various business and political successes. Frodo knew this road led nowhere; if it led out of the city into the suburbs, it led from a flat soul in a Bronx flat to a flat soul in a Westchester high rise. Even if the soul was taken out of the flat, the flat was not taken out of the soul.

Frodo's escape was inner, and it consisted largely of poetry. He was not clever enough to be either a poet or a teacher, and much of what he read he could not comprehend; but amid the great poets he frequently found "hauntings" that shot into his soul like steel arrows and remained. The little he saw, he saw with a piercing clarity. There was no middle ground, no merely scholarly or dilettantish competence, no understanding without actually standing under the poet's vision, being overarched by it, included in it, overwhelmed by it.

Poetry was passion to Frodo. His friends who were keeping themselves puritanically busy having "passionate affairs" seemed to lead a life that was a quite passionless affair. Frodo's passion for poetry was in fact only a part, though a large part, of a more general passion: Frodo loved any kind of exploring. He did not see the city as worth exploring, and he lacked the money to travel, so he turned to the world of thoughts, feelings, and imaginings. He found "acres of diamonds" in his own mental backyard. He especially loved exploring extremes, *ends* of things. The sources and mouths of rivers fascinated him, as did the source and mouth of life, birth and death. As a small boy, he had sought out-of-the-way corners and secret hiding places; then he read all he could find about small, unusual countries. When he discovered chess, he studied only eccentric and unusual openings. (He loved to surprise opponents by playing 1. P-KN4 and conquer their contempt for such a duffer's opening by an occasional victory; he preferred this to twice as many victories from using conventional, sounder openings.)

One of the most fascinating ideas he ever ran across was the idea of the flat earth. For a flat earth has an end, an edge. That is why he was so fascinated by the mystery of death: death was an end, an absolute end in time, a compensation for the roundness of the real world and its lack of any absolute end in space. He hated the book of Ecclesiastes, with its vision of cyclic time; he hated also the thought of reincarnation. But his fascination with death was not morbid; it was the opposite of morbid, for it was his love of life, his passion, that led him to explore endings, especially the ending of life. But he found very little light on this particular journey of exploration.

Like so many poets, he spontaneously saw the sea as symbolizing death and felt a strange awe and even longing for it. But he loved rivers even more, for their ends were discernible. He saw life as a river, and he loved the sea only because it lay at the end of the river. He loved life, not the end of life; yet he loved it because it had an end.

Frodo had longed to travel far from the city to explore a river from end to end but never did. Somehow the heavy inevitabilities of his life seemed always to make such a trip impossible, as it did all his other dreams. He saw the city as a monstrous spider living off the blood of its victims and himself as a tiny fly trapped in its sticky web, not yet eaten but not able to escape and fly free either. Perhaps this was only self-pity and weak will on his part, for which he conveniently blamed the city; or perhaps it was his charity coupled with others' insensitivity to his real needs, for whenever he contemplated such a trip of escape, someone else's need seemed to prevent it. In any case, he had seldom traveled outside the city, but he had often traveled in his dreams.

One day the great idea dawned: A city street was also like a river! Even if he could not explore a river, he could explore a street. Suddenly, and for no apparent reason, a street appeared to him as something different than it had, as a natural thing, like a river. For, he thought, a street is a road; and life is a road; and nothing is more natural than life. Therefore a street too is a natural thing and not just an artificial thing. Yet he had never bothered to explore a street. He especially wanted to explore the beginning and the end of a street. Perhaps some streets had real ends; perhaps they did not merely end in other streets, like the spider's web, like the round earth. Perhaps a street might lead him Somewhere.

The idea, he knew, was irrational; of course all streets led nowhere, led only to other streets. At least that was so here in the web of the city. But today "of course" somehow had lost its force, its heavy inevitability. His mother's lightness seemed really present to him, and he to it; what he would dismiss as whimsey on other days seemed likely fact today. In his new lightness he dared even to hope his own street might lead Somewhere; he thought he should begin at home, practicing the "acres of diamonds in your own backyard" principle. Surprising as it may seem, he had never walked to the end of his own street.

This street was an almost remarkably unremarkable street in the Bronx called Morris Park Avenue. It was four lanes wide (like many other streets), full of traffic lights, buses, and double parkers (like many other streets), and lined with small stores and large apartment buildings throughout its two-mile length (like many other streets). He had classified it as "middle-dull". Frodo classified dull things into three categories of dullness (the classifying of dullness somehow relieved dullness). At one extreme were things only slightly dull, things on the brink of interestingness. At the other extreme were things so dull they were fascinating—like Iowa or paper clips. In the middle were the most irredeemably dull things of all, "middle-dull". Most of the city was like that: not quite interesting, yet not so spectacularly dull that its very dullness was spectacular. Morris Park Avenue fit perfectly into the middle of the middle category of "middle-dull". In fact, the whole world seemed to Frodo to be an extension of Morris Park Avenue, to be a middle-world in quite an opposite sense from Tolkien's Middle-Earth.

Yet today he felt the strange hope that even this most irredeemably dull thing of all might lead out of the spider's web if only he had the hope to follow it. And he did. In a quiet inner exultation, he began the most important walk of his life. There was no reason for the mounting sense of excitement he felt along the way; one building replaced another as it always had; nothing either was or seemed different—until the end. As he walked down an incline and saw the last block of Morris Park Avenue ahead of him, he saw that it did indeed have an end and led Somewhere.

After it crossed its last cross street, it ran for one last block, quite level, past the slick brick home of the ASPCA on the left and undistinctive flats on the right. Then it turned right—the only way a car could go at the end of Morris Park Avenue was right—and became another street. But a walker could do something a car could not at the end of Morris Park Avenue; he could go straight instead of turning right, and find himself in a wonderfully different little world. There was a patch of woods—bushes, really—about half a block square there, where the bull's eye would be if you saw the avenue as an arrow. There was just enough greenery to promise secrets inside. Best of all, through the little woods ran a path, a dirt path about five feet wide. The path led up a steep hill, and the steepness of the hill plus the foliage hid whatever lay at the top, at the end of the path. Frodo saw the path as the barb of the arrow, as part of Morris Park Avenue itself, and whatever lay at the top of the path was the end of Morris Park Avenue.

It was a thoroughly delicous little surprise for Frodo; he never expected to see such an invasion of wilderness in his part of the city. It was even better than the much larger patches of planned wilderness in the city's large parks, for it was natural and artless and forgotten. No one, apparently, had ever noticed it but Frodo; it was there for him alone, *his* woods, his friend. It was the culmination of all the other things he had noticed that no one else had. A surprising feeling gradually came upon him as he stood contentedly a block away and contemplated the woods; more than the first feeling of pleasure at finding his green woods in the brown city, he now felt something almost fearful, something magical or miraculous. At first he put it down to his imagination and wishful thinking; but even while this rational and critical thought dominated his mind, the magic remained unimpaired, it seemed undissolvable by doubt, for it seemed to be coming not from within himself but from without, from objective reality, from something in those woods.

With mounting excitement, he focused on the feeling. It was not coming from the woods, he found, but from the path. The greenery, lovely as it was, was there only for the sake of the path. It was just a brown dirt path, full of stones and some litter; yet it seemed to him to be more than a path now; it seemed to be the center of the world, the navel of his cosmic mother, and the very middle of Middle-Earth. His world, his mother, and his dreams were all that path. Archetypes welled up within his mind; and the path appeared as a birth canal, *the* birth canal, the central passageway of his life and even of the universe. Absurd as it was, it seemed not only true but obvious, indubitable, necessary with a necessity as strong in its soaring lightness as the necessities of the city had seemed strong in their heaviness. The thought that this path was the birth canal of the universe did not seem like a thought at all but like a thing, an unyielding, unarguable, and utterly reliable thing, with hard corners like a rock. There it was, right in front of him at the end of Morris Park Avenue: the central street of the universe!

He had long been fascinated by accounts of medically dead and then resuscitated patients telling what they had seen on "the other side"; one recurrent feature in such accounts that interested him was the long dark tunnel, the passage. That had burned itself into his memory, for he had always been fascinated by tales of a passage into another world, like the Narnia stories of C. S. Lewis. The rabbit hole and the looking glass in Alice were for him infinitely more wonderful than any of the wonders beyond them. For such passageways were like a birth canal: not just doors from one part of the world to another, but doors from one whole world into another, passages into other whole worlds, and wholly other worlds. His exploring instinct, his fascination for all things "other", leaped up in him. This was his path.

Though the path was brown, dusty, dry, and dirty, it seemed to him like a silver thread, wet and alive, like a snail's slimy trail of life. It was as if something unutterably great, as if Life itself, had gone up that path and left a trail, a relic of itseslf, behind. Brown as it was down at its bottom, the path went up, through the green and into the blue. *Up* was the magic direction; all other directions were relative on this cruelly round and relative earth; but *up* was absolute, and this path went to the Absolute. He just knew it did. He remembered and recited, as if in a solemn liturgy, a "haunting" from the end of Tolkien's *Silmarillion* about such a path:

> Avalonne is vanished from the Earth and the Land of Aman is taken away, and in the world of this present darkness they cannot be found. Yet once they were, and therefore they still are, in true being and in the whole shape of the world as at first it was devised. For the Dunedain held that even mortal Men, if so blessed, might look upon other times than those of their bodies' life; and they longed ever to escape from the shadows of their exile and to see in some fashion the light that dies not; for the sorrow of the thought of death had pursued them over the deeps of the sea. Thus it was that great mariners among them would still search the empty seas, hoping to come upon the Isle of Meneltarma, and there to see a vision of things that were. But they found it not. And those that sailed far came only to new lands, and found them like to the old lands, and subject to death. And those that sailed furthest set but a girdle about the Earth and returned weary at last to the place of their beginning; and they said: "All roads are now bent."
>
> Thus in after days, what by voyages of ships, what by lore of star-craft, the kings of Men knew that the world was indeed made round; and yet the Eldar were permitted still to depart and to come to the Ancient West and to Avallone, if they would. Therefore the loremasters of Men said that a Straight Road must still be, for those that

were permitted to find it. And they taught that, while the new world fell away, the old road and the path of the memory of the West still went on, as it were a mighty bridge invisible that passed through the air of breath and of flight (which were bent now as the world was bent), and traversed Ilmen [the atmosphere] which flesh cannot endure, until it came to Tol Eressea, the Lonely Isle, and maybe even beyond, to Valinor, where the Valar still dwell and watch the unfolding of the story of the world.[1]

Frodo thought of the Frodo of the old tale in *The Lord of the Rings, that* Frodo was one of those permitted to find a Straight Road, a road that led Somewhere. He had sailed out of Middle-Earth on the last elvish ship, with Gandalf the wizard and Cirdan the shipwright and the last Elves. Perhaps Frodo Grubb was also Frodo! Perhaps that path was a Straight Road.

As these thoughts and wild hopes came to him, he was shocked by their objectivity; they came not from within but from without. They were not rationalizations, wish fulfilments, ways of compensating for long-imbedded inner conflicts, projections, or anything of that sort. He was surprised by them, by their joy. But he was surprised not because he had not believed in the objective reality of the unseen—he had—but because now this magic was coming to *him*.

He had to fulfill his role, like Frodo Baggins. Even the small can do great things, he reminded himself, thinking of the other Frodo instead of himself. So he walked up to the beginning of the path, took a deep breath, and ascended. He felt like an exiled king returning to his

[1] J. R. R. Tolkien, *The Silmarillion* (Boston: Houghton Mifflin, 1977), pp. 281–282.

throne or a high priest leading a solemn liturgical procession. He felt both like a conqueror and like one conquered, both exploring and explored—as if some Presence were moving up him at the same time as he was moving up It.

As he walked through the woods and through the wonder, he felt as if he was indeed passing through a birth canal, being born. The path was not an object in his world but a passage between worlds. He was carried along it as on an escalator, not by his feet but by his destiny. As he went "farther up and farther in" (a "haunting" from Narnia), all the strange thoughts and feelings intensified. He anticipated something at the end wonderful beyond anticipation; he knew he would find something beyond knowledge, something "eye hath not seen, nor ear heard, nor hath it entered into the heart of man".

And he did. He found the City.

Topping the tiny knoll at the end of the path, he emerged with a start, like a baby popping out of its mother, into something infinitely more wonderful, awesome, and glorious than he had ever conceived in any fantasy, any science fiction dream of civilizations advanced millions of years in wisdom, or any ravishing wish fulfillment dream of ecstatic bliss. It hit him as light hits the womb-darkened eyes of the newborn. He saw the City for the first time.

It was his own city, not as the Bronx was his but as the woods and the path were his. Yet it was the Bronx. The path emptied him out onto a plain, middle-dull city street. But everything about it was infinitely different; this was another world, not part of the city he had come from. He was utterly convinced of this, of its objective truth; as before, it was not just a change in his subjective feeling or perception or attitude; this was a new City. For one thing, there were the colors. They transcended words as much as any mystical experience transcends words; yet they were physical, concretely real colors. By comparison, he had lived all his life until now in a world of blacks and whites—no, of grays and brown-grays.

The dirt—it was Perfect Dirt, Platonic Essence of Dirt. Its very word was perfect for the first time. He repeated it fifty times, and it never became meaningless: "Dirt, dirt, dirt, dirt, dirt, dirt, dirt. . . ." It was an incantation, not a curse. In fact, everything about this City was absolutely perfect, infinitely and exactly perfect, utterly what it ought to be, what it had to be, the fulfillment of its light necessity, the deliberate expression of the omniscient, wise, and joyful will of a Cosmic Artist, a nameless God, an inescapable presence haunting and determining every atom. Threads seemed to reach down from the stars to connect every atom on the earth with every other atom and with the sky. And the threads were also hands: wise and skillful hands of an Artist, not the hands of blind necessity or fate.

His attention returned to the colors. Most of the street at the top was brown or brownish-gray. He had always hated the color brown; yet this street was as beautiful as the path, which was also brown. Like the path, the street seemed to be at the same time brown and silver-blue. Blue had always been his favorite color; he had compared the blue of sky with the brown of earth and preferred the first; but now somehow the brown was part of the blue, as the earth was part of the sky. He had always longed to travel in outer space; and now he realized this dream too had come true; he already was in outer space, on the best of all spaceships, Spaceship Earth. The brown thing was part of the blue thing and brought him into the blue thing, as the path had brought him here to the top. Earth had brought him to heaven; earth was his mother; he had been born.

The blue was no less blue because it included the brown. In fact, though the blueness of the sky pervaded everything here in the new City, it was a bluer blue, a more lightsome (though not a lighter) blue than he had ever seen. By comparison the bluest thing he had seen in the old world was only a colorless thing with imitation blue paint covering its surface to hide its real, inner colorlessness. Here everything was blue through and through, from within; yet the blue did not obliterate other colors but revealed them. Brown was really brown now that it was blue within, and he loved it for the first time.

He turned to the path behind him. He had seen it as an escape *from* the world; now it had become his path *into* the world. He realized he had to go back down the path; but it would not be going *back*. He would never have to go back. The path led to the City, and everything in the City was perfect, including the things at the bottom of the path. The very trash was now perfect; it was "the evacuations of the City" and part of the City and therefore a joy; he understood the vision of Charles Williams in *All Hallows Eve* now. He would return to the trash, but it would not be a return, for the trash was here, too, at the top, in the sky. The City was in the sky, and whatever was in the sky was not trashy, and whatever was in the City was not trashy. The trash here was blue and the trash at the bottom of the path would be blue, too. For the old city *was* the new City. This realization was infinitely more surprising to Frodo than it could ever be to any outside observer who would see both halves of the path as "of course" the same city. It was no "of course" to Frodo, but as startling as the Incarnation of a God in a dying criminal. He saw That too as part of the same vision, the co-inherence.

He walked back down as liturgically and triumphantly as he had walked up, not as leaving a glory but as entering one. For his way down was a part of his way up, a "farther up and farther in". For he had been born, and birth, like death, was irreversible. He could not re-enter his mother's womb, as Nicodemus thought. Newborn, he was in a new world forever, for self and world were ecologically related: new self could live only in new world, not old.

When he stepped off the path onto Morris Park Avenue, it was an equal part of the City in the sky. The whole world below was as new as the world above because it was a part of, not apart from, the world above, just as the womb is part of the world. But the fetus does not know this until it is born. Frodo was born.

How wonderfully strange, he thought, that the whole old city he had thought to be so threateningly large was only a tiny and temporary part of the womb of his new world; and how strange that a whole new world was found within this little patch of bushes and this little path at the end of one street in his old world. He saw this as a mystery, but one which connected in a meaningful way with other mysteries: every mother's womb also contained the beginning of something larger than the world, a mind and heart which could contain the whole world. And once a Virgin's womb in one world had contained a God greater than all worlds. *That* now seemed no stranger than this.

Well, he was, he was born, he existed. He had being. Never again would he or could he return to his womb, his coffin, his old confined box in the earth. He had undone death, and his end was his beginning. At the end of Morris Park Avenue he now found his life beginning. His walk home would be real exploring, not fantasy. And when he reached his little flat he knew that it too would be bigger on the inside than on the outside because in this world everything is. And Frodo Grubb had finally come *in*.